NE BIS IN IDEM

MW00804745

Questions of the application and interpretation of the *ne bis in idem* principle in EU law continue to surface in the case law of different European courts. The primary purpose of the proposed book is to provide guidance and to address important issues in connection with the *ne bis in idem* principle in EU law. The development of the *ne bis in idem* principle in the EU legal order illustrates the difficulty of reconciling pluralism with the need for doctrinal coherence, and highlights the tensions between the requirements of effectiveness and the protection of fundamental rights in EU law. The *ne bis in idem* principle is a 'litmus test' of fundamental rights protection in the EU. This book explores the principle, and the way the CJEU has interpreted it, in the context of competition law and the areas of freedom, security and justice, human rights law and tax law.

BAS VAN BOCKEL is Senior Lecturer of EU law at Utrecht University, visiting professor at Universita Ca' Foscari in Venice, and honorary judge at the District Court at Amsterdam. Amongst other things, he was formerly visiting professor of EU law at Saarland University, lecturer of EU law at Leiden University, and Jean Monnet Fellow at the European University Institute. His main research interests lie in EU fundamental rights protection, competition law and EU criminal law.

NE BIS IN IDEM IN EU LAW

Edited by

BAS VAN BOCKEL

Utrecht University/Universita Ca' Foscari

CAMBRIDGE
UNIVERSITY PRESS

CAMBRIDGE
UNIVERSITY PRESS

University Printing House, Cambridge CB2 8BS, United Kingdom

One Liberty Plaza, 20th Floor, New York, NY 10006, USA

477 Williamstown Road, Port Melbourne, VIC 3207, Australia

314-321, 3rd Floor, Plot 3, Splendor Forum, Jasola District Centre, New Delhi - 110025, India

79 Anson Road, #06-04/06, Singapore 079906

Cambridge University Press is part of the University of Cambridge.

It furthers the University's mission by disseminating knowledge in the pursuit of
education, learning and research at the highest international levels of excellence.

www.cambridge.org
Information on this title: www.cambridge.org/9781107451841

© Bas van Bockel 2016

First published 2016
First paperback edition 2018

A catalogue record for this publication is available from the British Library

Library of Congress Cataloging in Publication data
Names: Bockel, Bas van, 1973–
Title: Ne bis in idem in EU law / edited by Bas van Bockel.
Description: Cambridge : Cambridge University Press, 2016. |
Includes bibliographical references and index.
Identifiers: LCCN 2016026421| ISBN 9781107087064 (Hardback) |
ISBN 9781107451841 (Paperback)
Subjects: LCSH: Double jeopardy–Euorpean Union countries.
Classification: LCC KJE9698 .N43 2016 | DDC 345.24/04–dc23 LC record available at
https://lccn.loc.gov/2016026421

ISBN 978-1-107-08706-4 Hardback
ISBN 978-1-107-45184-1 Paperback

CONTENTS

CONTRIBUTORS

ANGELICA ERICSSON Doctoral candidate, Lund University

XAVIER GROUSSOT Professor of EU law and pro dean, Lund University

RENATO NAZZINI Professor of Law, King's College, London

DANIEL SARMIENTO Professor of EU Law, Universidad Complutense de Madrid and Legal secretary at the European Court of Justice

BAS VAN BOCKEL Senior Lecturer of EU Law, Utrecht University and visiting professor, Universita Ca' Foscari

PETER J. WATTEL Professor of European Tax Law, ACTL, University of Amsterdam and Advocate-General, *Hoge Raad der Nederlanden* (Supreme Court of the Netherlands)

Introduction and Set-up of the Study

BAS VAN BOCKEL

The present study concerns the development of the *ne bis in idem* principle in EU law. One of the reasons for embarking on this study is that the interpretation and application of the *ne bis in idem* principle between the legal orders of the EU and the Member States, and across different EU policy areas, continues to raise questions that this study aims to address. Another is that the complex judicial interaction between the Court of Justice of the European Union (CJEU), the European Court of Human Rights (ECtHR) and national constitutional courts in the case law on the *ne bis in idem* principle discussed in this study has important implications for EU fundamental rights protection. A form of constitutional balancing moving beyond a mere judicial dialogue on the substance of the *ne bis in idem* principle is seen in the case law of these 'highest' European courts. This would not be so if those courts did not recognize that they are in different ways part of a common 'European' constitutional system, however fragmented and incomplete that system may be. Thus, the case law on the *ne bis in idem* principle discussed in the different chapters of this study serves as a kind of 'litmus test' bringing wider issues and developments in EU fundamental rights protection to light.

The set-up of this study is as follows. In the introductory chapter, the sources, scope and elements of the *ne bis in idem* principle are presented and discussed. Some of the more general questions arising in connection with the interpretation and application of the 'European' *ne bis in idem* principle are introduced in order to provide the necessary background for the subsequent chapters.

Chapter 2 addresses the relationship between the case law of the ECtHR and the European Court of Justice on the *ne bis in idem* principle, raising the question whether uniform interpretation is the 'sole cure' for the ailments of the system of European fundamental rights protection. The absence of a common European or international *ne bis in idem* standard and the consequences of this fragmentation for

the dynamic of European fundamental rights jurisprudence are discussed. Special attention is given to Article 52(3) of the Charter of
Fundamental Rights of the EU, which regulates the relationship
between the EU and the ECHR legal orders, and the case of *Åkerberg
Fransson*, which is paradigmatic for the relationship between the CJEU
and the ECtHR. Although the Convention is formally speaking not
binding upon the EU, the relationship between EU law and the Convention has become highly internalized in the EU legal order. The
Convention sets forth a minimum standard and therefore allows for
a degree of divergence in the interpretation of a fundamental right like
ne bis in idem as long as the Convention standard of protection is
respected. An important question is whether Article 52(3) of the
Charter allows for the same, or whether it obliges the CJEU to scrupulously follow the Strasburg case law. The CJEU has rejected the latter
position, and has found ways to safeguard its interpretative autonomy
where Charter rights corresponding to rights from the Convention are
concerned. In doing so, the CJEU has gone beyond Article 52(3) of the
Charter by interpreting that provision rather restrictively and by giving
a pluralist meaning to Article 53 of the Charter ('level of protection').
At the same time, the CJEU has taken an autonomous approach in
interpreting Article 50 of the Charter, often omitting references to the
case law of the ECtHR. The CJEU's minimalist interpretation of the
homogeneity clause of Article 52(3) contrasts both with its broad
reading of Article 51 in the *Åkerberg Fransson* judgment as well as
with its differentiated construction of Article 53 of the Charter. The
combined effect of this position has far-reaching constitutional implications for European human rights law.[1]

In competition cases, it appears that the CJEU avoids tackling the
question of the relationship between Article 50 of the Charter and Article
4 of Protocol no. 7 ECHR. This raises some complex issues in the light of
the circumstance that several Member States of the Council of Europe
have not ratified the 7th Protocol to the ECHR. The full application of
the so-called Engel criteria in the field of competition law as well as in
other EU policy areas might endanger the requirement of effectiveness
under EU law. The fact that the Charter rights form an integral part of
EU policies that aim to further European integration has important
consequences for the manner in which EU fundamental rights are

---

[1] See: Chapter 2, p. 82.

protected. The existence of strong constitutional principles like the principle of supremacy of EU law and the duty of loyal cooperation give EU fundamental rights much greater 'traction' within national legal orders than ECHR rights, the legal status of which varies considerably between the Member States of the Council of Europe. The *Åkerberg Fransson* judgment and the way in which that judgment was received in Sweden is an example of how a plurality of human rights standards may lead to higher levels of protection of human rights in a national legal order. If European standards of fundamental rights protection were entirely uniform, we likely wouldn't be seeing the same dynamic application of European human rights law. Although the absence of uniformity in European fundamental rights protection is in many ways regrettable, a surprising conclusion from this is that the plurality of sources and standards of human rights protection in Europe can therefore also form a driving force behind developments towards higher European standards of protection of some rights, like the *ne bis in idem* principle.

In Chapter 3, the developments in the case law of the CJEU are presented and discussed. The *ne bis in idem* principle touches on almost every EU policy area, but its scope and substance are still open to considerable discussion. Although the case law of the CJEU on the *ne bis in idem* principle is not coherent, a general 'vision' of the principle can be deduced from the individual decisions. The substance, scope and elements of the *ne bis in idem* principle are discussed in the light of the wording and scope of Article 50 of the Charter and the case law of the CJEU. After that, the genesis and further development of the *ne bis in idem* principle in the case law of the CJEU, first as a 'general requirement of natural justice' and later on as a general principle of EU law, are presented and discussed. An important and unresolved question is that of the relationship between the general principles and the rights from the Charter. In theory, if a rule constitutes a 'principle', this would render it autonomous from other rules and principles of the legal system – including the Charter. In practical terms however, the distinction between general principles and Charter rights would only appear to be relevant to the realization of those rights in situations falling *outside* of the scope of the Charter, but within the scope of EU law. Now that the CJEU has held in the *Åkerberg Fransson* judgment that all situations falling within the scope of EU law also fall within the scope of the Charter, the question of the relationship between the general principles and the rights from the Charter may have become moot.[2] The CJEU however has not so far shed further light on this point so the nature of the relationship between general principles and Charter rights remains unclear.

The CJEU has struggled in the past to develop a coherent doctrine governing the relationship between EU fundamental rights, the ECtHR and 'national constitutional traditions'.[3] The entry into force of the Treaty of Lisbon has added complexity to the relationship between the Charter and the Convention in this regard. In one line of case law the CJEU makes a rather standardized use of the Charter and the case law of the ECtHR highlighting its role as a source of interpretation, while in another the CJEU conspicuously omits all references to the Convention or the Strasburg case law, and the *ne bis in idem* principle features in both lines of case law. As long as the EU has not acceded to it, the CJEU thus maintains a relative autonomy *vis-à-vis* the Convention in interpreting and applying Charter rights. Where the constitutional traditions common to the Member States are concerned, the CJEU has made a pragmatic use of national experience in order to find an appropriate solution in the light of the goals of the policy area concerned.

The case law of the CJEU is conclusive in holding that the *ne bis in idem* principle concerns not to be *tried*, and not the right not to be *punished* twice. For the area of Justice and Home Affairs, this results from the fact that the *ne bis in idem* principle forms a corollary of the free movement rules in that area. In the cases concerning Article 54 of the Convention Implementing the Schengen Agreement (CISA), the Court (following the Opinion by Advocate General Sharpston in the *Gasparini* case) appears to construe the *ne bis in idem* principle in that provision both as the concrete expression of a more general principle, and as a reflection of the specific needs and characteristics of that policy area. This approach suggests that the contents and standard of protection of the principle are not necessarily the same across different policy areas.[4]

A difference between Justice and Home Affairs and competition law is that in competition matters, the Commission has exclusive competence to implement a single legal framework. National authorities have assumed broad enforcement powers and coordinate their efforts in an attempt to avoid *ne bis in idem* situations, but this does not rule out the possibility of violations of that principle. These issues are key in

---

[2] In addition, it would seem to make little sense to distinguish between the same right as a general principle and as codified in the Charter, see: Chapter 3, p. 111.

[3] See: Chapter 3, p. 113.   [4] See: Chapter 3, p. 122.

understanding the stance of the CJEU on the *ne bis in idem* principle in competition law.[5] As a result of these special characteristics, it could perhaps be argued that competition law forms an autonomous and self-sufficient area of law, but the peculiarity of competition law should not be over-emphasized. The stance of the CJEU in the matter is ambiguous to say the least, and invites criticism. The question is whether the lack of coherence in the case law can be justified, and the CJEU has not so far provided many arguments to this end in its case law.[6]

Chapter 4 examines the development and application of the *ne bis in idem* principle in competition law. The requirement of identity of the 'legal interest protected' which the CJEU has upheld in its *ne bis in idem* cases in competition matters would lead to the conclusion that an undertaking only benefits from the protection afforded by that principle when the EU competition rules – and not other EU rules, or national competition rules – are applied a second time in respect of the same infringement. In situations involving decisions from non-EU Member States in which the *ne bis in idem* principle does not apply, the protection against multiple decisions and/or sanctions is entirely left to the (voluntary) self-restraint of authorities and courts around the world in imposing only the sanctions which reflect the harm caused in that jurisdiction.[7] Within the EU, the system of EU competition enforcement is almost by design conducive to multiple proceedings in respect of the same conduct, although abuse is avoided as a matter of prosecutorial restraint. This is effectuated through a sensible administration of the (re-)allocation of cases within the European Competition Network (ECN), aimed at identifying the authority best placed to act in a given case. A risk inherent in this system is that the Commission and the national competition authorities (NCAs) may find it expedient to allocate different aspects of what may constitute a single infringement for the purpose of the application of the *ne bis in idem* principle to different authorities, and there have been several examples of such situations.[8] Another issue is that there is no mechanism within the ECN barring a second investigation after the first case was closed. This is particularly problematic because the CJEU has held in the *Tele2 Polska* judgment that national authorities do not have the power to (finally) *acquit* an undertaking of an infringement of EU competition law.[9] In addition, the Commission is under no duty to adopt a non-infringement decision if an investigation has not produced the

---

[5] See: Chapter 3, p. 129. [6] See: Chapter 3, p. 130. [7] See: Chapter 4, p. 134.
[8] See: Chapter 4, p. 138. [9] Case C-375/09, *Tele2 Polska*, ECLI:EU:C:2011:270.

sufficient evidence. Under those circumstances the only predictable way of limiting the proliferation of investigations and proceedings in competition cases is a robust and coherent application of the *ne bis in idem* principle, but this is impaired by its overly restrictive judicial interpretation of that principle in the competition case law of the CJEU.[10]

The requirement of the identity of the 'legal interest protected' in the Toshiba case seems difficult to justify.[11] In the light of the internal market rationale for the *ne bis in idem* principle in EU law, the need for a conduct-based interpretation of the concept of 'offence' is even stronger, given that the legal interest protected will by definition differ when considered from the perspective of different sovereign states. In competition cases, this results in a legal market fragmentation that the Court itself has held to be incompatible with the single market in other areas of EU law. The only possible justification for this appears to be that Article 50 of the Charter refers to the same 'offence' instead of the same 'acts' like Article 54 CISA, but this same terminology did not stop the ECtHR from adopting a factual approach to the definition of *idem* in the case of *Zolotukhin* v. *Russia*.[12]

For competition law, a related question is whether a complex or single continuous cartel consisting of several agreements and/or concerted practices which are 'inextricably linked' forms a single offence, or can be divided up into smaller segments, according to the markets affected. The answer is clear: if the authorities are left with full discretion to choose how they divide a single infringement up in smaller segments according to where the effects of the conduct are felt, this will rob the *ne bis in idem* principle of any substance or protective function. In addition, the effective enforcement of the competition rules does not require such segmentation, as both the Commission and national competition authorities have sufficient legal and other means at their disposal to deal with EU-wide cartels. Although the test for when the facts are the 'same' and/or 'inextricably linked' must be applied in the light of the circumstances of every case, complex or single continuous infringements in competition cases present no specific difficulty in this regard, and some examples are given.[13]

As regards the finality of the outcome of competition investigations and proceedings, the authorities also enjoy much discretion. In their case

---

[10] See: Chapter 4, p. 140.   [11] See: Chapter 4, p. 142.

[12] *Zolotukhin* v. *Russia*, ECtHR 10 February 2009 (appl. no. 14939/03).

[13] See: Chapter 4, p. 142.

law, both CJEU and the ECtHR by and large defer to the applicable national laws in determining when a decision is 'final'. For situations under Article 54 CISA it is both logical and necessary that the finality of a decision is assessed under national law. For EU competition law however this is a different matter, for several reasons. One reason is that the decisional powers of the Commission and the NCAs are entirely regulated in an instrument of EU secondary law (Regulation 1/2003), and EU secondary legislation must be interpreted in a manner consistent with the *ne bis in idem* principle as a hierarchically superior EU legal norm.[14] Another is that in EU competition law there are no issues of mutual trust along the lines of those found in the area of Police and Judicial Cooperation in Criminal Matters (PJCCM), which may call for a more deferential approach. In order to correct the resulting gap in protection, certain decisions in competition matters like commitment decisions under Article 9 of Regulation 1/2003 should by their nature be considered as 'final'. Similarly, it is argued that the grounds for considering the setting aside of an infringement decision on procedural grounds by the EU Courts as 'not-final' lack conviction. A test is proposed in such circumstances, balancing the protection of the right of the undertaking concerned with the need to safeguard the effective enforcement of EU law. This means that proceedings could only be resumed if: a) the procedural defect was not attributable to the competition authority, or, if it was, if: b) the competition authority was not acting in bad faith or grossly negligently. Finally, the *Walt Wilhelm* and *Boehringer* cases are discussed. It is argued that *Walt Wilhelm* is no longer 'good law', but that the grounds for the *Boehringer* judgment are still valid.[15]

Chapter 5 addresses a number of actual and potential *ne bis in idem* issues in EU tax law. Within the EU, questions of *ne bis in idem* may arise in three main types of situations in respect to both EU harmonized taxes (such as customs duties, VAT, excise duties and capital tax), and unharmonized tax in situations falling within the scope of the EU free movement rules.[16] An important difference with an area like competition law is that EU law does not confer any sanctioning powers on EU institutions in respect of contraventions of tax law, and the sanctioning powers of national authorities are found only in national law.

The different ways in which the two 'versions' of the *ne bis in idem* principle (*ne bis in idem puniri* and *ne bis in idem vexari*) can be

---

[14] See: Chapter 4, p. 144.   [15] See: Chapter 4, p. 161.   [16] See: Chapter 5, p. 169.

operationalized are discussed: the 'credit' or 'accounting' system versus the possibility of cancelling out the previous penalty for *ne bis in idem puniri*; and the '*una via* system' versus the 'finality system' for *ne bis in idem vexari*.[17] It is established case law before the ECtHR that Article 4 of Protocol no. 7 ECHR must be understood as *ne bis in idem vexari*, therefore in accordance with the finality system.

For *ne bis in idem*, a problem in applying the homogeneity rule of Article 52(3) of the Charter is the limited ratification of the 7th Protocol ECHR. It appears that a number of Member States wanted to reserve the possibility of imposing administrative penalties like tax surcharges first, and subsequently bringing criminal proceedings in respect of the same tax offences later on.

The case law of the ECtHR leaves no doubt that tax surcharges are 'criminal' for the purpose of Article 6 ECHR, and therefore also for those of the *ne bis in idem* principle of Article 4 Protocol no. 7 ECHR. In the *Jusilla* judgment, the ECtHR introduced a distinction between the 'hard core' of criminal law and the periphery where less stringent requirements apply under the criminal head of Article 6 ECHR. For the *ne bis in idem* principle of Article 4 of Protocol no. 7 ECHR, however, it appears unlikely that it could be applied with anything less than its 'full stringency', as this would mean that it would not be applied at all.[18] Turning to the implications of the *Åkerberg Fransson* judgment for tax law, it now appears that in respect of penalties for evasion of indirect taxes the scope of the Charter is much wider than in respect of penalties for evasion of unharmonized direct taxes. However, the CJEU did observe in the *Åkerberg Fransson* judgment that the fact that VAT forms part of the EU's own resources provides a 'direct link between the collection of VAT in compliance with the European Union law applicable and the availability to the European Union budget of the corresponding VAT resources'.[19] If that link is deemed sufficient for a situation to enter into the scope of application of EU law, the same will logically apply to any situation in connection with national taxation because the EU's budget is paid out of national tax revenue.[20] The difference with VAT is therefore not the link with the EU budget, but the fact that direct taxation is not in any way harmonized.[21] Direct taxation therefore does not enter the scope of EU law unless there is a cross-border 'element'.

---

[17] See: Chapter 5, pp. 172–173.   [18] See: Chapter 5, p. 190.
[19] See: Chapter 5, p. 193.   [20] See: Chapter 5, p. 200.
[21] Apart from a few directives on certain forms of corporate taxes which are very narrow in scope, see: Chapter 5, p. 202.

It has been pointed out by in the past that Article 50 of the Charter to some extent 'sets aside' the non-ratification of Article 4 of Protocol no. 7 ECHR. It should however not be forgotten that this only applies in situations falling within the scope of the Charter itself. By consequence, this has little or no impact in respect of penalties for direct taxes.[22]

A question that is left open after the *Åkerberg Fransson* judgment is that of the relationship between the *ne bis in idem* principle of Article 50 of the Charter and the principle of effectiveness of EU law. What if the tax penalty imposed on the subject in that case would be considered insufficiently 'effective, proportionate and dissuasive' in order to protect the EU budget and dissuade entrepreneurs from further evasion of VAT duties?[23] At present, it appears that the requirements of effectiveness under EU law may require Member States to bring a second prosecution under certain circumstances, in violation of Article 4 of Protocol no. 7 ECHR. It is submitted that where enforcement considerations and fundamental rights clash, the latter should prevail over the former. Otherwise, it cannot be said that EU fundamental rights protection is 'effective'.[24]

Finally, a parallel is drawn between *ne bis in idem* and the issue of double taxation. Similarly to Article 54 CISA double taxation occurs in situations between different states. Due to disparities and mismatches in the applicable instruments dealing with double taxation it persists, also between EU Member States. Although it is obvious that double taxation hampers free movement, the provision in the former EC Treaty (which called for negotiations between the Member States to take measures) has disappeared in the Lisbon Treaty. It is at present unclear if any further measures will be taken to combat double taxation in the EU, and by whom. The chapter concludes by observing that double taxation may form a much more serious form of double jeopardy for the EU than *ne bis in idem* itself, as far as tax matters are concerned.

In Chapter 6, the potential for *ne bis in idem* situations under the Single Supervisory Mechanism (SSM) is discussed. The powers of the European Central Bank (ECB) under the SSM Regulation (SSM-R) are extensive. The ECB has the competence to ensure compliance with the minimum capital requirements, to safeguard the adequacy of internal capital in relation to the risk profile of a credit institution, and to enforce compliance with provisions on leverage and liquidity. To this end the

---

[22] See: Chapter 5, p. 204.　　[23] *Ibid*　　[24] See: Chapter 5, p. 205.

ECB has a wide range of measures at its disposal, including the power to impose fines directly upon credit institutions. All the while, national supervisory authorities play a significant role, and EU financial regulation takes shape in a joint effort between the ECB and national supervisory authorities. In the end however, the ECB alone is responsible for the effective and consistent functioning of the SSM. A comparison with competition law shows that although the architecture of enforcement of the SSM and Regulation 1/20033 are somewhat comparable in spirit, the problems that present themselves in the context of the SSM differ from those found in competition law, and there are some potential *ne bis in dem* issues which are identified. Where violations of the *ne bis in idem* principle are avoided in the relation between enforcement measures under the SSM-R and national (criminal) law, this is only due to the gaps in the system of fundamental rights protection in the EU.

In the Conclusions, the various observations from the previous chapters are brought together. The case law of the CJEU on the *ne bis in idem* principle illustrates the difficulty of reconciling pluralism with the need for doctrinal coherence, and highlights the tensions between the requirements of effectiveness and the protection of fundamental rights in EU law. The CJEU has struggled in the past to develop a coherent doctrine governing the relationship between EU fundamental rights, the ECtHR and national 'constitutional traditions'. Whilst it may be deemed opportune or necessary to differentiate in the interpretation of a right like the *ne bis in idem* principle according to the specific characteristics of EU policy areas, the CJEU will have to find some doctrinal justification for the inconsistencies that were identified at several points in this study. Otherwise, the national judiciary may not always be persuaded to follow the CJEU, especially in situations in which national constitutional rights or Convention rights are at stake.

It appears increasingly difficult to maintain that the requirement of the 'identity of the legal interest protected' from the competition law cases can mean anything other than 'the scope of EU law' as laid down in Article 51 of the Charter. In the *Åkerberg Fransson* judgment, it was held that the scope of the Charter coincides with that of EU law itself. In the light of the requirement of the 'identity of the legal interest protected', this raises the question of what other 'legal interest' could be at stake other than that of EU law in situations falling within the scope of the Charter. The same follows *mutatis mutandis* from the *Walt Wilhelm* judgment, in which the requirement of the identity of the protected legal interest was originally introduced by the CJEU. It is observed that if there is indeed only one possible 'legal interest' to be considered for the purposes of '*idem*' in situations falling within the scope of EU law (and this conclusion appears inevitable) this causes the 'threefold requirement' from the competition cases to collapse into the twofold *Zolotukhin* test – that is, unless the CJEU finds some other acceptable doctrinal justification for its differentiated interpretation of the element of *idem*, capable of withstanding the weight of this doctrinal logic.

An observation from the cases discussed in this study is that considerations of judicial autonomy and conditionality (along the lines of *Solange II*, *Bosphorus* and *Åkerberg Fransson*) as well as undeniable interdependence steer the jurisprudential developments in different, sometimes opposing directions.[25] The notion of a 'constitutional balance' may go some way in explaining both the attracting and the opposing forces seen at work in the case law.[26]

Returning to the question from Chapter 2 whether uniformity is the sole cure for the ailments of the system of EU fundamental rights protection, the *Zoran Spasic* case is discussed,[27] which should be understood against the background of the earlier judgment of the *Bundesverfassungsgericht* in the case of *Boere*, the shadow of which may have loomed over *Spasic*. In many ways, the *Spasic* case is paradigmatic for the dynamic interaction between the CJEU, the ECtHR and the German *Bundesverfassungsgericht*, which doesn't necessarily contribute to greater uniformity or coherence in the substantive interpretation of fundamental rights. The (perhaps surprising) conclusion is, however, that this peculiar 'judicial competition' doesn't necessarily erode fundamental rights protection in the EU, and may even contribute to a higher level of protection of fundamental rights (or at least, in some cases), as suggested in Chapter 2. In keeping with the idea of a constitutional balance, this is likely so due to a legal and institutional

---

[25] In Opinion 2/13, the Court's objections primarily concern its judicial autonomy and its guardianship of the 'specific characteristics' of the EU's legal order. Amongst other things, the Court argues that the draft accession agreement is likely to have an adverse impact on the 'autonomy' of EU law and its 'specific characteristics': Opinion 2/13, paras. 164–177.

[26] A few exceptions aside, the idea of 'EU constitutional balance' has not received much scholarly attention so far. One exception is M. Dawson and F. de Witte, 'Constitutional Balance in the EU after the Euro-crisis', (2013) *Modern Law Review* 76(5), pp. 817–844.

[27] CJEU, Case C-129/14 PPU, *Zoran Spasic*, ECLI:EU:C:2014:586.

situation of mutual interdependence in which each judicial actor enjoys a limited degree of interpretative autonomy *vis-a-vis* the others, whilst none really has the final say. Although this is in many ways perhaps not ideal for a system of fundamental rights protection due to the complexity and legal uncertainty that results from it, it does make for a particularly fascinating and dynamic area of law.

The 'European' *Ne Bis in Idem* Principle

Substance, Sources, and Scope

BAS VAN BOCKEL

1 Introduction

The principle of *ne bis in idem* is a fundamental principle of law, which restricts the possibility of a defendant being prosecuted repeatedly on the basis of the same *offence, act or facts*. The principle has a long history and exists in national systems of law in different forms: as a constitutional guarantee, as a rule of criminal procedure, and as a guarantee in extradition law. In continental law traditions, a distinction is often made between the principle's role as an individual right and its function as a guarantee for legal certainty, although these two aspects are intrinsically linked. In the former sense, the principle protects the individual from abuses of the state's *ius puniendi* (right to punish). Several logically linked *rationale* are identified in this regard. For one, the guarantee ensures the fair administration of criminal justice, as the additional burdens arising out of the repeated prosecution of a subject 'include the duplicated costs of legal representation, coercive measures to the person and property, and psychological burdens associated with the extended procedures and the absence of finality'.[1] Another *rationale* is found in the requirement that a prosecution must be based on pre-existing legislation (principle of legality), which would become illusory if a defendant could be prosecuted continually for various legal aspects of the same act or facts. In its function as a guarantee for legal certainty the principle serves to protect the authority of the judgment by upholding the final authority of judicial

Many thanks are owed to Belle Beems for her assistance and to prof. J. Gerards for her comments on an earlier draft of parts of this chapter.

[1] Such burdens form part and parcel of law enforcement, it is their repetition that is by definition 'unfair': M. Fletcher, 'The problem of multiple criminal prosecutions: building an effective EU response', *Yearbook of European Law* (Glasgow: 2007), 10.

decisions. This is also important because a court cannot be impartial unless its decisions bind not only on the subject, but also other organs of the State and other courts.[2] The guarantee therefore touches on both the 'very essence of the right to a fair trial' and the legitimacy of the state.[3] In spite of the determinacy of legal rules and doctrines and the disciplining force of legal procedure, the legal process itself would become entirely arbitrary if legal proceedings could be repeated indefinitely.[4] A final *rationale* commonly identified in connection with the *ne bis in idem* principle is that of proportionality, which is also an important principle in EU law.[5]

The principle's traditional appropriation as a 'principle' rather than a 'rule' appears to form a customary expression of its importance; according to most contemporary distinctions between legal rules and principles, the *ne bis in idem* principle would belong in the 'rule' rather than the 'principle' category.[6]

There is no generally accepted customary rule of international law or *ius cogens* offering international protection against double jeopardy in international situations. The international and transnational application of the *ne bis in idem* principle therefore depends on specific instruments offering protection from double jeopardy, usually in connection with extradition or other forms of mutual assistance in criminal matters.

2 The Reception of *Ne Bis in Idem* in the EU Legal Order

Ne bis in idem provision entered into the EU legal order in different ways, and for different reasons. The Treaties establishing the European

---

[2] With the exception of the possibility of appeal.

[3] *Nikitin* v. *Russia*, ECtHR 20 July 2004, appl. no. 50178/99, para. 57.

[4] Selznick conceives the function of the rule of law as the restraint of public authority through what he calls the 'rational principles of civic order', which 'aim to minimize the arbitrary element in legal norms and decisions'. P. Selznick, P. Nonette, and H. Vollmer, *Law, Society and Industrial Justice*, (Transaction Publishers, 1980), 11. This observation arguably reveals a bias in Dworkin's 'right answer thesis' towards substantive rather than procedural aspects of legal decision-making, which equally determine the legal validity ad even moral content of a judgment. Absent the requisite legal safeguards, Judge Hercules' decision, although it is the 'right answer' is not of *legal* value.

[5] The principle of proportionality in EU law is a multifaceted principle which plays a pivotal role in EU legal order. See, amongst others: T.-I. Harbo, 'The Function of the Proportionality Principle in EU Law', (2010) 16 *European Law Journal*, 2, 158–185.

[6] The influential rule/principle distinction proposed by Dworkin shares sufficient common ground on this point with other distinctions such as those proposed by Raz and Schauer. See: Ronald M. Dworkin, 'The Model of Rules', 35 *U. Chi. L. Rev.* 25 (1967); Joseph Raz, 'Legal Principles and the Limits of Law', 81 *Yale L. J.* 823 (1972).

Communities did not provide for a *ne bis in idem* rule or any other provisions guaranteeing the protection of fundamental rights.[7] The absence of a fundamental rights instrument on the Community level, however, proved problematic in view of the growing extent to which the Community showed itself to be capable of raising fundamental rights issues.[8] This led to the development of a body of fundamental rights including the *ne bis in idem* principle through the case law of the Court of Justice of the European Union (CJEU) as 'general principles of EU law', later codified in the Charter of Fundamental Rights of the EU. In addition a number of instruments of Community and EU law, such as for example the European Arrest Warrant, were adopted over time containing *ne bis in idem* rules. Some of these instruments were modeled after similar initiatives and instruments within the Council of Europe, resulting in the coexistence of a number of differently worded *ne bis in idem* provisions in different parts of EU law as well as in Conventions within the legal framework of the Council of Europe and other international instruments. Perhaps the most significant development for the reception of the *ne bis in idem* principle in EU law has been the incorporation of the Schengen agreements into the EU legal order by way of a Protocol to the Treaty of Amsterdam. With the coming into force of the Treaty of Amsterdam the necessity to provide for a transnational *ne bis in idem* principle in the Area of Freedom, Security and Justice (AFSJ) was increasingly felt. Provisions in existing instruments were considered too varied in substance and scope to provide effective *ne bis in idem* protection, in keeping with the aim of free movement. A solution was found in the form of Article 54 of the 1990 Convention on the Implementation of the Schengen Agreement (CISA).[9] As discussed at several points in this

---

[7] The initial absence of a fundamental rights instrument in Community law may reflect a decision to leave the protection of European citizens in the hands of the Member States, assuming that economic integration would not carry any real fundamental rights relevance.

[8] B. De Witte, 'The past and future role of the European Court of Justice in the Protection of Human Rights', in *The EU and Human Rights*, ed. P. Alston with N. Bustelo and J. Heenan (Oxford: Oxford University Press, 1999), 878 *et seq.*

[9] Convention of 19 June 1990 implementing the Schengen Agreement, [2000] OJ L239/19. The first Schengen agreement had been concluded in 1985 outside of the legal framework of the (then) Communities as an intergovernmental instrument between five Member States: Agreement between the Governments of the States of the Benelux Economic Union, the Federal Republic of Germany and the French Republic on the gradual abolition of checks at their common borders (1985), [2000] OJ L 239/13.

chapter, Art. 54 CISA has been a turning point for the establishment of the *ne bis in idem* in the EU and has spawned a sizeable body of case law.

2.1 Provisions

2.1.1 Article 4 of Protocol no.7 to the European Convention for the Protection of Human Rights and Fundamental Freedoms ('Art. 4 of Protocol no. 7 ECHR')

Article 4 of Protocol no. 7 to the ECHR reads as follows:

1. No one shall be liable to be tried or punished again in criminal proceedings under the jurisdiction of the same State for an offence for which he has already been finally acquitted or convicted in accordance with the law and penal procedure of that State.
2. The provisions of the preceding paragraph shall not prevent the reopening of the case in accordance with the law and penal procedure of the State concerned, if there is evidence of new or newly discovered facts, or if there has been a fundamental defect in the previous proceedings, which could affect the outcome of the case.

Although Art. 4 of Protocol no. 7 ECHR forms a later addition to the ECHR, it is placed amongst those guarantees that cannot be derogated from even in time of war or other public emergency, which forms an indication of its importance. The draft provision was prepared by the Steering Committee for Human Rights and finally adopted and opened for signature by the Member States of the Council of Europe at the 374th meeting of the Ministers' Deputies on 22 November 1984.[10] The reason for including the 7th Protocol was, that 'problems might arise from the coexistence of the European Convention on Human Rights and the United Nations Covenants'.[11] In Recommendation 791,[12] the Assembly urged the Committee of Ministers to 'endeavour to insert as many as possible of the substantive provisions of the Covenant on Civil and Political Rights in the Convention', and the influence of Article 14(7) ICCPR on Art. 4 of Protocol no. 7 ECHR is clear. The 7th Protocol has not been ratified by all of the Member States of the Council of Europe. In

---

[10] The Explanatory Report is available from: http://conventions.coe.int/Treaty/en/Reports/Html/117.htm.

[11] Explanatory Report, at point 1.

[12] Recommendation 791 (1976) on the protection of human rights in Europe, http://assembly.coe.int/Main.asp?link=/Documents/AdoptedText/ta76/EREC791.htm.

Ponsetti and Chesnel, the European Court of Human Rights (ECtHR) confirmed that the *ne bis in idem* principle 'is embodied solely in Article 4 of Protocol no. 7 (and) the other provisions of the Convention do not guarantee compliance with it either expressly or implicitly'.[13] For the Member States of the EU this gap is partially filled by the applicability of Article 50 of the Charter, in situations falling within the scope of EU law.

According to the Explanatory report, Art. 4 of Protocol no. 7 ECHR does not 'prevent the reopening of the proceedings in favour of the convicted person or any changing of the judgment to the benefit of a convicted person', and therefore only applies in situations in which proceedings are brought in order to secure a conviction.[14] Art. 4 of Protocol no. 7 ECHR refers to 'criminal proceedings', mirroring the term 'criminal charge' found in Article 6 par. 1 ECHR, but does not require that the offence is 'criminal' in nature. According to the Explanatory Report:

> It has not seemed necessary ... to qualify the offence as "criminal".
> Indeed, Article 4 already contains the terms "in criminal proceedings"
> and "penal procedure", which render unnecessary any further specifica-
> tion of the text of the article itself.

The Report goes on to state that Article 4 does not prevent a person from being subjected to an action of a different 'character'.[15] In spite of these reassurances, the ECtHR has in its case law concerning Art. 4 of Protocol no. 7 interpreted the terms 'criminal proceedings' in Art. 4 of Protocol no. 7 ECHR and 'criminal charge' in Art. 6 ECHR broadly and autono-mously, as will be discussed in more detail later on in this chapter. As a result, the scope of application of Art. 4 of Protocol no. 7 ECHR has expanded into other areas of law, including administrative and tax law, and disciplinary proceedings of different kinds.

Art. 4 of Protocol no. 7 refers to both the right not to be tried, and the right not to be punished again for an 'offence' for which the subject has been finally acquitted or convicted. This may give rise to some confusion, as these two guarantees differ considerably from one another. The prohibition of double punishment on the one hand merely prohibits the accumulation of penalties in respect of the same offence, but does not in itself preclude the possibility of bringing a second prosecution if

---

[13] *Ponsetti and Chesnel* v. *France* (dec), ECtHR 14 September 1999, appl. nos. 36855/97 and 41731/98, para. 6.
[14] Explanatory Report at point 31.   [15] Explanatory Report at point 28.

this doesn't lead to the imposition of a 'double' penalty on the same subject. This offers only very limited protection as the bringing of a second prosecution itself already places a considerable burden on the subject, regardless of the outcome.[16] The right not to be prosecuted twice or 'prohibition of double prosecution' on the other hand bars any further proceedings once the outcome of the first set of proceedings has become final. This guarantee bars the bringing of any new proceedings, regardless of whether a penalty was imposed in the first proceedings, or of the manner in which that penalty was calculated. In *Franz Fischer*, the ECHR confirmed that the *ne bis in idem* principle of Art. 4 of Protocol no. 7 primarily sets forth the prohibition of double prosecution and 'is not confined to' the prohibition of double punishment.[17] In the decision of the Grand Chamber in the case of *Zolotukhin*, the Court confirmed this, and identified a third 'distinct' guarantee contained in Art. 4 of Protocol no. 7: 'that no one shall be ... liable to be tried' for an offence for which that person has been finally acquitted or convicted.[18] Although the Court has not shed any further light on when it is precisely that a subject is 'liable to be tried', it must be assumed from this that, similarly to Article 6 ECHR, the protection afforded by Art. 4 of Protocol no. 7 extends into the pre-trial stages of the prosecution.

Art. 4 of Protocol no. 7 ECHR requires that the subject is 'finally acquitted or convicted', but does not require that the penalty imposed has been enforced or is being enforced. Furthermore, Art. 4 of Protocol no. 7 ECHR contains an exception to the *ne bis in idem* rule allowing for a second trial where there are new or newly discovered facts (*novum*), or if there has been a fundamental defect in the previous proceedings affecting the outcome of the case. This includes new or newly discovered evidence, including new means of proof.[19]

---

[16] In some legal systems, this guarantee finds expression in a procedural rule which stipulates that only the highest penalty is actually enforced in the event that several penalties are imposed in respect of the same event, or course of events.

[17] In the *Franz Fischer* judgment, the ECtHR expressly held that Art. 4 of Protocol no. 7 'is not confined to the right not to be punished twice but extends to the right not to be tried twice', *Franz Fischer* v. *Austria*, ECtHR 29 May 2001, appl. no. 37950/97. See also: *Sergey Zolotukhin* v. *Russia*, ECtHR (GC) 10 February 2009, appl. no. 1493/03.

[18] *Sergey Zolotukhin* v. *Russia*, ECtHR (GC) 10 February 2009, appl. no. 1493/03, para. 110.

[19] Explanatory Report at point 31.

2.1.2   Article 50 of the Charter of Fundamental Rights of the European Union

Article 50 of the Charter of Fundamental Rights of the European Union ('the Charter') reads as follows:

> No one shall be liable to be tried or punished again in criminal proceedings for an offence for which he or she has already been finally acquitted or convicted within the Union in accordance with the law.

The Charter was proclaimed on 7 December 2000 in Nice and

> reaffirms, with due regard for the powers and tasks of the Community and the Union and the principle of subsidiarity, the rights as they result, in particular, from the constitutional traditions and international obligations common to the Member States, the Treaty on European Union, the Community Treaties, the European Convention for the Protection of Human Rights and Fundamental Freedoms, the Social Charters adopted by the Community and by the Council of Europe and the case law of the Court of Justice of the European Communities and of the European Court of Human Rights.[20]

According to Annex IV to the Conclusions of the Presidency of the Cologne European Council of 3–4 June 1999, the aim was 'to establish a Charter of fundamental rights in order to make their overriding importance and relevance more visible to the Union's citizens'.

The Venice Commission concluded that the Charter is 'obviously inspired by the ECHR', but that there 'exist however significant differences between the two instruments, relating to both the wording and the scope of the rights guaranteed':

> In respect of the rights which are also listed in the ECHR, the Charter has taken as an example the text of the latter, but has often modified it with a view to rendering it simpler, more up-to-date, and at times broader. Possibilities for limitations of the rights guaranteed by the Charter are not enumerated right-by-right, like in the ECHR, but are contained in a general provision (Article 52 of the Charter), without an exhaustive enumeration of the grounds for limitation. Further, certain rights guaranteed by the Charter are not listed in the ECHR, but have been recognised by the case-law of the European Court as being encompassed by it.[21]

---

[20] Preamble, at para. 5.

[21] European Commission for Democracy through law ('Venice Commission'), Opinion 256/2003, 18 December 2003, www.venice.coe.int/webforms/documents/?pdf=CDL-AD (2003)022-e.

The Explanatory Memorandum provided by the Bureau of the Convention, the body which drafted the Charter, states that:

> in accordance with Article 50, the "non bis in idem" principle applies not only within the jurisdiction of one State but also between the jurisdictions of several Member States. That corresponds to the *acquis* in Union law; see Articles 54 to 58 of the Schengen Convention, Article 7 of the Convention on the Protection of the European Communities' Financial Interests and Article 10 of the Convention on the fight against corruption.[22]

Art. 50 Charter is succinctly worded when compared to the provisions cited in the Explanatory Memorandum. Like many Charter rights, Art. 50 captures the essence of the *ne bis in idem* principle, possibly in order to avoid conflict with other *ne bis in idem* provisions. Now that the Charter has become legally binding primary EU law, an important question is whether this economy of words intentionally gave Art. 50 Charter stronger protective force than other European *ne bis in idem* provisions (*inter alia* by not including the exception possibility from Art. 4 (2) of Protocol no. 7 ECHR or the enforcement condition from Art. 54 CISA) or whether Art. 50 Charter should be interpreted 'in accordance with' the other provisions mentioned in the Explanatory Memorandum, so that particular features of pre-existing *ne bis in idem* provisions in EU law will remain unaffected by the wording of Art. 50 Charter. In essence, the question is therefore how discrepancies between Charter rights and other fundamental rights provisions in EU law should be dealt with, and this question presents itself for many other Charter rights. In theory, there are different methods available to the Court when dealing with possible conflict between different provisions in EU law: by way of recourse to the hierarchy of legal norms in the EU legal order and/or Art. 52 of the Charter, or by way of 'integrative' interpretation between different provisions. For the *ne bis in idem* principle these questions were addressed by the Court for the first time in the *Zoran Spasic* judgment discussed later in this chapter (Section 2.1.4).

---

[22] www.europarl.europa.eu/charter/pdf/04473_en.pdf.

2.1.3 Articles 54–58 of the Convention Implementing the Schengen Agreement[23]

Articles 54–58 of CISA read as follows:

Article 54: A person whose trial has been finally disposed of in one Contracting Party may not be prosecuted in another Contracting Party for the same acts provided that, if a penalty has been imposed, it has been enforced, is actually in the process of being enforced or can no longer be enforced under the laws of the sentencing Contracting Party.

Article 55: 1. A Contracting Party may, when ratifying, accepting or approving this Convention, declare that it is not bound by Article 54 in one or more of the following cases:

(a) where the acts to which the foreign judgment relates took place in whole or in part in its own territory; in the latter case, however, this exception shall not apply if the acts took place in part in the territory of the Contracting Party where the judgment was delivered;

(b) where the acts to which the foreign judgment relates constitute an offence against national security or other equally essential interests of that Contracting Party;

(c) where the acts to which the foreign judgment relates were committed by officials of that Contracting Party in violation of the duties of their office.

2. A Contracting Party which has made a declaration regarding the exception referred to in paragraph 1(b) shall specify the categories of offences to which this exception may apply.

3. A Contracting Party may at any time withdraw a declaration relating to one or more of the exceptions referred to in paragraph 1.

4. The exceptions which were the subject of a declaration under paragraph 1 shall not apply where the Contracting Party concerned has, in connection with the same acts, requested the other Contracting Party to bring the prosecution or has granted extradition of the person concerned.

Article 56: If a further prosecution is brought in a Contracting Party against a person whose trial, in respect of the same acts, has been finally disposed of in another Contracting Party, any period of deprivation of liberty served in the latter Contracting Party arising from those acts shall be deducted from any penalty imposed. To the extent permitted by national law, penalties not involving deprivation of liberty shall also be taken into account.

Article 57: 1. Where a Contracting Party charges a person with an offence and the competent authorities of that Contracting Party have

---

[23] Convention of 19 June 1990 implementing the Schengen Agreement, [2000] OJ L239/19.

reason to believe that the charge relates to the same acts as those in respect of which the person's trial has been finally disposed of in another Contracting Party, those authorities shall, if they deem it necessary, request the relevant information from the competent authorities of the Contracting Party in whose territory judgment has already been delivered.

2. The information requested shall be provided as soon as possible and shall be taken into consideration as regards further action to be taken in the proceedings underway.

3. Each Contracting Party shall, when ratifying, accepting or approving this Convention, nominate the authorities authorised to request and receive the information provided for in this Article.

Article 58:The above provisions shall not preclude the application of broader national provisions on the *ne bis in idem* principle with regard to judicial decisions taken abroad.

Although the 1985 Schengen-agreement and the 1990 CISA (together: the 'Schengen-agreements') were concluded outside of the Community framework between the original five 'Schengen-group States',[24] they were drafted with European integration in mind and are functionally linked to the objective of free movement of persons. Around the same time as the Schengen-agreements were adopted, the 1987 'Convention between the Member States of the European Communities on Double Jeopardy' was opened for ratification by the Member States. Although it was never adopted, the 1987 Convention was very similar in wording to the 1990 CISA on the point of the *ne bis in idem* principle, but was more supranational in design due to the fact that it lacked the more intergovernmental exceptions of Art. 55 CISA. At the EU Intergovernmental Conference (IGC) of 1996, the Deputy Minister of Foreign Affairs of the Netherlands submitted a proposal for the integration of the Schengen *acquis* into the framework of the (then) 'Third Pillar' of the EU, enabling the EU to benefit from the progress that had been made within the 'Schengen-framework'. Three years later, the Schengen *acquis* was successfully 'hijacked' by the EU with the entry into force of the Treaty of Amsterdam, and became (secondary) EU law.

The aim of the Schengen-agreements is twofold: to establish free circulation of persons by abolishing border checks, while at the same time implementing countervailing measures facilitating the cross-border enforcement of criminal law through police cooperation, mutual assistance in criminal matters, extradition,[25] transfer and enforcement of

---

[24] The Netherlands, Belgium, Luxemburg, Germany and France.

[25] The European Arrest Warrant has since replaced the extradition provisions of the Schengen-agreements.

judgments, and the Schengen Information System (SIS). Art. 54 CISA is regarded as the most developed expression of an internationally applicable *ne bis in idem* rule in force in the way it is worded, although its protective force is watered down in Art. 55 CISA. As discussed at several points in this study, the case law on this provision has greatly contributed to the development of the 'European' *ne bis in idem* principle.[26] At the same time it is clear from the context of the Schengen Agreements that the wording of Art. 54 CISA does not necessarily reflect any particular supranational human rights ambitions on the part of the drafters. The CISA is closely linked to extradition and was in many ways drawn up in a spirit of intergovernmental, rather than supranational enforcement cooperation between states. *Inter alia*, this may be evidenced by the way in which the Schengen-agreements were adopted outside of the EU framework, by the scope of application of Art. 54 CISA (applying *between* the Schengen states), by the exception possibilities laid down in Art. 55 CISA, and by the requirement that the previous penalty must have 'been enforced, or can no longer be enforced' from Art. 54 CISA. In jurisdictions in which foreign *res iudicata* is legally recognized and accepted this enforcement requirement applies only in relation to *foreign* judgments. Arguably, the wording of Art. 54 CISA where it refers to the same 'acts' (instead of 'offences') also follows from the same because the legal qualification of the same acts will necessarily vary between jurisdictions. The need for a clearly worded and broad *ne bis in idem* rule such as Art. 54 CISA is clear, given the aim of the extradition provisions in the Schengen-agreements.[27] At the same time however, the majority of national *ne bis in idem* rules emphasize the objective, historical facts over their legal qualification, also in domestic situations. On the one hand, the specific context of the Schengen-agreements could therefore justify some interpretative differences in case law of the CJEU. In national systems of law, extradition is procedurally distinct from the actual trial in which the full bill of national procedural and constitutional rights protects the subject, so that different standards of protection may be deemed acceptable. On the other hand, however, a transnational fundamental right like Art. 54 CISA does not exist in interpretative

---

[26] Although it must be admitted that this is to a significant degree due to the fact that it refers to 'acts' rather than 'offences'.

[27] These provisions aimed to simplify and expedite extradition procedures between the Member States much in the same way as the European Arrest Warrant that later replaced them.

isolation from other *ne bis in idem* provisions in different legal orders once it has come about. The CJEU will therefore have to provide some justification for any interpretative differentiation beyond that what can be distilled from a literal reading of the provisions, both in the light of the specific goals of the EU in the AFSJ, as well as in view of the overall need to secure a coherent and consistent body of fundamental rights jurisprudence in the EU.

2.2   Connecting the Dots? The Boere and Spasic Judgments

In addition to the case law on the *ne bis in idem* principle itself, the case law of the CJEU on Arts. 51–53 Charter increasingly co-shapes the interpretation and application of the n*e bis in idem* principle in the EU legal order, and this case law is discussed at different points in this study. The relationship between Charter and Convention rights is governed by Art. 52(3) of the Charter (the so-called homogeneity clause). As discussed in Chapter 3, paragraphs 2–4, the CJEU has so far adhered to a 'minimalist' interpretation of this provision amongst other things by not addressing the question of the relationship between Charter and Convention rights directly, and by omitting references to the case law of the ECtHR in some judgments. The CJEU has thus carved out ample discretionary room *vis-à-vis* the case law of the ECtHR in interpreting Charter rights.

In the *Spasic* judgment the CJEU addressed the relationship between Arts. 54 CISA and 50 Charter.[28] In order to get a sense of the direction that the case law of the CJEU is taking, it is useful to discuss this judgement in somewhat more detail. The questions referred by the *Oberlandesgericht* (higher regional court) at Nurnberg in the main proceedings against Mr Spasic specifically concerned the requirement of the enforcement of the previous penalty from Art. 54 CISA. As previously discussed, this requirement does not feature in Art. 50 Charter and questions were consequently raised on the point of its compatibility with the latter. The case concerned Mr Spasic, a Serbian national, who was prosecuted before the regional court in Regensburg, Germany for organised fraud committed against a German national, and the German authorities issued a European Arrest Warrant with a view to his surrender. He had previously been tried in Italy for these same facts and was

---

[28] Case C-129/14 PPU, *Spasic, EU:C:2014:586.*

sentenced *in absentia* to imprisonment, as well as a modest fine. In the meanwhile, he was being held in custody in Austria on grounds not directly connected to those at issue in the case German courts. After Mr Spasic was surrendered to the German authorities and was remanded in custody there, he paid the Italian fine. In the proceedings before the German regional court, his lawyers argued *inter alia* that although he never served his prison term in Italy, his sentence had consequently been 'enforced' within the meaning of Art. 54 CISA through the payment of the fine, and that he should be released from custody. When this plea was rejected by the court, Mr Spasic appealed to the higher regional court in Nurnberg on the grounds that the requirement of the enforcement of the enforcement of the previous penalty would violate Art. 50 of the Charter. This court thereupon stayed proceedings and referred questions to the CJEU asking whether the enforcement requirement from Art. 54 CISA is compatible with Art. 50 Charter.

Before discussing the judgment of the CJEU, it is worth noting that the questions referred by the German court in this case may not have come as a surprise, or at least not to some. In 2011 the German Federal Supreme Court (*Bundesverfassungsgericht*) had already held in its *Boere* judgment that the enforcement requirement from Art. 54 CISA forms a limitation of Art. 50 Charter, compatible with Art. 52(1) Charter.[29] The *Bundesverfassungsgericht* further more ruled there was 'no doubt' as to these findings, and therefore no need to refer any questions to the CJEU in a reference for a preliminary ruling. The higher regional court at Nurnberg was therefore entirely right in referring questions to the CJEU in the *Spasic* case in order to verify the validity, as a matter of EU law, of the approach taken by the *Bundesverfassungsgericht* in *Boere*. At the same time however, this may have presented the CJEU with the choice of whether or not to second-guess the *Bundesverfassungsgericht* that may perhaps have been awkward in view of the dynamic relationship between those two courts. It is helpful to briefly sketch the facts and backgrounds of this case in order to better appreciate how the *Boere* judgment may have foreshadowed the *Spasic* judgment.

The case of *Boere* concerned a former Dutch national who was a member of the so-called *Kommando-Silbertanne*, an elite SS squad that carried out executions of citizens in the Netherlands in retaliation for actions by the resistance during WWII. After the end of the war,

---

[29] Judgment (ECLI): DE:BVerfG:2011:rk20111215.2bvr014811.

Mr Boere was sentenced to death *in absentia* in the Netherlands but escaped to Germany where he remained free from prosecution during the decades that followed. When he was finally prosecuted for his actions in the Netherlands during WWII before a German court in 2009, his lawyers relied on the transnational *ne bis in idem* principle in EU law in view of Boere's previous conviction in the Netherlands. Although both the facts of the case as well as the first judgment predate the project of European integration itself, this does not stand in the way of the application *ratione temporis* of Arts. 54–58 CISA if the second prosecution was brought at a time that the CISA had entered into force as also confirmed by the CJEU in the case of *Bourquain*.[30] Mr Boere however was prevented from relying directly on Art. 54 CISA in this case because his earlier sentence in the Netherlands had never been enforced against him. In his defence before the German courts his lawyers argued that the enforcement requirement from Art. 54 CISA would form an unlawful limitation of Art. 50 of the Charter, and that Boere's prosecution therefore violated the *ne bis in idem* principle in EU law, but this plea was thrown out by subsequent German courts. The case reached the *Bundesverfassungsgericht*, which confirmed that the enforcement requirement from Art. 54 CISA forms a 'limitation' of the *ne bis in idem* principle of Art. 50 of the Charter, but held this limitation to be compatible with Art. 52(1) of the Charter.

In its *Spasic* judgment the CJEU followed the approach of the *Bundesverfassungsgericht* (although without reference to the latter). The CJEU based its approach mainly on the Explanations relating to the Charter. Point 54 of the judgment in particular is of interest in this regard:

> The explanations relating to the Charter as regards Article 50 — which, in accordance with the third subparagraph of Article 6(1) TEU and Article 52 (7) of the Charter, were drawn up in order to provide guidance in the interpretation of the Charter and must be duly taken into consideration both by the Courts of the European Union and by the courts of the Member States — *expressly mention Article 54 CISA among the provisions covered by the horizontal clause in Article 52(1) of the Charter.*[31] (italics added)

This last phrase is remarkable, because the Explanations to Art. 50 of the Charter do *not* actually mention Art. 54 CISA as being 'among the

---

[30] Case C-297/07, *Bourquain*, EU:C:2008:708.   [31] *Spasic*, at 54.

provisions covered by the horizontal clause in Article 52(1) of the Charter'. The Explanations do not, in fact, mention any specific provisions but merely refer to the 'very limited exceptions' found in the relevant Conventions:

> In accordance with Article 50, the 'non bis in idem' rule applies not only within the jurisdiction of one State but also between the jurisdictions of several Member States. That corresponds to the acquis in Union law; see Articles 54 to 58 of the Schengen Convention and the judgment of the Court of Justice of 11 February 2003, C-187/01 Gözütok [2003] ECR I-1345, Article 7 of the Convention on the Protection of the European Communities' Financial Interests and Article 10 of the Convention on the fight against corruption. *The very limited exceptions in those Conventions permitting the Member States to derogate from the 'non bis in idem' rule are covered by the horizontal clause in Article 52(1) of the Charter concerning limitations.* (Italics added)

For the CISA, the exceptions are found in Art. 55, which provision allows a Member State to declare that it is not bound by Art. 54 in respect of certain previously specified categories of offences. It's a limited list of acts with a strong link to the sovereignty and territorial integrity of the state: acts which took place in the territory of the State, offences against national security or other important interests of the State, and acts committed by the state's officials. Although it can be concluded that the Explanations provide less support for the Court's reasoning in *Spasic* than it would appear from that judgment seems justified, there is no doubt that the enforcement requirement from Art. 54 features among the more intergovernmental aspects of the CISA and places certain restrictions on the exercise of the *ne bis in idem* in that provision. The developments in the AFSJ that followed the conclusion of the CISA and its incorporation into the EU's legal order may justify a re-examination of some of its provisions, amongst other things in the light of the provisions of the Charter and the objectives of the EU in the AFSJ. Art. 52(1) of the Charter reads a follows:

> Any limitation on the exercise of the rights and freedoms recognised by this Charter must be provided for by law and respect the essence of those rights and freedoms. Subject to the principle of proportionality, limitations may be made only if they are necessary and genuinely meet objectives of general interest recognised by the Union or the need to protect the rights and freedoms of others.

The first sentence mentions the 'essence' of Charter rights, a suitable measure of the compatibility of an expression or aspect of a fundamental right in EU law (in this case: the enforcement requirement from Art. 54 CISA) with the provisions of the Charter, as many Charter rights could be seen as expressions of the 'essence' of those rights. In *Spasic*, however, the Court stopped short of examining what the 'essence' of the *ne bis in idem* entails, merely holding that:

> (T)he execution condition laid down in Article 54 CISA does not call into question the *ne bis in idem* principle as such. That condition is intended, *inter alia*, to avoid a situation in which a person definitively convicted and sentenced in one Contracting State can no longer be prosecuted for the same acts in another Contracting State and therefore ultimately remains unpunished if the first State did not execute the sentence imposed.[32]

It is worth exploring the question of what an actual examination of the 'essence' of a Charter rights could have looked like if the Court would have gone so far as to carry out in *Spasic*. A quick comparison of some national *ne bis in idem* provisions in the legal orders of the Member States shows that, contrary to for example the possibility of an exception in the case of new or newly discovered evidence (*novum*), the enforcement requirement only features in jurisdictions which recognize *ne bis in idem* effect of foreign *res iudicata*, and only applies in respect of those foreign *res iudicata*.[33] There appears to be no *ne bis in idem* provision in existence in any of the Member States that contains any requirements similar to that found in Art. 54 CISA as far as the enforcement of the previous penalty in domestic situations is concerned. It could be concluded from this that the enforcement requirement from Art. 54 CISA does not reflect any part of the 'essence' of national *ne bis in idem* rules, and this may be evidenced also by the wording of Art. 4 of Protocol no. 7 ECHR as well as that of other provisions in international conventions like Art. 14(7) ICCPR. From there, it is a small step to reason that that condition does not *respect* the essence of the *ne bis in idem* principle.[34] In his View, the Advocate General also went on to examine what the 'essence' of the *ne bis in idem* principle entailed based on 'the development of the international and national protection of that fundamental right', but came to somewhat different findings without further explaining the method applied or the reasoning that led to the identification of different elements of the principle.[35]

---

[32] *Spasic*, at 58.   [33] As is the case in Belgium and the Netherlands, amongst others.
[34] The Court merely held that the enforcement requirement 'does not call into question the *ne bis in idem* principle as such'.
[35] View of Advocate General Jaaskinen in *Spasic*, at 88.

The Court went on to examine whether the enforcement requirement can be regarded as fulfilling an objective of general interest and whether it respects the principle of proportionality. As regards the former, the Court observed that the enforcement condition is 'necessary to meet the objective of general interest of preventing, in the area of freedom, security and justice, the impunity of persons definitively convicted and sentenced in one EU Member State', which almost appears a truism.[36] Further down, the judgment rightfully holds that 'the system established by Art. 54 CISA, such prosecutions would take place only in cases where the system currently provided by EU law was — for whatever reason — not sufficient to prevent the impunity of persons definitively convicted and sentenced in the European Union'.[37] Based on this, the Court arrived at the finding that the principle of proportionality is respected. Unsurprisingly, the Court ruled that the fact that Mr Spasic paid the fine was not sufficient to fulfil the enforcement requirement.

Some comments to the judgment are in order. One is that, due to their particularly wide and potentially vying nature, any reasoning based on an interpretation of the objectives of the EU in the AFSJ or on a particular ranking order between them will necessarily be open to debate. This is a problem that the EU legal order faces in many policy areas due to its strongly purposive nature, but it is perhaps particularly obvious in the AFSJ. At the root of this problem are two main problems: i) the open-ended, non-legal and potentially vying nature of policy objectives and ii) the fact that those objectives come before the legal rules that are subsequently adopted in order to realize them. Paragraphs 62 and 63 of the judgment are particularly illustrative in this regard:

> As can be seen from Article 67(3) TFEU, in order to achieve its objective of constituting an area of freedom, security and justice, the European Union endeavours to ensure a high level of security through measures to prevent and combat crime, and through measures for coordination and cooperation between police and judicial authorities and other competent authorities, as well as through the mutual recognition of judgments in criminal matters and, if necessary, through the approximation of criminal laws. The execution condition laid down in Article 54 CISA is to be seen in that context since it is intended, as noted in paragraph 58 of the present judgment, to prevent, in the area of freedom, security and justice, the impunity of persons definitively convicted and sentenced in an EU Member State.

---

[36] Para. 65 of the judgment.   [37] Para. 71 of the judgment.

Here, it appears the Court could equally have come to the opposite finding based on *inter alia* the principle of mutual recognition in the AFSJ, and the necessary implication that a 'high level of trust' exists between the Member States. There is an important although at times difficult to make distinction between the *objectives* of the EU (in this case in the AFSJ), and the *principles* that have been established in its connection. One could speculate that the Court may have failed to sufficiently distinguish between the relevant policy objectives (here: a 'high level of security', or in the same connection the 'prevention of impunity') and the underlying principles (here: mutual recognition and mutual trust). The manner in which the CJEU appears to give precedence to the objective of 'security' over that of 'freedom' (or 'justice') here appears fortuitous.

In the end, the Court stopped short of fundamentally addressing the relationship between Arts. 50 Charter and 54 CISA in *Spasic*, and this is perhaps understandable given the special background of the case. Although there are without doubt valid reasons for the Court to uphold the enforcement requirement in Art. 54 CISA (as may be illustrated by the *Boere* case) the reasoning of the Court in *Spasic* lacks conviction on a number of points. The manner in which the Court develops the proportionality test from Art. 52(1) Charter in the judgment is summary, and appears to be based solely on the objective of maintaining a 'high level of security' or that of the 'prevention of impunity' within the AFSJ. Arguably, that isn't really a proportionality test at all. In his View, the Advocate General came to the opposite conclusion, arguing that the enforcement requirement was indeed disproportionate in view of the aim of preventing impunity. It can be expected that questions of the relationship between the provisions of the Charter and other fundamental rights provisions in EU law will resurface in the case law.

3   Scope of Application of the *Ne Bis in Idem* Guarantee

There are several aspects to the scope of application of the *ne bis in idem* principle in EU law which are discussed at different points in this study. The *Åkerberg Fransson* judgment[38] on the scope of the Charter as laid down in Art. 51 Charter is discussed in more detail *inter alia* in Chapter 2, Section 4.2 *et seq*. In Chapter 5 the tax implications of that judgment are gauged. Chapter 4 discusses the questions raised by the *Walt Wilhelm*

---

[38]   Case C-617/10, *Åkerberg Fransson*, EU:C:2013:280.

and *Toshiba* judgments. Among other things it is argued there that the Court has so far avoided addressing the relationship between its inter-pretation of *ne bis in idem* principle in the competition cases and in its case law on the CISA. As discussed further down in this paragraph, these questions tie in closely with the scope of the Charter as laid down in Art. 51 Charter (*Åkerberg Fransson* and *Melloni*[39] judgments).

The following (sub)paragraphs of this chapter provides an overview of different aspects of the scope of application of the *ne bis in idem* principle. Particular attention is given to the scope of application of the guarantee *ratione materiae* in the case law of the ECtHR, which raises many potential questions and issues for EU law. This paragraph con-cludes with some remarks on the subjective and temporal scope of application of the *ne bis in idem* principle. Although kept to a minimum, some overlap with the other chapters of this study cannot be fully avoided without compromising the overall structure of this study.

3.1   Objective Scope of Application of the Guarantee

The application of the *ne bis in idem* principle is traditionally limited to situations within one and the same state. This limitation is not a condition for the application of the *ne bis in idem* principle as such, but a consequence of the unwillingness of states to accept the negative enforce-ment consequences of foreign *res iudicata*. Several reasons have been cited for this in legal literature. Among those are the fact that accepting the negative enforcement consequences of foreign decisions requires a high degree of confidence in the other states, that self-interest may incite states to reconsider criminal prosecution (in particular if the crime was committed on their own territory or affects their important national interests, as for example reflected in Art. 55 CISA) and furthermore that the *ne bis in idem* principle itself varies significantly from one state to another. If one considers the issue of the international non-application of the *ne bis in idem* principle in the light of the general criminal law aims of punishment and deterrence, the problem lies with the general lack of confidence of states have in the ability of other states to achieve a level of punishment and deterrence that is comparable to their own. This is understandable, for example in situations in which the litigious act has cross-border elements if certain aspects of the infringement can

---

[39]   *Ibid.*; Case C-399/11, *Melloni*, EU:C:2013:107.

consequently not be taken into account in the proceedings in another state. This can be so due to a lack of jurisdiction, or due to practical restraints in setting up an international investigation, gathering the necessary evidence, and restraining the subject. Under those circumstances, a foreign prosecution will (usually) lead to a lower sentence than what is deemed desirable. In the EU, these and similar issues have been addressed *inter alia* through the adoption and implementation of mutual recognition instruments like the European Arrest Warrant and the European Evidence Warrant,[40] and by furthering cooperation between national authorities cooperation instruments[41] and networks like Eurojust and Europol. Another important issue in the EU is that the differences between national criminal laws and procedures in the Member States continues to place some limitations on the willingness of Member States to mutually accept the full *ne bis in idem* consequences of each others' judicial decisions, as may be evidenced for example by the exception clauses in the European Arrest Warrant Framework Directive and the CISA. Here, the role of the EU is limited to harmonization in the field of so-called Euro-crimes,[42] as well as harmonization of (national) criminal law with regard to some EU policies based on the competence provided for in Art. 83 TFEU. The further development of an AFSJ in the

---

[40] Council Framework Decision 2008/978/JHA on the European evidence warrant for the purpose of obtaining objects, documents and data for use in proceedings in criminal matters. Other mutual recognition instruments include Council Framework Decision 2008/909/JHA of 27 November 2008 on the application of the principle of mutual recognition to judgments in criminal matters imposing custodial sentences or measures involving deprivation of liberty; Council Framework Decision 2008/947/JHA of 27 November 2008 on the application of the principle of mutual recognition to judgments and probation decisions with a view to the supervision of probation measures and alternative sanctions; and Council Framework Decision 2003/577/JHA on the execution in the European Union of orders freezing property or evidence.

[41] Among these are: Council Decision 2009/316/JHA of 6 April 2009 on the establishment of the European Criminal Records Information System (ECRIS) in application of Article 11 of Framework Decision 2009/315/JHA; Council Decision 2005/671/JHA of 20 September 2005 on the exchange of information and cooperation concerning terrorist offences; Council Framework Decision 2006/960/JHA of 18 December 2006 on simplifying the exchange of information and intelligence between law enforcement authorities of the Member States of the European Union, and Council Framework Decision 2008/977/JHA on the protection of personal data processed in the framework of police and judicial cooperation in criminal matters.

[42] Such as: Directive 2011/36/EU of the European Parliament and of the Council of 5 April 2011 on preventing and combating trafficking in human beings and protecting its victims and Directive 2011/93/EU of the European Parliament and of the Council of 13 December 2011 on combating the sexual abuse and sexual exploitation of children and child

EU, the implementation of the mutual recognition principle in that Area and the necessity of building a high level of mutual trust between the Member states are therefore intrinsically linked to the 'full' application of the *ne bis in idem* principle in EU law, and none of these have been fully realized so that some limitations on the application of the *ne bis in idem* principle in EU law may be considered as justified, as also confirmed by the Court in the aforementioned *Spasic* judgment.

It is worth mentioning here that there is increasing criticism of the international non-application of the *ne bis in idem* principle. If an offence was satisfactorily adjudicated in another jurisdiction, any further enforcement action harms both the states that channel their state resources towards unnecessary prosecutions, as well as the subjects who are disproportionally affected by double prosecution and penalties. However self-evident this may appear, if the possibility of accepting the negative enforcement consequences of foreign *res iudicata* is framed as a question of the sovereignty of states, the argument becomes impenetrable given the difficulty of weighing the interests of 'sovereignty' against those of 'justice', or of 'the individual'.

As further discussed in Chapter 2, Section 4.2 *et seq* of this study, the CJEU has held in the *Åkerberg Fransson*[43] judgment that the scope of the Charter coincides with that of EU law itself but goes no further than that. In the case of *Pfleger*, the CJEU confirmed that this also covers the so-called *ERT*-type of situation in which a Member State *derogates* from EU law.[44] The *Siragusa* judgment and the order in *Sindicato dos Bancários do Norte*[45] further clarify that not every connection with EU law is sufficient to trigger the application of the Charter.[46] The case of *Sindicato dos Bancários do Norte* concerned bank personnel in Portugal litigating against a nationalized bank which had significantly reduced wages as from January 2011 to comply with the national budget law providing for wage reduction in respect of all civil servants with a view to meeting the requirements of the EU Stability and Growth Pact (SGP). Even though the national legislation was adopted in order to comply with Portugal's

---

pornography, Council Framework Decision 2008/919/JHA of 28 November 2008 amending Framework Decision 2002/475/JHA on combating terrorism, and Council Framework Decision 2008/841/JHA of 24 October 2008 on the fight against organized crime.

[43] Case C-617/10, *Åkerberg Fransson*, EU:C:2013:280.
[44] Case C-390/12, *Pfleger*, EU:C:2014:281.
[45] Case C-128/12, *Sindicato dos Bancários do Norte*, EU:C:2013:149.
[46] Case C-206/13, *Siragusa*, EU:C:2014:126; see also: *Sindicato dos Bancários do Norte*.

obligations under the SGP, the CJEU ruled that it was not competent to address the questions referred to it by the Portuguese court as there was no 'implementation of EU law' in the sense of Art. 51 Charter. The relationship between the *Åkerberg Fransson* and *Sindicato dos Bancários do Norte* judgments is not entirely clear and there remains a degree of uncertainty as regards the question how 'strong' the link between national and EU law must be in order for the Charter to apply. Notwithstanding the importance of questions of the applicability of the Charter for the EU legal order, the actual impact of Charter rights in proceedings before national courts may for now prove limited. One reason for this is that large parts of the Charter remain untouched by the case law of the CJEU, so that much is left to the attitude of the national judiciary when applying Charter rights, or referring questions to the CJEU. Another is that in cases like *Åkerberg Fransson*,[47] the CJEU leaves the actual determination of whether there has been an infringement of a Charter right to the referring court. This may be part of a wider judicial strategy on the part of the CJEU aimed at ceding as little as possible of its exclusive role as the EU's highest constitutional court to the ECtHR, while at the same time leaving the national judiciary some space to make its own determination of fundamental rights issues where its citizens are concerned in situations under the Charter.

In competition matters, questions of the objective scope of application of the *ne bis in idem* principle in EU law have long featured in the case law of the EU courts under the guise of a particular interpretation of the element of '*idem*'. By consequence, the question of the objective scope and the interpretation of the element of *idem* in that case law have been mixed up. This makes aspects of this case law difficult to categorize for the purposes of a study like the present. The jurisprudential developments in the field of competition law are seminal for the development of the *ne bis in idem* principle in the EU legal order *inter alia* because the judgments in *Walt Wilhelm*[48] and *Boehringer*[49] were the first judgments in which the *ne bis in idem* principle was considered by the Court, and the applicability of the principle in the EU context was henceforth accepted by implication.[50]

---

[47] Case C-617/10, *Åkerberg Fransson*, EU:C:2013:280.
[48] Case 14–68, *Walt Wilhelm and others v. Bundeskartellamt*, EU:C:1969:4.
[49] Case 7/72, *Boehringer Mannheim v. Commission*, EU:C:1972:125.
[50] It is worth noting that the first judgment in which the application *ratione materiae* of the *ne bis in idem* principle in competition matters was explicitly confirmed was the

The *Walt Wilhelm* judgment which is also discussed in Section 3.5 of Chapter 4 concerned an agreement between a group of German undertakings. The German Competition Authority (*Bundeskartellamt*) had initiated proceedings under German competition law, after the Commission had done the same on the basis of (then) Article 85 EC (now: Article 101 TFEU). The Competition Chamber (*Kartellsenat*) of the Berlin Court (*Kammergericht Berlin*) referred several questions to the (then) European Court of Justice (ECJ) in preliminary ruling proceedings asking whether national authorities are at liberty to 'apply to the same facts the provisions of national law' after the Commission has initiated proceedings in the same case. In addition, the ECJ was asked whether 'the risk of its resulting in a double sanction imposed by the Commission . . . and by the national authority with jurisdiction in cartel matters renders impossible the acceptance for one set of facts of two parallel procedures'.[51] The Court replied that Regulation 17/62 only dealt with the competence of the authorities of the Member States in so far as they are authorized to apply the Treaty provision in situations in which the Commission has not taken action, and did not apply to situations in which national authorities apply *national* competition laws. According to the Court, 'Community and national law on cartels consider cartels from different points of view. Whereas Article . . . 85 (now: Article 101 TFEU, *red.*) regards them in the light of obstacles which may result for trade between the Member States, each body of national legislation proceeds on the basis of the considerations peculiar to it and considers cartels only in that context.' Therefore, although the 'economic phenomena and legal situations' concerned may well be 'interdependent', 'one and the same agreement may, in principle, be the object of two sets of parallel proceedings'.[52] In the judgment, the Court emphasized that Article 83 EC (now: Article 103 TFEU) authorizes the Council 'to determine the relationship' between national competition laws and the competition provisions from the Treaty, but that the Council had not availed itself of this particular competence in adopting Regulation 17/62. This left the Member States free in the application of national competition laws, with the important proviso that 'if the ultimate general aim of the Treaty is to be respected, this parallel application of the national system can only be

---

judgment of the CFI in the PVC cartel cases (Joined Cases T-305/94, T-306/94, T-307/94, T-313/94, T-314/94, T-315/94, T-316/94, T-318/94, T-325/94, T-328/94, T-329/94 and T-335/94 PVC, EU:T:1999:80).

[51] Para. 3 of the judgment.   [52] Para. 3 of the judgment.

allowed in so far as it does not prejudice the uniform application throughout the common market of the Community rules on cartels and of the full effect of the measures adopted in implementation of those rules'.[53]

In its later judgments in the *Cement cartel* cases, the Court followed the Opinion of the Advocate General in formulating a 'threefold identity' for the application of the *ne bis in idem* principle in competition matters: the 'identity of the facts, unity of offender and unity of the legal interest protected'.[54] By the time these cases were brought, however, the legal situation was quite different than at the time of *Walt Wilhelm*. By then, the Member States had adopted competition laws along the lines of the Treaty provisions although they were never under any formal EU legal obligation to do so. For this reason, the Advocate General argued in his Opinion that there can be no doubt as to the unity of the legal interest at stake as far as competition matters are concerned because 'the rules which guarantee free competition within the European Union do not allow a distinction to be drawn between separate areas, the Community area and the national areas, as though there were watertight compartments'.[55] The Court did not go so far as to confirm this, as it found that the material facts at issue were not identical, and that there had consequently been no breach of the *ne bis in idem* principle.

In *Toshiba*[56], the Court reiterated this approach. The case concerned a worldwide cartel on the market for gas insulated switchgear (GIS) which was active between 1988 and 2004. The companies involved were fined by the Commission and the Czech competition authority. The cartel formed a single continuous infringement. The Commission decision only concerned the implementation of the cartel within the EU in the period prior to accession of the Czech republic (1 May 2004). The decision of the Czech competition authority concerned the implementation of the cartel within the Czech Republic in two periods before the date of accession: 'up and until' 30 June 2001 under the 'old' Czech competition law, and between 30 June 2001 and 3 March 2004 under the Czech

---

[53] Para. 4 of the judgment.

[54] Joined Cases C-204/00 P, C-205/00 P, C-211/00 P, C-213/00 PC-217/00 P and C-219/00 P, *Aalborg Portland and others* v. *Commission*, EU:T:1999:80, para. 338; Opinion of Advocate General Colomer delivered on 11 Feb. 2003 in Case C-217/00 P, *Buzzi Unicem* v. *Commission*, EU:C:2003:85, para. 171.

[55] Para. 173 of the Opinion.

[56] Case C-17/10, *Toshiba and Others*, EU:C:2012:72, para. 99.

competition law as amended.[57] Both decisions were adopted *after* the date of accession of the Czech Republic and after the entry into force of Regulation 1/2003, but before the entry into force of the Lisbon Treaty (1 December 2009), and therefore before the Charter acquired its legally binding status. The Court held that the parallel procedures by the Czech competition authority and the Commission did not infringe the *ne bis in idem* principle, given that:

> the Commission's decision refers specifically, in many of its passages, to the consequences of the cartel at issue in the main proceedings within the European Community and the EEA [European Economic Area], referring expressly to the 'Member States of the time' and the States 'which were contracting parties' to the EEA Agreement. Next . . . that decision does not penalise the possible anti-competitive effects produced by that cartel in the territory of the Czech Republic during the period prior to the accession of that State to the Union. Finally, it is apparent from the methods of calculation of the fines that, in its decision, the Commission did not take account of the States which acceded to the Union on 1 May 2004. According to point 478 of the grounds of the Commission's decision, the latter used as the basis for calculation of the fines the turnover figures achieved by the members of the said cartel in the EEA during 2003.[58]

Holding that 'it is settled case-law (that) EU law and national law on competition apply in parallel', and that '(t)hat situation has not been changed by the enactment of Regulation No 1/2003', the Court came to the conclusion that there had been no infringement of the *ne bis in idem* principle.

The judgment arguably raises many more questions than it answers. As the Court rightly points out, both decisions were adopted after accession of the Czech republic to the EU, so that there can be no doubt the situation falls within the scope of application *ratione temporis* of the *ne bis in idem* principle in EU law.[59] It appears however that neither the Commission's decision nor that of the Czech competition authority had become final at the time of the judgment, so that there was no

---

[57] The reason for this was the entry into force of the Czech competition law as amended in the light of accession to the EU.

[58] Para. 101 of the judgment.

[59] See ECtHR, *Gradinger* v. *Austria*, 23 October 1995, appl. no. 15963/90; Case C-436/04, *Leopold Henri van Esbroek*, EU:C:2006:165; Case C-297/07, *Bourquain*, EU: C:2008:708.

infringement of the *ne bis in idem* principle to begin with. The problem
here is one of parallel procedures addressing different periods during
which the cartel was in operation which, as discussed further down in
this chapter, are not a problem of *ne bis in idem* as such because that
principle requires finality of the previous decision. Such situations may
however trigger protection from double fines under the prohibition of
double punishment. Indeed, where the Court states that 'that decision
does not *penalise* (emphasis added) the possible anti-competitive effects
produced by that cartel in the territory of the Czech Republic during the
period prior to the accession of that State to the Union', the Court refers
to the prohibition of double *punishment* and not to the *ne bis in idem*
principle because the latter applies regardless of any risk of double
punishment. In addition, the Court fails to explain why the entry into
force of Regulation 1/2003 did not change anything in the way of the
regulation of the relationship between national and EU competition law
in view of the fact that the *Walt Wilhelm* judgment expressly refers to the
fact that the Council had not availed itself of the competence laid down
in (now) Article 103 TFEU in bringing about Regulation 17/62, and this
same competence *was* used by the Council in bringing about Regulation
1/2003.

   Now that the Charter has become legally binding, the 'unity of the
legal interest protected' can hardly mean anything else than the 'scope of
EU law' as further clarified by the Court in the *Åkerberg Fransson*[60]
judgment. Otherwise, the Court will have to find some way to distinguish
between *the scope of EU law* itself, and *the scope of the 'legal interest
protected' by EU law*, something which may prove rather difficult to do.
The question that remains is the same question now found anywhere in
EU law: whether a given situation falls within the scope of the Charter or
not. For national competition law, this question has not so far been
addressed in the case law of the EU courts. It would appear from the
Åkerberg Fransson and *Melloni*[61] judgments that at least for Art. 101
TFEU there can be little or no doubt that national competition law does
fall within the scope of the Charter, even in situations not affecting trade
between the Member States. The reasons for this are essentially the same
as those already given by Advocate General Colomer in his Opinion in
the *Cement cartel* cases, cited earlier. Although it cannot be said that
national competition law 'implements' EU law directly it certainly does

---

[60] Case C-617/10, *Åkerberg Fransson*, EU:C:2013:280.
[61] Case C-399/11, *Melloni*, EU:C:2013:107.

so indirectly and in doing so creates a 'level playing field'. As a result, substantively the same competition rules apply across the board and throughout the EU, as was expressly intended in drafting Regulation 1/2003. A combined reading of the *Melloni*[62] and *Åkerberg Fransson* judgments furthermore shows that the Charter applies to national law falling within the scope of EU law, regardless of the *degree to which national law is determined by* EU law. For Art. 101 TFEU, Art. 3 Regulation 1/2003 entirely 'determines' national competition law in situations where there is an effecting on trade between the Member States, but not in situations without effect on trade between the Member States. There is by consequence a *partial determination* of national competition law in regulation 1/2003, and this alone is sufficient to trigger the applicability of the Charter. In addition, it must be said that in reality Regulation 1/2003 *does* determine national competition law in its entirety as far as the cartel prohibition is concerned given that it is not feasible or desirable, in view of the need for a level playing field, for a Member States to have two separate competition acts in force with different substantive cartel rules for situations with and without effect on trade between the Member States. That would appear to be precisely the kind of situation that the painstaking drafting of Art. 3 Regulation 1/2003 aims to avoid. For Art. 102 TFEU this may be another matter given the clear difference in treatment given to that provision in Art. 3 of Regulation 1/2003 when compared to Art. 101 TFEU. It cannot however be presumed given general requirements such as the primacy, unity and effectiveness of EU law that this gives the Member States a 'carte blanche' to adopt and enforce laws prohibiting unilateral conduct in a manner contrary to the substance of Art. 102 TFEU, so it must be assumed that EU law determines national law at least to some degree, also where Art. 102 TFEU is concerned. There is however at present no case law available on this point.

3.2 *Scope of Application* Ratione Materiae *of the Guarantee: the* Engel *Doctrine*

As regards the material scope of application of the guarantee, the ECtHR has consistently held that:

> the legal characterization of the procedure under national law cannot be the sole criterion of relevance for the applicability of the principle of non

---

[62] *Ibid.*

bis in idem under Article 4 § 1 of Protocol No. 7. Otherwise, the application of this provision would be left to the discretion of the Contracting
States to a degree that might lead to results incompatible with the object
and purpose of the Convention.[63]

In the first paragraph, Art. 4 of Protocol no. 7 refers to 'criminal proceedings', which echoes the term 'criminal charge' from Article 6 ECHR. The
scope of application of Art. 4 of Protocol no. 7 is accordingly determined as
an autonomous concept under the Convention by reference to three
criteria, commonly known as the *'Engel* criteria', which were similarly
adopted by the CJEU in the *Bonda* judgment.[64] The *Engel* criteria are:

   i) the legal classification of the offence under national law,
  ii) the nature of the offence,
 iii) the degree of severity of the penalty that the person concerned risks
     incurring.

The *Engel* doctrine leads to a presumption that the charges against a
subject are 'criminal', 'a presumption ... which can be rebutted entirely
exceptionally, and only if the deprivation of liberty cannot be considered
appreciably detrimental given their nature, duration or manner of execution'.[65] In applying these criteria it is the maximum potential penalty for
which the relevant law provides which must be taken into account here;
the sentence that was actually imposed 'cannot diminish the importance
of what was initially at stake'.[66]

   The first Engel criterion, the legal classification as 'criminal' under
national law is of little consequence. If an offence is classified as criminal
under national law it will automatically be likewise classified for the
purposes of the Convention. According to the Court, the second and
third Engel criteria are 'alternative and not necessarily cumulative. This,
however, does not exclude a cumulative approach where separate analysis of each criterion does not make it possible to reach a clear conclusion
as to the existence of a criminal charge.'[67] In applying the second Engel

---

[63] *Sergey Zolotukhin* v. *Russia*, ECtHR (GC) 10 February 2009, appl. no. 1493/03, para. 78.
[64] *Engel and Others* v. *Netherlands*, ECtHR 8 June 1976, (Series A-22); Case C-489/10,
   Bonda, EU:C:2012:319. In the *Bonda* judgment the CJEU gave its own rendering of the
   Engel doctrine with particular emphasis on the need to protect the own financial means of
   the Union.
[65] *Sergey Zolotukhin* v. *Russia*, ECtHR (GC) 10 February 2009, appl. no. 1493/03, para. 56.
[66] *Ibid.*
[67] *Putz* v. *Austria*, ECtHR 22 February 1996, (Reports 1996, 312), para. 31; *Sergey Zolotukhin* v. *Russia*, ECtHR (GC) 10 February 2009, appl. no. 1493/03, para. 53.

criterion, the Court will amongst other things have regard to the seriousness of the conduct itself, and the manner in which the misconduct is
classified in other Member States.[68] In doing so, the Court examines
amongst other things whether the rule at issue is of a 'general character',
applicable to all citizens and therefore belonging to the realm of criminal
law in the wider sense, or a disciplinary rule which specifically aims to
protect the qualities and/or integrity needed for the exercise of certain
professions. The more specific a rule is in terms of the persons it
potentially applies to (the case law provides examples of doctors, jour-
nalists, politicians), the greater the likelihood that the Court will consider
that a measure is disciplinary, rather than 'criminal' in nature. In *Demicoli* it was held that if the subject is in a particular position (in this case: a
politician), this does not remove the prosecution from the criminal
sphere if the same legal provision *could*, by its nature also apply to
others.[69] Similarly, in the case of *Grande Stevens*, the Court held that
the Italian rules prohibiting market manipulation generally aim to safeguard the proper functioning and transparency of financial markets and
to protect the confidence of the general public in the functioning of those
markets.[70]

The third *Engel* criterion raises questions because the Court has not set
a lower limit for its application, and this is perhaps necessarily so as it
may be difficult for the Court to justify the setting of any particular
amount of a fine as a 'minimum threshold' due to the differences in
circumstances between individual cases. Because of this, the third Engel
criterion all but obliterates the second one in practice. This points to a
weakness in the *Engel* doctrine as a whole, and could tempt the Court to
set the threshold for a minimum 'criminal' fine ever lower in cases where
it is more difficult to adopt a more principled stance on a particular
aspect of the second Engel criterion. The case law so far shows that not

---

[68] In *Öztürk* the Court for instance held it to be sufficient that the charges brought against
the subject under provisions of administrative law were part of the criminal law in many
Member States.

[69] *Demicoli v. Malta*, ECtHR 27 August 1991, appl. no. 13057/87.

[70] *Grande Stevens v. Italy*, ECtHR 4 March 2014, appl. nos. 18640/10, 18647/10, 18663/10,
18668/10 and 18698/10, at paras. 96 and 97. According to the Court, these market rules
serve the 'general interests of society' normally protected by criminal law, and therefore
belong to the sphere of criminal law for the purposes of the Convention. It follows that
the Court focuses on the nature of the rule at issue and on the question whether the *rule* is
of a specific character rather than on the question whether the *subject* belongs to a specific
group, or profession in applying the second Engel criterion.

only the deprivation of liberty, but even a relatively modest fine can be sufficient to bring a case within the criminal law sphere for the purposes of the Convention.[71] The possibility of the withdrawal of a license falls under the third Engel criterion. In *Nilsson* v. *Sweden*, the Court found that the temporary suspension of a driving license belonged to the criminal law sphere in that case because the suspension was not an 'automatic' or 'immediate and foreseeable' consequence of the subject's conviction for a serious road traffic offence. Because some time passed between the time of the subject's conviction and the moment his driving license was suspended, the Court concluded that the measure must have been, at least in part, punitive in nature. It held that 'prevention and deterrence for the protection of the safety of road users could not have been the only purposes of the measure; retribution must also have been a major consideration'.[72] In the *Haarvig* case, the temporary revocation of a medical license was considered not to be of a 'criminal law nature' given that the provision in question laid down a professional standard and did not aim to punish and deter, but only to prevent further damage to the subject's patients.[73] Similarly, minor disciplinary proceedings against lawyers merely leading to a warning have been held to fall outside of the scope of the notion of 'criminal charge'. A finding of a criminal charge may be based on a combination of factors. In the *Matyjek* case, the Court considered that a ban from taking certain government positions was sufficiently serious to constitute a criminal charge, even though not accompanied by a fine or any other form of punishment.[74] The reason for this was, according to the Court, that 'the prohibition on practicing certain professions (political or legal) for a long period of time may have a very serious impact on a person, depriving him or her of the possibility of continuing professional life. . . . This sanction should thus be regarded as having at least partly punitive and deterrent character.'[75]

The extension of the *Engel* doctrine to the *ne bis in idem* principle has potentially far-reaching consequences for national systems of law. The *ne bis in idem* principle entails no rule of conflict or priority between different legal rules or different types of proceedings within different

---

[71] The Court has consistently held that 'the relative lack of seriousness of the penalty cannot divest an offence of its inherently criminal character': *Ruotsalainen* v. *Finland*, ECtHR 16 June 2009, appl. no. 13079/03, para. 43.

[72] *Nilsson* v. *Sweden*, ECtHR 13 December 2005, appl. no. 73661/01.

[73] *Knut Haarvig* v. *Norway*, ECtHR 11 December 2007 (admissibility), appl. no. 11187/05.

[74] *Matyjek* v. *Poland*, ECtHR 30 May 2006 (admissibility), appl. no 38184/03.

[75] Para. 55 of the judgment.

jurisdictions, so that the application of the *Engel* doctrine to the *ne bis in idem* principle in practice requires full procedural coordination and/or concentration of administrative, tax and criminal proceedings. In practice, the unwanted consequences thereof are usually mitigated through *una via* rules, or by way of the coordination of enforcement efforts through a judicial network or government database. A second problem is that this may require a level of *ne bis in idem* protection under the Charter that the CJEU may deem to be not in conformity with the requirement of effectiveness of EU law under circumstances.[76]

3.3 Subjective and Temporal Scope of Application of the Guarantee

As regards the temporal scope of Art. 54 CISA, the CJEU held in its judgment in *Van Esbroeck* that if the first prosecution was brought before the entry into force of the CISA in that Member State, but the CISA was in force in the Member State where the second prosecution was brought by the time it was brought, Art. 54 CISA will apply *ratione temporis*.[77] This was confirmed in *Bourquain*, the facts of which case predated the project of European integration.[78] The ECtHR adopted essentially the same approach in its judgment in *Gradinger*, where it was held that Art. 4 of Protocol no. 7 ECHR applies if the second proceedings reached their conclusion at a later date than the entry into force of Art. 4 of Protocol no. 7 ECHR.[79] A minor difference appears to be that in *Van Esbroeck*, the CJEU appears takes into account the time at which the second proceedings *were brought*, whereas in *Gradinger* the ECtHR held that Art. 4 of Protocol no. 7 ECHR applied if the second proceedings *reached their conclusion* after the date of entry into force of that provision.

Gasparini has so far been the only case before either court on the point of the subjective scope of application of the guarantee; in other words: the question who can rely on the guarantee – at least as far as natural persons are concerned.[80] In the judgment, the Court confirmed that only those persons who were *actually prosecuted* and had stood trial – and not any accomplices or others who escaped the attention of the authorities – benefit from *ne bis in idem* protection under Art. 54 CISA.

---

[76] The *Åkerberg Fransson* judgment has provided one example of this.
[77] Case C-436/04, *Van Esbroek*, EU:C:2006:165; see also: Case C-297/07, *Bourquain*, EU:C:2008:708.
[78] *Bourquain*.   [79] ECtHR, *Gradinger v. Austria*, 23 October 1995, appl. no. 15963/90.
[80] Case C-467/04, *Gasparini*, EU:C:2006:610.

4 Finality (*Res Iudicata*)

The principle of finality is an important legal principle in its own right, apart from its function as a requirement for the application of the *ne bis in idem* principle. It has been the subject of litigation before the CJEU on a number of occasions. This case law particularly concerns the question of which *parts* of a judgment acquires (formal) finality. Although it is beyond the scope of this study to discuss this case law in more detail, it is useful for the purposes of this study to summarily take this case law into account. The CJEU has summarized its own case law on this point as follows:

> (T)he principle of *res judicator* extends only to the matters of fact and law actually or necessarily settled by the judicial decision in question.[81]

Not all types of judicial decisions are, in their nature, capable of acquiring finality. Some types of judicial decisions do not aim to settle a matter that is the subject of a prosecution finally, but serve a different legal purpose. The case law before both Courts revolves in different ways around the question how to properly distinguish such decisions from decisions that do, or must be considered to bring proceedings to a (final) end. It is established case law before the ECtHR that a judicial decision is *final* when it is has acquired *res iudicata* in reference to the applicable rules under national law, and has become irrevocable.[82] This is the case when there are no more ordinary remedies available under the law, when all available remedies are exhausted, or when the time limits for bringing such remedies have expired.[83] Decisions against which an ordinary appeal may still be brought are therefore excluded from the application of the *ne bis in idem* principle. The possibility of bringing extraordinary remedies under national law however does *not* affect the final nature of the decision.[84] The question whether the decision in question concerns an acquittal or conviction is irrelevant; the only question is whether that decision has become final.[85] Art. 4 of Protocol no. 7 does not stand in the way of the reopening of a case if there is still a possibility to resume proceedings.

---

[81] Case C-462/05, *Commission* v. *Portugal*, EU:C:2008:337.

[82] *Sergey Zolotukhin* v. *Russia*, ECtHR (GC) 10 February 2009, appl. no. 1493/03, para. 107.

[83] *Ibid.*; see also: *Nikitin* v. *Russia*, ECtHR 20 July 2004, appl. no. 50178/99, para. 107.

[84] *Sergey Zolotukhin* v. *Russia*, ECtHR (GC) 10 February 2009, appl. no. 1493/03, para. 107.

[85] *Ibid.*, para. 111.

Some differences in emphasis, rather than substance could be pointed out between the case law of the ECtHR and that of the CJEU as far as the requirement of the finality of the previous decision is concerned, but these have not led to any obvious discrepancies or incompatibilities between the two. In keeping with the principle of mutual recognition, the CJEU has developed in its case law a semi-autonomous approach to the question which types of decisions should be considered as decisions 'finally disposing of someone's trial' within the meaning of Art. 54 CISA. In the seminal *Gözütok and Brügge* judgment, the CJEU held in this regard that:

> Article 54 of the CISA can not play a useful role in bringing about the full attainment of that objective unless it also applies to decisions definitively discontinuing prosecutions in a Member State.[86]

The CJEU has held that regardless of the nature or content of the decision, there must at least have been a 'substantive determination' of the facts and the pleas of the case in order for a decision to be able to acquire finality, except where it concerns decisions discontinuing the prosecution for reasons of a time bar.[87] At the same time, the mere fact that a decision involves some determination of the facts is in itself not sufficient for it to acquire finality. A decision by the police to discontinue the investigation does not trigger *ne bis in idem* protection if that decision does not have the effect of barring further prosecution under national law, even if that decision was based on an assessment of the facts of the case.[88]

The CJEU has confirmed that in competition matters an annulment of a Commission decision by the Community courts on formal grounds does not prevent the Commission from adopting a second decision in the same case which cures the formal defect in the previous decision, as such a formal annulment cannot be regarded as an 'acquittal within the meaning given to that expression in penal matters'.[89] Not all types of settlements in competition proceedings lead to a final outcome. Both the settlement procedure introduced by Article 10a of Commission Regulation 773/2004[90] and applications for leniency can lead to decisions that

---

[86] Joined Cases C-187/01 and C-385/01, *Gozutok and Brugge*, EU:C:2003:87.
[87] Case C-469/03, *Miraglia*, ECLI:EU:C:2005:156.
[88] Case C-419/07, *Criminal proceedings against Vladimir Turansky*, EU:C:2008:768.
[89] Joined Cases C-238/99 P, C-244/99 P, C-245/99 P, C-247/99 P, C-250/99 P to C-252/99 P and C-254/99 P, *Limburgse Vinyl Maatschappij*, EU:C:2002:582.
[90] 2004 OJ L 123/18; see also the Commission Notice on the conduct of settlements in cartel cases.

are conditional and enforceable against the subject, and that bar further prosecution if the conditions are met. The commitments procedure under Article 9 Regulation 1/2003 however does not lead to a final outcome. Although commitments can be made binding on the undertaking by a Commission decision, that decision is not a substitute for a decision by the Commission imposing a fine. Furthermore, Article 9(2) Regulation 1/2003 provides that the case may be reopened by the Commission under certain conditions, and that the national competition authorities (NCAs) or national courts may subsequently come to a finding of an infringement in respect of the same conduct.

In its case law, the ECtHR has been faced with a wide variety of questions of finality, *inter alia* in connection with extraordinary remedies provided for in the laws of many states, which were formerly in the sphere of influence of the Soviet Union. In the case of *Nikitin v. Russia*, the applicant was acquitted from charges of 'treason through espionage' and 'aggravated disclosure of an official secret'.[91] The Russian Procurator General filed a request with the presidium of the Supreme Court to review the acquittal in supervisory proceedings, but this request was refused. The applicant himself thereupon challenged the Russian legislation, which allowed for a re-examination of a closed case and the quashing of an acquittal in supervisory review proceedings before the Russian constitutional court. His appeal was successful and the relevant legislation was declared unconstitutional. The applicant also complained to the ECtHR that the request for supervisory review proceedings by the Procurator General breached Art. 4 of Protocol no. 7 because it had rendered him *liable* to be tried again by creating the potential for a new prosecution. In the judgment that followed, the ECtHR noted that within the Russian legal system at the time, an acquittal such as that in the case of *Nikitin* did not become 'final' until the time limit for a request for supervisory review (one year) had expired. However, because supervisory review could be seen as an extraordinary appeal in that was not accessible to the defendant in a criminal case and its application depended on the discretion of the authorised official, the ECtHR assumed that the actual acquittal had become final for the purposes of Art. 4 of Protocol no. 7.[92] The ECtHR observed that Art. 4 of Protocol no. 7

> draws a clear distinction between a second prosecution or trial, which is prohibited by the first paragraph of that Article, and the resumption of a

---

[91] *Nikitin v. Russia*, ECtHR 20 July 2004, appl. no. 50178/99.   [92] *Ibid.*, para. 39.

trial in exceptional circumstances, which is provided for in its second paragraph. Article 4 § 2 of Protocol No. 7 expressly envisages the possibility that an individual may have to accept prosecution on the same charges, in accordance with domestic law, where a case is reopened following the emergence of new evidence or the discovery of a fundamental defect in the previous proceedings.[93]

The ECtHR however held that, in this instance, the mere *attempt* by the prosecution to secure a supervisory review was in itself not sufficient to consider that it had rendered the applicant liable to be tried again. After all, this request was refused. Furthermore, the prosecution's request should be seen as an attempt to have the proceedings reopened, rather than an attempt to hold a second trial.[94]

5   The Identity of the Facts (*Idem*)

As discussed at various points in different chapters of this study, the element of *idem* is perhaps the most contentious aspect of the *ne bis in idem* principle. Discrepancies remain between the case law of the CJEU in competition matters and the cases on Art. 54 CISA. The competition cases have been discussed earlier in this chapter, where it was argued that 'threefold requirement' is not actually an '*idem*' in the real sense, but a limitation of the objective scope of application of the *ne bis in idem* principle. In this paragraph, some developments in the case law of the ECtHR will be discussed, followed by the case law of the CJEU on Art. 54 CISA.

Before the judgment of the Grand Chamber in *Zolotukhin*, the case law of the ECtHR on the interpretation of the notion of 'the same offence' contained in Article of Protocol no. 7 ECHR was riddled with questions and uncertainties. Several different approaches to the interpretation of the notion of '*idem*' could be identified in the case law. After some initial, vying judgments in *Gradinger* and *Oliveira*, the ECtHR adopted an autonomous approach to the interpretation of 'the same offence' by taking into account the question whether two or more offences share the same *essential elements* in *Franz Fischer* and several subsequent judgments.[95] This approach weakened the protection offered by the *ne*

---

[93] *Ibid.*, para. 45.   [94] *Ibid.*, para. 47.
[95] *Gradinger v. Austria*, ECtHR 23 October 1995, appl. no. 15963/90; *Olivieri v. Switzerland*, ECtHR 30 July 1998, appl. no 25711/94. *Franz Fischer v. Austria*, ECtHR 29 May 2001, appl. no. 37950/97.

bis in idem principle contained in Art. 4 of Protocol no. 7 and gave rise to legal uncertainty.[96] In particular, it was far from clear from the case law of the Court how the phrase 'the same essential elements' should be interpreted and applied. In *Zolotukhin*, the Grand Chamber expressly denounced the earlier case law on this point, considering that 'the existence of a variety of approaches to ascertaining whether the offence for which an applicant has been prosecuted is indeed the same as the one of which he or she was already finally convicted or acquitted engenders legal uncertainty incompatible with a fundamental right'.[97] Following, amongst others, the *Van Esbroeck* judgment of the CJEU on Art. 54 CISA, the Grand Chamber embraced a broad, objective approach to the interpretation of the element of *idem*. It held that 'Article 4 of Protocol no. 7 must be understood as prohibiting the prosecution or trial of a second "offence" in so far as it arises from identical *facts or facts* which are substantially the same.' The case concerned a Russian national who had displayed disorderly behaviour towards several public officials. He was placed in detention for three days for the administrative offence of 'minor disorderly acts'. Shortly afterwards, he was prosecuted for the criminal offences of 'disorderly acts', 'use of violence against a public official', and 'insulting a public official' on the basis of substantially the same facts. He lodged an application with the ECtHR, which was declared (partly) admissible and in which a Chamber found a violation of Art. 4 of Protocol no. 7.[98] At the request of the Russian government, the case was referred to the Grand Chamber for review. In the judgment, the Grand Chamber held that:

> the use of the word 'offence' in the text of Article 4 of Protocol No. 7 cannot justify adhering to a more restrictive approach. It reiterates that the Convention must be interpreted and applied in a manner which renders its rights practical and effective, not theoretical and illusory. . . .
>
> The Court further notes that the approach which emphasises the legal characterisation of the two offences is too restrictive on the rights of the individual, for if the Court limits itself to finding that the person was prosecuted for offences having a different legal classification it risks

[96] See: S. Trechsel, with the assistance of S.J. Summers, *Human Rights in Criminal Proceedings* (Oxford University Press, 2005), p. 394. See also: U.K. Law Report Commission, Law Com. No. 267, Cm. 5048, London 2001, pp. 29–32; and B. van Bockel, *The Ne Bis In Idem Principle in EU Law*, (Alphen aan de Rijn: European Monographs, Kluwer Law International, 2010), pp. 191–201.

[97] *Sergey Zolotukhin v. Russia*, ECtHR (GC) 10 February 2009, appl. no. 1493/03, para. 78.

[98] *Sergey Zolotukhin v. Russia*, ECtHR 7 June 2007, appl. no. 1493/03.

undermining the guarantee enshrined in Article 4 of Protocol No. 7 rather than rendering it practical and effective as required by the Convention .... Accordingly, the Court takes the view that Article 4 of Protocol No. 7 must be understood as prohibiting the prosecution or trial of a second 'offence' in so far as it arises from identical facts or facts which are substantially the same.[99]

The importance of this statement lies in the fact that the Court has fundamentally rejected any recourse to more formal (and therefore more arbitrary) criteria that tie in with the legal qualification of the act or facts, such as the 'essential elements' of an offence as defined in national criminal law. A more 'objective' approach, based on the historical rather than the legal act or facts offers stronger protection for the individual and strengthens legal certainty by rendering the *ne bis in idem* principle more predictable in its application. All the while, however, the facts underlying the prosecution of a subject inevitably derive their significance from the constitutive elements of the relevant offence as it is codified in law. For this reason, the degree of objectivity of 'legal facts' cannot be equated to that of 'facts' in empirical scientific research. The judgment can therefore only be understood as requiring the highest possible *degree* of objectivity in assessing the underlying facts of the case.

As previously mentioned, in *Zolotukhin* the Grand Chamber followed (*inter alia*) the case law of the CJEU on Art. 54 CISA. As pointed out in Chapter 5 (paragraph 3.2.2) of this study, this must have been 'both pleasing and displeasing' to the CJEU. The CJEU must have been pleased that the approach previously taken by it in the case law on Art. 54 CISA convinced the ECtHR and prompted it to radically change its course and to harmonize its various approaches in a single doctrine, but also displeased because this approach ignores that the CJEU's case law on Art. 54 CISA is purposive, driven by the specific aims of the EU (in this case) in the context of the Schengen *acquis*, and strongly reliant on the precise wording of Art. 54 CISA. This case law is discussed later.

The general rule that the Court formulated in the *Van Esbroeck* judgment is that the element of *idem* is to be understood solely as the 'identity of the material acts, understood in the sense of the existence of a set of concrete circumstances which are inextricably linked together'. The legal classification of the act(s) and the nature of the 'protected legal interest' are therefore of no consequence. This was subsequently

---

[99] *Sergey Zolotukhin* v. *Russia*, ECtHR (GC) 10 February 2009, appl. no. 1493/03, paras. 82 and 83.

confirmed and further elaborated by the ECJ in, *inter alia*, the *Van Straaten* and *Kraaijenbrink* judgments.[100] The *Van Straaten* case concerned the question whether such requires that the quantities of forbidden substances and the identities of accomplices are the same. In his Opinion in that case, Advocate General Colomer reiterated the *Van Esbroeck* judgment, where the ECJ had held that 'the same acts' must be understood as meaning: 'one single timeframe, one single space, but also one single intent', which must be inextricably linked. According to the Advocate General, the objective element of *idem* therefore refers both to the relevant space and time where the facts took place, as well as to the subjects' intentions. It would follow from this that not all facts have to be exactly identical; the fact that the quantities as well as the identities of the accomplices varied would not change the objective action itself. The ECJ followed the Opinion. In the judgment, it called to mind the relevant considerations from *Van Esbroeck*, and the fact that the wording of Art. 54 CISA refers to the same 'acts'. According to the judgment, this 'shows that that provision refers only to the nature of the acts in dispute and not to their legal classification'. The Court held that this is confirmed by the nature of Art. 54 CISA as a fundamental right and its purpose within the context of the Schengen *acquis*, and that the central question is 'whether a situation constitutes a set of facts which are inextricably linked together'.[101] It held that consequently, the quantities of narcotic drugs or the identity of accomplices are not required to be identical, in order for there to be identity of facts.

In the *Kraaijenbrink* judgment the ECJ was asked by the referring court to provide guidance on the question of to what extent the subjective intentions of the subject are relevant for a finding of '*idem*'.[102] The case concerned Mrs Kraaijenbrink who had been sentenced by a local district court in the Netherlands for 'several offences under Article 416 of the Netherlands Penal Code of receiving and handling the proceeds of drug trafficking between October 1994 and May 1995 in the Netherlands'. Three years later, she was sentenced by the criminal court at Ghent (Belgium) for the offence of 'exchanging in Belgium sums received from trading narcotics in the Netherlands between November 1994 and February 1996'. In appeal, the Belgian court of cassation, stayed proceedings in order to ask the ECJ, firstly, whether the conduct on the basis of which Mrs Kraaijenbrink was convicted in Belgium and the Netherlands should

---

[100] Case C-150/05, *Van Straaten*, EU:C:2006:614.   [101] Para. 41 of the judgment.
[102] Case C-367/05, *Kraaijenbrink*, EU:C:2007:444.

be regarded as 'the same acts' within the meaning of Art. 54 CISA in view of the fact that the underlying intentions were the same, and secondly, whether this would bar a second conviction on a 'subsidiary' basis, taking into account therefore earlier convictions for different acts, committed with the same intentions. Although very little could be inferred by the CJEU from the order for reference as regards the relevant facts of the case, the Belgian court of cassation submitted that if the defendant had been prosecuted for these same acts on both counts in Belgium, these acts would have been interpreted as a 'single act' for the purpose of the application of the *ne bis in idem* principle under Belgian criminal law. In its judgment, the ECJ held that the questions posed by the referring court

> must be understood as seeking, in essence, to ascertain whether the notion of 'same acts' within the meaning of Article 54 of the CISA must be construed as covering different acts consisting, in particular, first, in holding in one Contracting State the proceeds of drug trafficking and, second, in the exchanging at exchange bureaux in another Contracting State of sums of money having the same origin, where the national court before which the second criminal proceedings are brought finds that those acts are linked together by the same criminal intention.

Following the Opinion of the Advocate General, the ECJ held that the 'same acts' within the meaning of Art. 54 CISA 'must be understood as a set of concrete circumstances which are inextricably linked together', and held that this inextricable link does not depend solely on the intentions of the defendant. The same criminal intention 'does not suffice to indicate that there is a set of concrete circumstances which are inextricably linked together covered by the notion of "same acts" within the meaning of Art. 54 of the CISA'. The rule from *Kraaijenbrink* is that, where the historical facts may provide the objective link between a given set of circumstances, the intentions of the subject may provide a subjective link. The mere fact that there is a subjective link between a set of concrete circumstances is however in itself insufficient.

6 Exceptions

Out of the provisions discussed in this chapter, only Art. 4 (2) of Protocol no. 7 ECHR allows for 'the reopening of the case . . . if there is evidence of new or newly discovered facts, or if there has been a fundamental defect

in the previous proceedings that could affect the outcome of the case'.[103]
It appears from the Explanations that this exception is only relevant in
instances in which a conviction or harsher sentence is sought, and that
the reopening of a case to the benefit of the subject does not infringe
Art. 4 of Protocol no. 7 ECHR. Case law on this paragraph of the
provision is very scarce. In its case law the possibility of 'supervisory
review', which possibility of exists in many legal systems of the states who
were formerly within the sphere of influence of the Soviet Union, the
ECtHR has repeatedly examined whether the power to reopen the case
was 'exercised by the authorities so as to strike, to the maximum extent
possible, a fair balance between the interests of the individual and the
need to ensure the effectiveness of the system of criminal justice'. It has
however *consistently done so under the heading of Art. 6 ECHR*, rather
than under that of Art. 4 of Protocol no. 7 ECHR.[104] In the case of
Zigarella, the Court held that new proceedings may be brought in error,
without knowledge that the defendant has been previously tried. Art. 4
(2) of Protocol no. 7 ECHR only applies to instances in which proceedings were brought in the knowledge that the defendant has already been
tried, and that the bringing of proceedings in error does not infringe the
ne bis in idem principle if those proceedings are subsequently
discontinued.[105]

---

[103] *Nikitin* v. *Russia*, ECtHR 20 July 2004, appl. no. 50178/99, para. 56.
[104] *Ibid.*, para. 57.
[105] *Zigarella* v. *Italy* (decision on admissibility), ECtHR 3 October 2002, appl. no. 48154/99;
     Falkner v. *Austria* (decision on admissibility), ECtHR 30 September 2004, appl.
     no. 6072/02.

2

Ne Bis in Idem in the EU and ECHR Legal Orders

A Matter of Uniform Interpretation?

XAVIER GROUSSOT AND ANGELICA ERICSSON

1 Introduction

Never has the European Court of Justice (ECJ) delivered so many human rights judgments, and never have the concerns as to the lack of uniformity of the European human rights law been so big. But is uniform interpretation the sole cure to all these qualms? The *ne bis in idem* principle and its dynamic jurisprudence from both the ECJ and the European Court of Human Rights (ECtHR) offers in that sense a perfect field for studying the interaction between the EU and European Convention on Human Rights (ECHR) legal orders. As the title suggests, this chapter will focus on the relationship between *ne bis in idem* in the EU and the ECHR legal orders. This will be done mainly through a quest to unlock the mysteries of the so-called homogeneity clause of Article 52(3) in the EU Charter of Fundamental Rights (the Charter or EUCFR), a clause that seems to be the key to the relationship between the two legal orders, but which has been given an understated role in the latest jurisprudence of the ECJ on *ne bis in idem*. This chapter will not only discuss the relationship between the EU and the ECHR from within these particular international legal orders, but we will also take a closer look at the concrete consequences of this active interface in the national legal orders. To be more specific, we will provide a detailed examination of the effects brought about by the ECJ's recent *Åkerberg* judgment in the Swedish legal order.[1]

In this case, the *Haparanda tingsrätt* asks the Court, in essence, whether the *ne bis in idem* principle laid down in Article 50 of the Charter should be interpreted as precluding criminal proceedings for tax evasion from being brought against a defendant where a tax penalty

---

[1] Case C-617/10, *Åklagaren v. Åkerberg Fransson*.

has already been imposed upon him or her for the same acts of providing false information.[2] This new decision is in our view paradigmatic for understanding the relationship between the EU and the ECHR legal orders as it shows not only its complexity but also reveals the position of the ECJ on this matter. Does the ECJ really aspire to ensure a uniformity of the European human rights law as it is mandated by the text of Article 52(3) of the Charter when the rights are corresponding between the two legal orders? This chapter is divided into four sections. The first section analyses the complexity of the *ne bis in idem* principle by looking at the lack of uniformity surrounding its interpretation in the laws of the Member States of the EU (Section 2). Second, we gauge the impact of the homogeneity clause (Article 52(3) of the Charter) in the ECJ case law and look whether there is an obligation to respect the ECtHR case law (Section 3). The third section examines the place and role given to Article 52(3) EUCFR and to the ECtHR case law by the ECJ in interpreting the *ne bis in idem* provision of the Charter, that is Article 50 EUCFR. It is argued that the ECJ went beyond the 'homogeneity clause' of Article 52(3) of the Charter by interpreting this provision very restrictively and by giving, in turn, a 'pluralist' meaning to Article 53 (level of protection) of the Charter. This interpretation of the horizontal provisions goes hand to hand with an autonomous interpretation of Article 50 of the Charter where there is no direct reference to the ECtHR case law. This position has also serious constitutional implications on the European human rights law and the competences of Member States of the EU (Section 4). Finally, to complete the picture of the relationship between the Charter and the ECHR, in particular the respective interpretations of *ne bis in idem* connected to each of these documents, it is useful to take stock of how they are perceived in the national legal systems. The difference in status and function of these documents is bound to affect the way in which the national courts take on board the principle of *ne bis in idem*, as interpreted by the ECJ and the ECtHR respectively. However, in regard to their effects on the national interpretation of *ne bis in idem*, it is interesting to explore not just the differences but also the interplay between the Charter and the ECHR (Section 5).

---

[2] Article 6(1) third sentence 3 of the TEU states: 'the rights, freedoms and principles in the Charter shall be interpreted in accordance with the general provisions in Title VII of the Charter governing its interpretation and application and with due regard to the explanations referred to in the Charter, that set out the sources of those provisions'.

2   The 'Commonality' of *Ne Bis in Idem* in the Laws of Europe

Is *ne bis in idem* a common principle of the laws of Europe? As discussed in the previous chapter of this study, the *ne bis in idem* principle, in general terms, entails that a party cannot be prosecuted, tried and convicted twice for the same behaviour.[3] In its original sense, the principle can be traced back to Greek and Roman laws and evidence shows that it traveled from there into Canon law and on into civil and common law.[4] However, the rationales[5] of this principle have changed completely over time and even its status as a 'principle' was doubted until quite recently.[6] Today, the *ne bis in idem* principle is enshrined in several international instruments, the relevant ones for the purpose of this chapter on the relationship between ECHR and EU laws being Article 4 of Protocol no. 7 to the European Convention of Human Rights, Article 50 of the EU Charter of Fundamental Rights and Article 54 of the Convention Implementing the Schengen Agreement (CISA).[7] The principle is intended to guarantee the proper administration of justice and to protect the individual's private sphere.[8] It is considered to contribute to efficient law enforcement in that it prevents over-punishment, prevents vexatious multiple prosecutions and creates incentives for proficient coordination between prosecutors.[9]

---

[3] J. Vervaele, 'The Application of the EU Charter of Fundamental Rights (CFR) and its *Ne Bis In Idem* Principle in the Member States of the EU' (2013) 6 *Review of European Administrative Law*, 1, 114. According to Vervaele, '[t]he *ne bis in idem* principle is a general principle of (criminal) law in many national legal orders, sometimes even codified as a constitutional right, such as in article 103 of the German Constitution. Historically the *ne bis in idem* principle only applies nationally and is limited to criminal justice, this means precluding application to punitive administrative enforcement. There is also no general rule of international law that imposes an obligation to comply with *ne bis in idem*'.

[4] B. van Bockel, *The Ne Bis In Idem Principle in EU Law* (Alphen aan de Rijn: European Monographs, Kluwer Law International 2010), p. 30.

[5] *Ibid.*, pp. 25–30. There are many rationales to the *ne bis in idem* principle in national systems of law such as e.g. legal certainty, due process, proportionality, protection of *res judicata* or protection of human rights.

[6] R. Lööf, '54 CISA and the Principles of *Ne Bis In Idem*' (2007) 15 *European Journal of Crime, Criminal Law and Criminal Justice*, 3, 309.

[7] CISA of 14 June 1985 between the Governments of the States of the Benelux Economic Union, the Federal Republic of Germany and the French Republic on the gradual abolition of checks at their common borders, Schengen, 19 June 1990, in force 1 September 1993, OJ 2000 No. L239/19.

[8] G. di Federico, 'EU Competition Law and the Principle of *Ne Bis in Idem*' (2011) 17 *European Public Law*, 2, 243.

[9] W. Wils, 'The Principle of *Ne Bis in Idem* in EC Antitrust Enforcement: A Legal and Economic Analysis' (2003) 26 *World Competition*, 2, 136.

As discussed in Chapter 1, the ECHR does not contain a specific provision establishing the *ne bis in idem* as an individual right. In fact, the former European Commission on Human Rights denied the existence of the principle as such under Article 6 ECHR, or any other provision of it for that matter.[10] The principle has been instead incorporated into the Convention framework by Article 4 Protocol no. 7 to the ECHR.[11] At this stage, forty-three out of forty-seven States of the Council of Europe have ratified Protocol no. 7. It is worth noting that Belgium ratified Protocol no. 7 on 13 April 2012. However, Germany and the Netherlands have not yet ratified it and many States which are also part of the European Union, such as Austria, France, Italy and Portugal have made reservations as to the application of Article 4 of Protocol no. 7 and the definition of 'criminal offence' that must be determined under their respective national law.[12] The United Kingdom has not even signed it. The conclusion to which we are inescapably drawn is that the recognition of *ne bis in idem* in the ECHR system does not reflect a solid consensus among the western European democracies which are also part of the European Union. As put by Vervaele, 'neither ECtHR practice, nor the application of the *ne bis in idem* principle in the framework of the multilateral treaties in criminal matters of the Council of Europe have led to a common *ne bis in idem* standard in Europe'.[13] It is true that the case law of the ECtHR, notably on the definition of the '*idem*', has been extremely split with cases such as *Gradinger, Oliveira* and *Fischer*.[14]

---

[10] J. Vervaele, 'The Transnational *Ne Bis in Idem Principle* in the EU: Mutual Recognition and Equivalent Protection of Human Rights' (2005) 1 *Utrecht Law Review*, 2, 102.

[11] The Protocol was opened for signature on 22 November 1984 and entered into force on 1 November 1988.

[12] Germany has also made a reservation as to the application of Article 4.

[13] Vervaele, 'The Transnational *Ne Bis in Idem* Principle in the EU', 110.

[14] ECtHR, *Gradinger* v. *Austria*, 23 October 1995 (Appl. No. 15963/90); ECtHR, *Oliveira* v. *Switzerland*, 30 July 1998 (Appl No. 2571/94); ECtHR, *Franz Fischer* v. *Austria*, 29 May 2001 (Appl. No. 37950/97). *See* for comments on these cases, B. Van Bockel, cited in note 4, at pp. 190–200. *Gradinger* (breach of Article 4 of Protocol no. 7) and *Oliveira* (no breach of Article 4 of Protocol no. 7) are considered to be cases reflecting a lack of consistency as to the definition of the *idem* in the context of road safety offences. The *Franz Fissher* case added to the confusion with the creation of the doctrine of 'the essential elements of the offences'. In this decision, the ECtHR came to the conclusion that there was no breach of Article 4 of Protocol no. 7 as the administrative and criminal offences only partially overlap. There was no obvious overlap of the essential elements of the offences (*ibid.*, Van Bockel, at p. 195).

It is important to highlight that the *Zolothukin* case delivered by the Grand Chamber of the ECtHR in 2009 has eventually united the definition of the *'idem'*. Interestingly, the reasoning of this case as to the definition of the *'idem'*, which is based on the identity of the material acts or factual situation irrespective of the legal classification under national law,[15] is clearly inspired by Article 54 CISA[16] and the related interpretative case law of the ECJ, for example *Van Esbroeck* and *Van Straaten*.[17] This provision, in contrast to Article 4 of Protocol no. 7, only concerns a prohibition of double prosecution and has a cross-border application. This last specificity reflects the main purpose of the Schengen Agreement, which is the abolition of physical borders among the countries that are members to it, or in other words, the enhancement of the right to freedom of movement. In its case law on Article 54 CISA, the ECJ puts its emphasis mostly on the provision's function of promoting freedom of movement. It is interesting to note that it does not much refer to other and more general reasons for the application of the principle, such as legal certainty, the right to a fair trial or respect for *res judicata*. Through its case law, the Court of Justice has therefore created a strong link between the application of Article 54 CISA and the ultimate objective of the EU, which is the internal market. Importantly in the EU, the CISA case law is not applicable to Ireland and the United Kingdom since they are not parties to the Schengen Agreement. Again, the full consensus as to the application of *ne bis in idem* falls short.

Notwithstanding this lack of full consensus, it is worth noting that the principle of *ne bis in dem* has been recognized in the ECJ case law before the entry into force of both Protocol no. 7 in 1988 and Article 54 CISA in 1995. Already in *Gutman* (1965), the Court of Justice in a staff case recognized the existence of *ne bis in idem*.[18] In this ruling, the applicant

---

[15] *See* Section 5 of this chapter.

[16] According to Article 54 CISA, '[a] person whose trial has been finally disposed of in one Contracting Party may not be prosecuted in another Contracting Party for the same acts provided that, if a penalty has been imposed, it has been enforced, is actually in the process of being enforced or can no longer be enforced under the laws of the sentencing Contracting Party'.

[17] Case C-436/04, *Van Esbroeck* [2006] ECR I-2333 and Case C-150/05, *Van Straaten* v. *Staat der Nederlanden and Republiek Republiek Italië* [2006] ECR I-9327. *See also* Joined Cases C-187/01 *and* C-385/01, *Gözütok and Brugge* [2003] ECR I-1345; Case C-469/03, *Miraglia* [2005] ECR I-2009; Case C-467/04, *Gasparini and Others* [2006] ECR I-9199; Case C-297/07, *Bourquain* [2008] ECR I-9425 and Case C-491/07, *Turansky* [2008] ECR I-11039.

[18] Joined Cases 18/65 and 35/65, *Gutman* v. *Commission* [1966] ECR 103.

complained that the decisions of 20 and 21 January 1965, which ordered a fresh disciplinary inquiry to be held concerning him, violated the principle *ne bis in idem*. The Court found a violation by stating that neither in the terms of the contested decision nor in the items in the file submitted to it has the Court been able to find any assurance that the principle *ne bis in idem* has been respected. The application of the principle spilled over in the context of competition law with the judgment in *Walt Wilhelm* (1969), which concerns the parallel application of Community competition rules and those of the national authorities.[19] The Court stated that the acceptability of a dual procedure which can result in concurrent sanctions follows from the special system of the sharing of jurisdiction between the Community and the Member States with regard to cartels.[20] However, in the case of consecutive sanctions (and the Court saw no means of avoiding such a possibility in the general principles of Community law), it must be demanded that any previous punitive decision must be taken into account in determining any sanction which is to be imposed.[21] In support of this, the Court did not refer explicitly to the *ne bis in idem* principle, but instead relied on a more general concept of 'natural justice'.[22]

These two cases are significant in order to understand the position of the Court of Justice towards *ne bis in idem*. In that respect, the Court made an implicit reference in one case and referred to the principle of *ne bis in idem* in the other. However, there is no explicit reliance on a 'general principle' of Community law that might have reflected a consensus between the laws of the Member States. This is in fact not

---

[19] Case 14/68, *Walt Wilhelm and Others* v. *Bundeskartellamt* [1969] ECR 1. Cited in note 9.

[20] *See* Wils, 'The Principle of *Ne Bis in Idem* in EC Antitrust Enforcement', 143. When considering *Walt Wilhelm*, it is important to keep in mind that at that time the Commission had a monopoly on enforcing the EC competition rules in cases that affected trade between Member States. This was during the time of the old situation under Regulation No. 17/62. Back then, the Member States only rarely prosecuted infringements under EU law, but rather applied only their national competition law. Thus, the reasoning of the Court in this case is built on the fact that EC competition law and national competition laws pursued different ends and in that sense protected different legal interests.

[21] *Ibid.*, para. 11.

[22] The Court's reference to a 'general requirement of natural justice' in para. 11 may be seen to correspond with the argument of AG Cruz Villalón in the recent case of *Åkeberg*, para. 95 (*see* Section 4 in this chapter), where he states that the principle of proportionality, and the principle of the prohibition of arbitrariness, preclude a criminal court from exercising jurisdiction in a way which completely disregards the fact that the facts before it have already been the subject of an administrative penalty.

surprising since the first (laconic) reference to the 'general principles of Community law' was made the same year as *Walt Wilhelm* in *Stauder* (1969). At this stage, there was no methodology associated to the recognition and elaboration of the general principles. After cases such as *Nold* (1974), *Rutili* (1975) and *Johnston* (1984),[23] it was clear that the ECHR had become a significant source of inspiration for the Luxembourg judges for elaborating the 'general principles'. Nowadays, Article 6(3) Treaty on European Union (TEU) explicitly recognizes the ECHR as a (informal) source of inspiration for the 'general principles'. The ECHR will even become a formal source of inspiration after the entry into force of the accession agreement of the EU to the ECHR.

As to the relation of the EU *ne bis in idem* with the ECHR, the so-called *PVC II* case (2002) is paradigmatic.[24] This competition case post-Protocol no. 7 made clear in its paragraph 59 that 'the principle of *ne bis in idem* ... is a fundamental principle of Community law also enshrined in Article 4(1) of Protocol no. 7 to the ECHR'.[25] Two points should be made here. First, the Court of Justice of the European Union (CJEU) relies expressly on Article 4 of Protocol no. 7 to the ECHR. Second, it makes reference to *ne bis in idem* as a 'fundamental principle' of Community law but not as a 'general principle'. What is the dividing line between a 'fundamental principle' and a 'general principle'? The term 'fundamental principle' has often been used in the context of the rights of the defence. Notably, it has been used in the '*Orkem*' line of case law at the end of the 1980s in relation to the principle against self-incrimination, which at the time was not a principle common to the laws of the Member States of the EU. It is argued here that the use of the expression 'fundamental principle' by the CJEU instead of 'general principle' precisely reflects the lack of consensus between the laws of the Member States as to the application of the *ne bis in idem* principle.

Yet the principle of *ne bis in idem* is now enshrined in Article 50 of the binding EU Charter of Fundamental Rights – an instrument mirroring as such the highest level of consensus between the States of the Union – and

---

[23] Case C-222/84, *Johnston* v. *Chief Constable of Royal Ulster Constabulary* [1986] ECR I-1651.

[24] Joined Cases C-238/99, C-244/99, C-245, C-247, C-250 to C-252 and C-254/99, *Limburgse Vinyl Maatschappij and Others* v. *Commission* [2002] ECR I-8375, para. 59. Accordingly, the Court of Justice has confirmed that 'the principle of *non bis in idem* ... is a fundamental principle of Community law also enshrined in Article 4(1) of Protocol no. 7 to the ECHR'.

[25] *Ibid.*, *PVC II*, and Case C-289/04, *Showa Denko* [2006] ECR I-5859, para. 50.

therefore should also be seen as a general principle of EU law. According to Article 50 EUCFR, 'No one shall be liable to be tried or punished again in criminal proceedings for an offence for which he or she has already been finally acquitted or convicted within the Union in accordance with the law.' Similarly to Article 4 of Protocol no. 7 to the ECHR, this provision protects the individual against both double prosecution and double punishment. Nevertheless, in contrast to Protocol no. 7, its scope is wider since it covers not only internal situations but also cross-border situations as envisaged under Article 54 CISA. This interpretation is confirmed by the non-binding legal explanations[26] that states that,

> the *non bis in idem* principle applies not only within the jurisdiction of one State but also between the jurisdictions of several Member States. That corresponds to the acquis in Union law; see Articles 54 to 58 of the Schengen Convention, Article 7 of the Convention on the Protection of the European Communities' Financial Interests and Article 10 of the Convention on the fight against corruption. The very limited exceptions in those Conventions permitting the Member States to derogate from the "non bis in idem" principle are covered by the horizontal clause in Article 52(1) of the Charter concerning limitations.

Going further, the legal explanations emphasize that concerning the situations referred to by Article 4 of Protocol no. 7, namely the application of the principle within the same Member State, the guaranteed right has the same meaning and the same scope as the corresponding right in the ECHR. This means that Article 50 of the Charter when it applies in the so-called internal situation (application within the same Member State) should respect the ECHR case law in the light of Article 52(3) EUCFR, which regulates the relationship between the EU and ECHR legal orders or what we can call '*the Law between the legal orders*'.[27]

After the entry into force of the Charter, the ECJ delivered two Grand Chamber cases, namely *Toshiba* (2012) and *Åkerberg* (2013),[28] as to the application of *ne bis in idem* in EU law in respectively EU competition law and EU tax law. In *Toshiba*, a competition case concerning the application of Regulation 1/2003 (which under its recital 37 clearly links

---

[26] Explanations relating to the complete text of the Charter (December 2000), (OJ C 303, 14.12.2007, pp. 17–35) OJ 2007 No. C303/17–35 available at http://ue.eu.int/df/docs/en/EN_2001_1023.pdf.

[27] Editorial, 'The Law of the Laws – Overcoming Pluralism' (2008) 4 *European Constitutional Law Review*, 3, 397.

[28] Case C-617/10, *Åkerberg Fransson*, cited in note 1.

its application and interpretation to the EUCFR), the CJEU, in sharp contrast with its previous case law, where it methodically referred to Article 4 of Protocol no. 7 to the ECHR, and contrary to the Opinion of Advocate General (AG) Kokott, which insisted on the need for uniform interpretation of EU and ECHR law, has dropped the reference to the ECHR. As rightly put by Devroe, 'the explanation for the deletion of the reference to the ECHR cannot possibly be a desire to "update" fundamental rights protection from the ECHR to the Charter as indeed any mention of Article 50 of the Charter is equally lacking in the *Toshiba* judgment. The Charter is mentioned in relation to the *lex mitius* principle,[29] which makes its absence in relation to *ne bis in idem* even more striking.'[30]

In *Åkerberg*, a tax case concerning an 'internal application' of *ne bis in idem*, the CJEU did not refer either to the ECHR or its case law. The Opinion of AG Cruz Villalón is here very instructive and thus necessitates to be fully scrutinized.[31] As to the scope of application of Article 50 EUCFR *en préliminaire*, the AG was of the opinion that the Court of Justice did not have jurisdiction to give a ruling on the substance of the case since it should be considered to fall outside of the scope of EU law. However, he decided to propose an answer to the questions referred to the court, for the court to consider if it did decide to rule on the issue. He first looked into Article 4 of Protocol no. 7 to the ECHR and the relevant case law of the ECtHR, and pointed out that there had been considerable lack of agreement between the Member States of the EU regarding the problems resulting from the imposition of both administrative and criminal penalties in respect of the same offence. This lack of agreement he finds to be clearly revealed in the fact that not all Member States have been willing to ratify Protocol no. 7 to the ECHR and some have done so with reservations to the application and interpretation of Article 4 of that Protocol.[32] The AG traced the lack of agreement back to the importance of measures imposing administrative penalties in a large number of States, in addition to the special significance also afforded to criminal prosecution and penalties in those

---

[29] Case C-17/10, *Toshiba* v. *Commission* [2012].

[30] W. Devroe, 'How General Should General Principles Be? Ne Bis in Idem in EU Competition Law', in U. Bernitz, X. Groussot and F. Schulyok (eds.), *General Principles of EU Law and European Private Law*, European Monographs (Aphen aan de Rijn: Kluwer, 2013), vol. 84, paras. 105–107.

[31] Opinion of AG Cruz Villalón in *Åkerberg*, cited in note 1, delivered on 12 June 2012.

[32] *Ibid.*, para. 68.

Member States. The interest in maintaining a dual – administrative and criminal – power to punish, he said, explained why many Member States are holding on to this system even though the case law of the ECtHR has developed in a direction which practically excludes that duality.[33]

When looking into the case law of the ECtHR, with regard to Article 4 of Protocol no. 7 to the ECHR, the AG shows that, at the moment, Article 4 of Protocol no. 7 to the ECHR precludes measures imposing both administrative and criminal penalties in respect of the same acts, thereby preventing the commencement of a second set of proceedings, whether administrative or criminal, when the first penalty has become final.[34] When having established the meaning of the *ne bis in idem* principle in the context of Article 4 of Protocol no. 7 to the ECHR, the AG proceeded to look at the *ne bis in idem* principle in Union law, that is Article 50 of the EU Charter of Fundamental Rights and its interpretation in the light of Article 4 of Protocol no 7. to the ECHR. The AG maintained that the ECHR, as referred to in primary Union law, is the Convention as its stands now, and that notice must be taken of the fact that the *ne bis in idem* principle is not guaranteed in the same way as the core principles of the ECHR are guaranteed and by which all States are bound.[35] He then pointed out that in *Åkerberg* a lack of agreement concerning a right in the system of the ECHR clashes with the widespread existence and established nature in the Member States of systems in which both an administrative and a criminal penalty may be imposed in respect of the same offence. That widespread existence and well-established nature could even be described as a common constitutional tradition of the Member States. The view of the AG is thus that Article 50 of the Charter calls for a partially autonomous interpretation. Regard must be had to the current state of the case law of the ECHR, but the ECJ must independently interpret Article 50 of the Charter, basing its interpretation exclusively on the wording and scope of the provision itself.[36]

Similarly as in *Toshiba*, the CJEU again refrained from referring to the ECHR case law. It is argued that this reflects a conscious choice of the Luxembourg judges. According to Devroe,

---

[33] *Ibid.*, para. 74.   [34] *Ibid.*, para. 79.   [35] *Ibid.*, para. 84.

[36] *Ibid.*, paras. 86–87. The AG then goes on to discuss Article 50 of the Charter and the imposition of both an administrative and a criminal penalty for the same offence. With support of the established case law of the Court of Justice on the *ne bis in idem* principle, the AG finds that the tax surcharge of the case indeed represents a substantive criminal penalty and that the acts being penalized in the case were indeed 'same acts' within the meaning of *ne bis in idem*.

[s]ome may have believed that the deletion of a reference to the ECHR was a one-time '*accident de parcours*'. However, the recent *Fransson* [Åkerberg] judgement of the ECJ proves otherwise. It confirms – unfortunately again only implicitly – that the deletion of a reference to the ECHR very much translates as a deliberate choice of the ECJ. The ECJ is no longer willing to interpret the EU *ne bis in idem* requirement in Article 50 of the Charter in conformity with the ECHR's *ne bis in idem* requirement as interpreted in *Zolotukhin*. From now on, it seems that the EU and ECHR *ne bis in idem* principles will diverge in large areas of the law.[37]

If this is true, it means that there is no obligation to interpret Article 50 of the Charter in conformity with Article 4 Protocol no. 7 ECHR and its related case law. In the end, it appears that, after the entry into force of the EU Charter of Fundamental Rights and its incorporation in its Article 50, the principle of *ne bis in idem* can be viewed as a general principle of the EU legal order. Yet this incorporation does not lead to a uniform interpretation in the laws of Europe but instead reinforces the autonomous character of EU law towards the ECHR legal order. This autonomous interpretation of *ne bis in idem* clashes in our view with the so-called homogeneity clause enshrined in Article 52(3) EUCFR, which imposes an obligation to respect the ECtHR case law when the rights are corresponding between the Charter and the ECHR.

3   Interpretation of *Ne Bis in Idem* and the Homogeneity Clause

In light of Article 50 of the Charter, *ne bis in idem* is now a principle common to the laws of the Member States of the EU. But does this mean that *ne bis in idem* must be interpreted uniformly in both the EU and ECHR legal orders? Should the ECtHR case law apply, in all circumstances, to the interpretation of Article 50 EUCFR? Apparently, this uniform interpretation would be stimulated if the ECHR were a formal source of EU law. Nevertheless, as put by the former President of the ECtHR, Jean-Paul Costa, 'it is of course true that formally speaking the Convention is not binding under Union law'.[38] However, the relationship between the ECJ and the ECtHR has become so internalized into the EU

---

[37] *See* Devroe, 'How General Should General Principles Be? *Ne Bis in Idem* in EU Competition Law', paras. 105–107, cited in note 30.

[38] J. P. Costa, 'The Relationship between the European Convention on Human Rights and European Union Law – A Jurisprudential Dialogue between the European Court of Human Rights and the European Court of Justice', Lecture on 7 October 2008 at King's College London, available online, at p. 21.

legal system that it can no longer be considered an external policy matter.[39] In that sense, Article 52(3) of the Charter appears to be the key provision when it comes to assess the interaction between the two Courts and gauge whether there is an obligation of uniform interpretation of *ne bis in idem* in the laws of Europe.

3.1   Corresponding Rights, ECHR Case Law and Uniformity

With the entry into force of the Lisbon Treaty, as stated in the joint communication of Presidents Costa and Skouris, '[t]he Charter has become the reference text and the starting point for the CJEU's assessment of the fundamental rights . . . It is thus important to ensure that there is the greatest coherence between the Convention and the Charter in so far as the Charter contains rights which correspond to those guaranteed by the Convention.'[40] During the drafting of the Charter, its relationship with the ECHR was a matter of constant consideration.[41] It is apparent that one of the problems that a binding Charter could raise is that of diverging interpretations with the Convention. It may be argued, in that sense, that the Charter could increase the risk of divergence and thus reinforce a lack of uniformity between the two systems, since the text of the Charter does not correspond exactly to the text of the ECHR. Lenaerts and de Smijter contended, however, that '*[w]here the text of the Charter departs from that of the ECHR, it can never be at the expense of the level of protection offered by the ECHR*'.[42] Furthermore, if the Convention is to be amended in the future, these amendments will automatically become the minimum standard for the protection of fundamental rights within the European Union.[43] The risk of diverging *interpretation* is in reality rather weak due to the 'subsidiary' character

---

[39] C. Timmermans, 'The Relationship between the European Court of Justice and the European Court of Human Rights' in A. Arnull, C. Barnard, M. Dougan and E. Spaventa (eds.), *A Constitutional Order of States? Essays in EU Law in Honour of Alan Dashwood* (Oxford: Hart Publishing, 2011), p. 151.

[40] *See also* Joint Communication from Presidents Costa and Skouris, 24 January 2011, para. 1, available online.

[41] *See* M. Lindfelt, *Fundamental Rights in the European Union: Towards Higher Law of the Land? A Study of the Status of Fundamental Rights in a Broader Constitutional Setting* (Turku: Åbo Akademi University Press, 2007), p. 144.

[42] K. Lenaerts and E. de Smijter, 'A Bill of Rights for the European Union' (2001) 38 *CMLRev*, 2, 297.

[43] T. Lock, 'The ECJ and the ECtHR: The Future Relationship between the Two European Courts' (2009) 8 *The Law and Practise of International Courts and Tribunals*, 3, 382.

of the ECtHR jurisdiction.[44] It will become even weaker with the EU's accession to the ECHR.[45] It is important to look now at the ECtHR case law related to the issue of *ne bis in idem* and, especially, how this case law has been integrated or rejected within the CJEU jurisprudence. Two areas related to the interpretation of Article 4 of Protocol no. 7 are of crucial importance: the definiton of the criminal offence or *criminal charge* and the defintion of the *idem*. In those two areas, we find diverging case law that reflects the lack of uniformity of the jurisprudence of the two Courts in the *ne bis in idem* context.

As regards the definition of a criminal offence, it appears that the ECJ relies on the ECHR case law, the so-called *Engel* criteria, but not in all areas of EU law. In *Engel and Others* v. *the Netherlands*,[46] the ECtHR stated that for determining the real nature of a conduct one should look not only to the legal qualification of the offence under the internal law of a given State, but also to the very nature of the offence, together with the repressive and deterring character of the penalty, and the type and the degree of affliction (severity) of the penalty for which a given individual is liable.[47] In the application of these criteria the ECtHR has attributed a greater importance to the second and third criterion, which eventually has outweighed the first criterion, that is the formal classification of the offence under national law.[48]

The ECJ has been relying on the *Engel* criteria to assess whether sanctions required by EU law in order to implement EU secondary legislation may be qualified as criminal sanctions. In *Spector* (2009), in

---

[44] By 'subsidiary' character we mean that the preliminary ruling procedure is integrated within the 'exhaustion of remedies' under Article 35 ECHR. The recourse for an individual to the ECtHR is always his/her last resort at the national level. Therefore, in this context, the ECtHR may have the last word on the interpretation of the ECHR rights. *See also* A. Rosas, 'Fundamental Rights in the Luxembourg and Strasbourg Courts', in C. Baudenbacher et al. (eds.), *The EFTA Court: Ten Years on* (Oxford: Hart Publishing, 2005). According to Rosas, 'The thesis, often put forward in the literature, that there is a tension or even conflict between Luxembourg and Strasbourg case law is somewhat exaggerated. Harmony rather than conflicts is a much likely scenario.'

[45] A risk of divergence will always exist even after accession since the Convention is a minimum standard. The argument often used that accession to ECHR will bring coherence to fundamental is thus nugatory.

[46] ECtHR, *Engel and Others* v. *the Netherlands*, 8 June 1976 (Appl. No. 5100/71).

[47] *Ibid.*, para. 82.

[48] P. Rosiak, 'The *Ne Bis in Idem* Principle in Proceedings Related to Anti-Competitive Agreements in EU Competition Law' (2012) 5 *Yearbook of Antitrust and Regulatory Studies*, 6, 116.

a reference concerning the interpretation of Articles 2 and 14 of Directive 2003/6/EC2003 on insider dealing and market manipulation (market abuse), the Court interpreted Article 14[49] in the light of the *Engel* criteria and came to the conclusion that the administrative sanctions imposed against the persons responsible may be qualified as criminal sanctions, in the light of the nature of the infringements at issue and the degree of severity of the sanctions which may be imposed, for the purposes of the application of the ECHR.[50] Three years after *Spector*, the Grand Chamber of the CJEU delivered the *Bonda* (2012) ruling.[51] This case concerns the interpretation of Article 138 of Regulation No 2988/95, which specifies the sanctions to be taken by Member States against fraudulent farmers in the context of the common agricultural policy.[52] The Court considered after an in-depth analysis in light of the *Engel* criteria that the administrative nature of the measures provided for by Article 138(1) of Regulation No 1973/2004 is not called into question by an examination of the case law of the ECtHR on the concept of 'criminal proceedings' within the meaning of Article 4(1) of Protocol no 7. In that respect, the Court stated that,

> according to that case-law, three criteria are relevant in this respect. The first criterion is the legal classification of the offence under national law, the second is the very nature of the offence, and the third is the nature and degree of severity of the penalty that the person concerned is liable to incur (see, inter alia, ECHR, *Engel and Others* v. *the Netherlands*, 8 June

---

[49] Case C-45/08, *Spector Photo Group* [2009] ECR I-12073. Article 14(1) of Directive 2003/6/EC of 28 January 2003 on insider dealing and market manipulation, OJ 2003 No. L096/16 provides: 'Without prejudice to the right of Member States to impose criminal sanctions, Member States shall ensure, in conformity with their national law, that the appropriate administrative measures can be taken or administrative sanctions be imposed against the persons responsible where the provisions adopted in the implementation of this Directive have not been complied with. Member States shall ensure that these measures are effective, proportionate and dissuasive.'

[50] *Ibid.*, para. 43.   [51] Case C-489/10, *Łukasz Marcin Bonda* [2012].

[52] According to Article 138(2), '[w]here differences between the area declared and the area determined result from irregularities committed intentionally, the aid to which the farmer would have been entitled shall not be granted for the calendar year in question. Moreover, where that difference is more than 20% of the area determined, the farmer shall be excluded once again from receiving aid up to an amount which corresponds to the difference between the area declared and the area determined. That amount shall be off-set against aid payments to which the farmer is entitled in the context of applications he lodges in the course of the three calendar years following the calendar year of the finding.'

1976, §§ 80 to 82, Series A no. 22, and *Sergey Zolotukhin* v. *Russia*, no. 14939/03, §§ 52 and 53, 10 February 2009).[53]

As to the first criterion, the Court observed that the measures provided for in Article 138(1) of Regulation No 1973/2004 are not regarded as criminal in nature by European Union law, which must in the present case be equated to 'national law' within the meaning of the case law of the ECtHR. As regards the second criterion, the ECJ ascertained whether the purpose of the penalty imposed on the farmer is punitive. The sanctions are to apply only to economic operators who have recourse to the aid scheme set up by that regulation, and that the purpose of those measures is not punitive, but is essentially to protect the management of European Union funds by temporarily excluding a recipient who has made incorrect statements in his or her application for aid. As to the third criterion, the Court considered that the sole effect of the penalties is to deprive the farmer in question of the prospect of obtaining aid. Consequently, those penalties cannot be equated to criminal penalties on the basis of the third criterion based on the nature and severity of the penalty.[54]

By contrast, the *Engel* criteria are not applied as such in EU competition law. Moreover, the EU courts have never validated that competition fines are of criminal nature.[55] This is perhaps not so strange since criminal law was not part of the competence of the EU. As a result, any suggestion that an EU sanction might be defined as a criminal charge had to be avoided.[56] This position contrasts with the ruling of the ECtHR in *Menarini* (2011),[57] which held that a fine imposed for a violation of national competition law was of criminal nature and related to a criminal charge within the sense of Article 6 ECHR.[58] Similarly, the European Free Trade Association (EFTA) court in *Posten Norge* (2012)[59]

---

[53] *Ibid.*, para. 37.   [54] *Ibid.*, paras. 38–45.
[55] *See*, to that effect, Case T-83/91, *Tetra Pak* v. *Commission* [1994] ECR II-755, para. 235, Joined Cases T-25/95, T-26/95, T-30/95 to T-32/95, T-34/95 to T-39/95, T-42/95 to T-46/ 95, T-48/95, T-50/95 to T-65/95, T-68/95 to T-71/95, T-87/95, T-88/95, T-103/95 and T-104/95, *Cimenteries CBR and Others* v. *Commission* [2000] ECR II-0491, para. 717 and Case T-9/99, *HFB and Others* v. *Commission* [2002] ECR II-1487, para. 390.
[56] *See* A. de Moor Van Vugt, 'Administrative Sanctions in EU Law' (2012) 5 *Review of European Administrative Law*, 5–41.
[57] ECtHR, *Menarini Diagnostics S.r.l* v. *Italy*, 17 September 2011 (Appl. No. 43509/08).
[58] *Ibid.*, paras. 38–45. The ECtHR also decided to look beyond the Italian statutes and focused upon the actual review undertaken by the Italian Administrative Courts. It was held that not just a mere legality control had been exercised, but instead a full review (*see* at para. 64).
[59] Efta Court, Case E-15/10, *Posten Norge AS* v. *EFTA Surveillance Authority*, judgment of 18 April 2012. In this case, the scope of the control of legality review of the EFTA Court

considered that proceedings for the imposition of fines in competition law fall as a matter of principle within the criminal sphere.[60] Even AG Sharpston in *KME* considered that, '[i]n the light of [the *Engel*] criteria, I have little difficulty in concluding that the procedure whereby a fine is imposed for breach of the prohibition on price-fixing and market-sharing agreements in Article 81(1) EC falls under the "criminal head" of Article 6 ECHR as progressively defined by the European Court of Human Rights.'[61]

Nonetheless, the CJEU has ensured that the procedural safeguards of the ECHR and the Charter with respect to criminal proceedings are respected in practice in the context of EU competition law.[62] Although Article 23(5) of Regulation 1/2003 expressly says that the decisions on financial penalties are not of a criminal law nature, the *ne bis in idem* principle still has succeeded to find its way into competition law. Indeed, the CJEU – which as said before has never expressly confirmed that the *Engel* criteria are to be applied in competition law cases[63] – has frequently examined the possibility of application of the *ne bis in idem* principle to proceedings involving the breach of competition law and for penalties imposed by the Commission in such cases. And other parallels have also been drawn by the CJEU between criminal proceedings and proceedings concerning competition law breaches.

---

in relation to Article 6 ECHR was at issue. The Court acknowledged that only where it would have full jurisdiction to quash ESA's decision in regard of both questions of fact and of law would the requirements of Article 6(1) be adhered to. ESA defended itself by falling back on the concept of complex economic assessment, thus requiring the applicant to show a manifest error of appraisal in the authority's assessment.

[60] *Ibid.*, para. 100. According to the EFTA Court, 'it must be recalled that Article 6(1) ECHR requires that subsequent control of a criminal sanction imposed by an administrative body must be undertaken by a judicial body that has full jurisdiction. Thus, the Court must be able to quash in all respects, on questions of fact and of law, the decision (*see*, for comparison, ECtHR, *Janosevic* v. *Sweden*, 1 November 2001 (Appl. No. 34619/971), para. 81 and *Menarini Diagnostics S.R.L.* v. *Italy*, cited in note 57, para. 59). Therefore, when imposing fines for infringement of the competition rules, ESA cannot be regarded to have any margin of discretion in the assessment of complex economic matters which goes beyond the leeway that necessarily flows from the limitations inherent in the system of legality review challenged.'

[61] Case C-272/09 P, *KME Germany and Others* v. *Commission* [2011], para. 64.

[62] *See* Recital 37 of the Regulation on implementation of the rules on competition, Council Regulation 1/2003, OJ 2003 No. L1/1.

[63] Rosiak, 'The *Ne Bis In Idem* Principle in Proceedings Related to Anti-Competitive Agreements in EU Competition Law', 122. Cited in note 48.

For instance, in *Toshiba*, the CJEU had to assess whether the *ne bis in idem* principle as enshrined in Article 50 EUCFR impedes a national competition authority to impose fines on an undertaking where the Commission has already fined that same undertaking for its participation in the same cartel. Also, it is worth underlining that the CJEU, in its case law related to a right to fair hearing, could benefit from the approach taken by the ECtHR in the *Jussila* case.[64] In this case, which concerned a fiscal surcharge for tax fraud imposed by the Finnish tax authorities, the ECtHR considered that a denial of public hearing under Article 6 ECHR is allowed by the ECtHR in those cases where a criminal charge does not add up to a signifcant degree of stigma.[65] In other words, if the sanction concerns a light criminal charge a less strict procedure can be allowed and, therefore, it may lead to a situation where the usual criminal law guarantees do not apply with their full stringency as they would in a situation falling within the hard core of criminal law.[66] The essential question remains whether this line of reasoning is applicable to EU competitition law.[67] If the answer is positive, the *Jussila* ruling may then

---

[64] See ECtHR, *Jussila* v. *Finland*, 23 November 2006 (Appl. No. 73053/01) For a discussion on *Jussila* and its relationship with EU competition law; *see* W. Wils, 'EU Antitrust Enforcement Powers and Procedural Rights and Guarantees: The Interplay between EU Law, National Law, the Charter of Fundamental Rights of the EU and the European Convention on Human Rights' (2011) 34 *World Competition*, 2, 205.

[65] Moor Van Vugt, 'Administrative Sanctions in EU law', p. 41. Cited in note 56.

[66] K. Lenaerts, 'Due Process in Competition Cases' (2013) 1 *Neue Zeitschrift für Kartellrecht*, 5, 175. Available at www.ikk-2013.de/pdf/Lenaerts.pdf. *See also* ECtHR, *Janosevic* v. *Sweden*, 21 May 2003 (Appl. No. 34619/97), para. 81. According to the ECtHR, the tax authorities are administrative bodies which cannot be considered to satisfy the requirements of Article 6(1) ECHR. However, the ECtHR considered that the Contracting States must be free to empower tax authorities to impose sanctions like tax surcharges even if they come to large amounts. Such a system is compatible with Article 6(1) ECHR provided the taxpayer can bring any such decision affecting him before a judicial body that has full jurisdiction, including the power to quash the challenged decision.

[67] This interpretation is of course very far-reaching and it is doubtful that the *Jussila* line of case law can be transposed in the context of double penalties in competition law by granting a wide margin of discretion to the decision taker. A restrictive interpretation based only on the stringency of the procedural guarantees required for a fair hearing in a 'criminal' case should be preferred. *See* ECtHR, *Jussila* v. *Finland*, 23 November 2006 (Appl. No. 73053/01), para. 43. Accordingly, '[n]otwithstanding the consideration that a certain gravity attaches to criminal proceedings, which are concerned with the allocation of criminal responsibility and the imposition of a punitive and deterrent sanction, it is self-evident that there are criminal cases which do not carry any significant degree of stigma. There are clearly "criminal charges" of differing weight. What is more, the autonomous interpretation adopted by the Convention institutions of the notion of a "criminal charge" by applying the Engel criteria have underpinned a gradual broadening

be relied on in order to justify a non-uniform interpretation of the principle of *ne bis in idem* in EU law according to the nature and gravity of the criminal charge by making a distinction between hard core criminal law and 'soft' criminal law (e.g. tax surcharge).[68] In that respect, it is worth mentioning that a divergence of interpretation – reflecting a lack of consistency – as to the definition of the *'idem'* between the CJEU and ECtHR has occured in the wake of *Zolothukin*.[69]

In this judgment, the ECtHR takes the opportunity to clarify its case law on the issue of identification of *'idem'*. The Court considers that the variety of approaches to determining the identity of the offences an individual is being prosecuted for engenders legal uncertainty and it therefore feels called upon to provide a harmonized interpretation of the notion of the *'idem'* element of the *ne bis in idem* principle.[70] The Court then compares several different international instruments incorporating the *ne bis in idem* principle, some (e.g. the CISA) referring to 'same acts' and 'same conduct' and others (Article 4 of Protocol no. 7) referring to 'same offence'. The Court then states that the use of the word 'offence' in the Protocol cannot justify adhering to a more restrictive approach than if the wording was 'same acts' or 'same conduct' since the

---

of the criminal head to cases not strictly belonging to the traditional categories of the criminal law, for example administrative penalties (Öztürk, cited above), prison disciplinary proceedings (Campbell and Fell v. the United Kingdom, 28 June 1984, Series A no. 80), customs law (Salabiaku v. France, 7 October 1988, Series A no. 141-A), competition law (Société Stenuit v. France, 27 February 1992, Series A no. 232-A), and penalties imposed by a court with jurisdiction in financial matters (Guisset v. France, no. 33933/96, ECHR 2000-IX). Tax surcharges differ from the hard core of criminal law; consequently, the criminal-head guarantees will not necessarily apply with their full stringency.'

[68] T-138/07, *Schindler Holding* [2011] ECR II-4819, paras. 50–53. Here the General Court relies clearly on the *Jussila* approach in the context of competition law. This position is not fully confirmed in appeal by the recent ruling of the ECJ delivered on 18 July 2013 in *Schindler* (Case C-501/11 P, *Schindler Holdings Ltd. and Others v. Commission* [2013], paras. 33–35). The ECJ, relying heavily on the *Menarini* case (cited in note 57) of the ECtHR but not mentioning the *Jussila* decision, considered that decisions adopted by the Commission imposing fines in competition matters are not in itself contrary to Article 6 of the ECHR as interpreted by the ECtHR. It is interesting to note that the appelant (para. 25) recall the criteria set out in the judgment of the ECtHR in *Engel* and maintain that the General Court was wrong in holding that the judgment of the ECtHR in *Jussila* v. *Finland* – according to which, for certain categories of infringements not forming part of the hard core of criminal law, the decision need not be adopted by a tribunal in so far as provision is made for full review of the decision's legality – was transposable to cartel proceedings.

[69] EctHR, *Zolotukhin v. Russia* 7 June 2007 (Appl. No. 14939/03).   [70] *Ibid.*, para. 78.

provisions of an international treaty such as the Convention must be construed in the light of their object and purpose and also in accordance with the principle of effectiveness. Finding the approach of the legal characterization of the relevant offences, i.e. the '*legal idem*', to undermine the guarantee of the principle and thus rendering the provision incorporating it impractical and ineffective, the ECtHR comes to the conclusion that Article 4 of Protocol no. 7 must be understood as prohibiting the prosecution or trial of a second 'offence' in so far as it arises from identical facts or facts which are substantially the same.[71]

The ECtHR emphasizes that it is irrelevant which parts of the new charges are eventually upheld or dismissed in the subsequent proceedings, because Article 4 of Protocol no. 7 contains a safeguard against being tried or being liable to be tried again in new proceedings rather than a prohibition on a second conviction or acquittal. It then finally states that its inquiry should therefore focus on those facts which constitute a set of concrete factual circumstances involving the same defendant and inextricably linked together in time and space, the existence of which must be demonstrated in order to secure a conviction or institute criminal proceedings.[72] The Court's reasoning in *Zolotukhin* was reaffirmed in even more recent case of *Tomasović* v.*Croatia*, delivered by the ECtHR on 18 October 2011.[73]

3.2   An Obligation of Uniformity under the Homogeneity Clause?

So it follows from the previous section that the ECJ case law does not follow scrupulously the ECHR decisions. But is there an obligation to apply the ECHR case law in the context of *ne bis in idem*? To put it differently, can we deduce such an obligation by interpreting Article 50 EUCFR in light of Article 52(3) EUCFR? In fact, Article 52(3) has the purpose to ensure the consistency between the Charter and the ECHR by establishing the rule that, insofar as the rights in the present Charter also correspond to rights guaranteed by the ECHR, the meaning and scope of those rights, including authorized limitations, are the same as those laid down by the ECHR. It goes on to add that this will not

---

[71] *Ibid.*, paras. 79–82.   [72] *Ibid.*, paras. 83–84.
[73] ECtHR, *Tomasović* v. *Croatia*, 18 October 2011 (Appl. No. 73053/01). *See also*, case ECtHR, *Björn Henriksson* v. *Sweden*, 19 January 2010 (Appl. No. 7396/10) and case ECtHR, *Lucky Dev.* v. *Sweden*, 27 November 2014 (Appl. No. 7356/10).

prevent union law providing more extensive protection.[74] AG Kokott in *Solvay* rightly considers that the first sentence of Article 52(3) contains a 'homogeneity clause'.[75] As it stems from the legal explanations of the *praesidium*, the meaning and the scope of the guaranteed rights are determined not only by the text of those instruments, but also by the case law of the ECtHR and by the CJEU. This paragraph is essential to make sure that the Charter's rights incorporate as a minimum the standards of the Convention.

As AG Trstenjak noted in *NS*,[76] under Article 52(3) of the Charter the CJEU must ensure that the protection provided by the Charter rights is no less than the protection granted by the corresponding ECHR rights.[77] In other words, by Article 52(3) the EU has committed itself to *secure to everyone within their jurisdiction the rights and freedoms defined in the Convention.*[78] To be sure, that commitment exists only in respect of matters that fall within the scope of EU law, and only in respect of those ECHR rights which find their correspondence in the Charter, but the key point to note is that the EU has committed itself to respect ECHR rights, that is to say, the rights *defined* in the ECHR. This commitment entails a legal duty, derived from EU primary law, on the part of all EU institutions (including the CJEU), as well as the member states when acting within the scope of EU law[79] to respect the relevant ECHR right. This

---

[74] According to Article 52(3) of the EU Charter of Fundamental Rights, '[i]nsofar as this Charter contains rights which correspond to rights guaranteed by the Convention for the Protection of Human Rights and Fundamental Freedoms, the meaning and scope of those rights shall be the same as those laid down by the said Convention. This provision shall not prevent Union law providing more extensive protection.' In that regard, the horizontal provisions of the EU Charter of Fundamental Rights are particularly interesting when it comes to regulating the relationship between the Charter and Convention's rights and offering a framework for preventing conflicts between the CJEU and the ECtHR. In that sense, Articles 52(3), and 53 of the Charter are of special significance since they essentially seek to guarantee a harmonious relationship between the Charter and the Strasbourg regime. These provisions have the ambition to prevent a conflict of interpretation between the various jurisdictions arising as a result of the plurality of the legal sources. Article 52 of the Charter aims at ensuring equivalent protection of rights between the Strasbourg and Luxembourg regimes (Article 52(3)). Article 53 of the Charter establishes the so-called non-regression clause of the rights enshrined in the Charter, ECHR and the national constitutions.

[75] AG Kokott in Case C-110/10 P, *Solvay* v. *Commission* [2011] ECR I-10439, para. 95.

[76] AG Trstenjak in Case C-411/10, *NS* v. *State Home Dept* [2011].   [77] *Ibid.*, at para. 145.

[78] Which is the duty set out in Article 1 ECHR.

[79] *See* X. Groussot, L. Pech and G. Petursson, 'The Scope of Application of Fundamental Rights on Member States' Action: In Search of Certainty in EU Adjunction' (2011) 1 *Eric Stein Working paper*.

legal duty to respect the Convention derives from the Charter, and is not contingent on any accession by the EU to the ECHR or on any power of the Council of Europe or the ECtHR to sanction the EU for breach of the ECHR.

Even though, during the drafting of the Charter, there were many attempts to include an explicit reference to the ECtHR case law, Article 52(3) does not provide any *explicit* reference to it. Is the CJEU, after the entry into force of the Charter, bound by the jurisprudence of the Strasbourg Court? One could argue that the rights contained in the Convention and interpreted in the case law of the Strasbourg Court form an integral part of the meaning, interpretation and scope of the guaranteed rights within the EU legal order.[80] By contrast, Article 52(7) of the Charter merely states that its official explanations 'shall be given due regard'. In the explanations, it is established that the reference to the ECHR in Article 52 (3) covers both the ECHR and the Protocols to it and that 'the meaning and the scope of the guaranteed rights are determined not only by the text of those instruments, but also by the case law of the ECtHR and by the Court of Justice of the European Union'.[81] But since the interpreter of the Charter only has to give due regard to the case law of the ECtHR, there is nothing in these explanations that imposes an explicit obligation to respect the ECtHR jurisprudence. This is perhaps so due to the fact that the Convention constitutes a minimum standard of protection as emphasized by Article 52(3) of the Charter. Also, in view of the recent case law of the CJEU on fundamental rights – based on the doctrine of general principles – it is possible to consider that the material content of the Convention has been incorporated into EU law.[82] If this is the scenario, one should not worry about the lack of unequivocal reference.[83]

---

[80] *See* K. Lenaerts and E. de Smijter, 'The Charter and the Role of the European Courts' (2001) 8 *Maastricht Journal of European and Comparative Law*, 1, 90.

[81] Explanations relating to the EU Charter of Fundamental Rights.

[82] J. Jacqué, 'The Accession of the European Union to the European Convention on Human Rights and Fundamental Freedoms' (2011) 48 *CMLRev.*, 4, 1000. Strasbourg case law must be taken into consideration.

[83] Lock, 'The ECJ and the ECtHR: The Future Relationship between the Two European Courts', 387. The author argues against the binding effect of the ECtHR case law. According to him, during the drafting of the Charter, there were many attempts to include an explicit reference to the ECtHR case law in the Charter's text. Nevertheless it was impossible to agree on such reference. Neither the wording of the provision nor the history of the drafting support the fact that the CJEU is to be bound by the case law of the Strasbourg Court.

Ibid., p. 387. Cited in note 43.

It may even be said that there has never been an instance in which the CJEU openly challenged the ECtHR's interpretation of the Convention. This is not so surprising since the case law of the Court of Justice often takes into consideration the case law of the ECtHR on the relevant provisions of the ECHR in interpreting the provisions of the EU Charter of Fundamental Rights.[84] And in that sense, one can state that 'the ECJ has not only helped to maintain a high standard of human rights protection in Europe but also contributed to the development of these human rights. It is to be expected that [after accession] the two Courts will keep an eye on the development of the other's case law.'[85] It can even be argued that – in light of Article 52(3) of the Charter and in so far the Convention is part of EU Treaty law[86] – since the entry into force of the Treaty of Lisbon, the EU has made itself unilaterally bound to the jurisdiction of the ECtHR.[87]

As put by AG Trstenjak in *NS*, '*Because the protection granted by the ECHR is constantly developing in the light of its interpretation by the European Court of Human Rights, the reference to the ECHR contained in Article 52(3) of the Charter of Fundamental Rights is to be construed as an essentially dynamic reference which, in principle, covers the case-law of the European Court of Human Rights.*' However, in the same case the AG made a remark which is important to address:

---

[84] *See* AG Trstenjak in Case C-411/10, para. 127. Cited in note 76. *See*, most recently, Joined Cases C-92/09 and C-93/09, *Volker and Markus Schecke* [2010] ECR I-11063, para. 43 et seq. *See also* Case C-465/07, *Elgafaji* v. *Staatsecretaris van Justitie* [2009] ECR I-0921, para. 44, in which the Court stressed as an *obiter dictum* that the interpretation given in that judgment of the relevant provisions of Directive 2004/83 was fully compatible with the ECHR, including the case law of the ECtHR relating to Article 3 of the ECHR. In Case C-400/10 PPU, *McB* v. *L. E.* [2010] ECR I-8965, para. 53, the Court expressly found, with regard to Article 7 of the EU Charter of Fundamental Rights, that that provision must be given the same meaning and the same scope as Article 8(1) of the ECHR, as interpreted by the case law of the ECtHR. See recently Joined Cases C-404/15 and C-659/15 PPU, *Aranyosi and Caldararu* [2016].

[85] T. Lock, 'EU Accession to the ECHR: Consequences for the European Court of Justice', EUSA Conference, Boston, USA, paper for EUSA conference, 3 March 2011. The case of *Kokkelvisserij* can thus be read as evidence of the two Courts' endeavour not to contradict each other.

[86] Convention is thus part of EU primary law and therefore have a higher status than is normally acquired by Treaties concluded by the Union, i.e. in between secondary and primary law.

[87] *See* C. Timmermans, 'Relationships between the Strasbourg Court and the ECJ', Intervention Round Table CCBE, Luxembourg, 20 May 2011, at p. 3. Quoting Volker and DEB.

> *It should be borne in mind in this connection that the judgments of the European Court of Human Rights essentially always constitute case-specific judicial decisions and not the rules of the ECHR themselves, and it would therefore be wrong to regard the case-law of the European Court of Human Rights as a source of interpretation with full validity in connection with the application of the Charter. This finding, admittedly, may not hide the fact that particular significance and high importance are to be attached to the case-law of the European Court of Human Rights in connection with the interpretation of the Charter of Fundamental Rights, with the result that it must be taken into consideration in interpreting the Charter.*[88]

This passage seems to depict the judgments of the ECtHR as *merely* case-specific judicial decisions which do not provide rules of general application, and as such they therefore cannot be determinative of the scope and application of the corresponding rights. We consider that, if that was the meaning intended by the AG, then it does not reflect the true nature of the judgments of the ECtHR. It is true that in its judgments, the ECtHR usually focuses on the specific issues at hand, and avoids laying down general standards of interpretation.[89] However, through the application of the Convention to the specific cases at hand the ECtHR does interpret the meaning and scope of the Convention rights, and of the concepts contained within those rights, and this interpretation will be autonomous.[90] And it seems obvious that especially in Grand Chamber judgments (such as the *Jussila* judgment) and in pilot judgments the ECtHR indeed often hands down general rulings that clearly go beyond the individual case at hand. *Jussila* is a fine example of the Court reflecting on its previous case law, identifying inconsistencies and stating its policy for the future.

In a related vein, the search for implications of the constitutional principles established by Article 52(3) EUCFR, questions concerning the system of corresponding rights can be identified in the academic literature. By recognizing the ECHR as the minimum standard of protection for corresponding rights in the Charter and in the ECHR, Lock

---

[88] *Ibid.*, 145–146.

[89] Cameron argues that this choice of approach is a deliberate move on the part of the ECtHR, which is aware of the fact that it would be open to attack if its judgments were overly 'legislative' in character. I. Cameron, *National Security and the European Convention on Human Rights* (Uppsala: Martinus Nijhoff Publishers, 2000), p. 22.

[90] *See* for instance ECtHR, *Chassagnou and Others* v. *France*, 29 April 1999 (Appl. Nos. 25088/94, 28331/95 and 28443/95), para. 100, where the ECtHR held that the term 'association' in Article 11 had an autonomous meaning which was not dependent on domestic classification.

raises the question whether it is actually obligatory to rely on the ECtHR case law when the corresponding rights in the Charter are being interpreted.[91] This author argues against the existence of such an obligation. In support for his argumentation Lock appears to be mostly concerned with the potential effect on the independence of the Union legal order, the so-called autonomy of the EU legal order.[92] He poses a scenario where the ECJ always would be obliged to follow the interpretation of the corresponding articles in the ECHR and thereby be subject to the judgments of the ECtHR.[93] Lock nevertheless seems to believe that the jurisprudence of the ECtHR on articles in the ECHR corresponding to the Charter is of major importance along with other sources of interpretation.[94] Yet, this interpretation of Article 52(3) EUCFR makes it *une coquille vide*. It is not certain that it was the original wish of the drafters of the Charter to give Article 52 Charter such a limited meaning. The thesis followed in this chapter is different and gives, by contrast, an important role to Article 52(3) EUCFR when it comes to the interpretation of EU fundamental rights in relation to the ECHR. In our view, this horizontal provision of the Charter constitutes the core provision of what can be called the constitutional interpretation of Article 52(3) EUCFR.

4   A Matter of Constitutional Interpretation

This section examines the place and role given by the ECJ to Article 52(3) EUCFR and to the ECtHR case law in interpreting the *ne bis in idem* provision of the Charter, that is Article 50 EUCFR. It is argued that the ECJ went beyond the 'homogeneity clause' of Article 52(3) of the Charter by interpreting this provision very restrictively and by giving, in turn, a 'pluralist' meaning to Article 53 (level of protection) of the Charter. This interpretation of the horizontal provisions goes hand-to-hand with an autonomous interpretation of Article 50 of the Charter where there is no direct reference to the ECtHR case law. This position has also serious constitutional implications on the European human rights law and the competences of Member States of the EU.

---

[91] Lock, 'The ECJ and the ECtHR: The Future Relationship between the Two European Courts', 383. Cited in note 43.
[92] *Ibid.*, In order to follow the complete argumentation, *see* pp. 383–387.
[93] *Ibid.*, p. 383.   [94] *Ibid.*, p. 383, 387.

4.1   The Toshiba and Åkerberg Problem – Non-Corresponding Rights, Core Rights and Peripheral Rights

In neither *Toshiba* nor *Åkerberg*, did the CJEU refer to the ECHR for the interpretation of the *ne bis in idem* principle enshrined in Article 50 of the Charter. In doing so, was the Court in breach of its (constitutional) obligations under Article 52(3) of the Charter? It should first be recalled that Article 50 of Charter corresponds to Article 4 of Protocol no. 7 to the ECHR, but its scope is extended to European Union level between the Courts of the Member States. In other words, it may be viewed in certain circumstances (when there is a cross-border element) as a *non-corresponding right*.[95] The practical consequence is that there is no obligation for the ECJ under Article 52(3) Charter to respect the ECtHR case law.

The situation regarding the application of the *ne bis in idem* principle in EU competition law cases, as it can be read from ECJ case law is that the principle indeed does apply. The determination of '*idem*' or 'the same' is subject to a three-fold test (the so-called *Aalborg* criteria),[96] considering the identity of the factual circumstances, the identity of the offender and the identity of the legal interest that is being protected. In the *Toshiba* case, AG Kokott – in the name of uniformity – questioned the requirement of identity of the legal interest being protected, attempting to bring the application of the *ne bis in idem* principle in EU competition law more in line with its application in other areas of law.[97] She did not succeed. The CJEU stuck to its previous definition of *idem* in competition law cases and the reality is that what is still required after the ruling of the Grand Chamber in *Toshiba* is based on '*legal idem*', not factual *idem*. This orthodox position of the CJEU may be defended by arguing that Article 52(3) of the Charter does only apply in relation to corresponding rights. Since the *Toshiba* situation was not a one-country situation, the ECtHR case law did not need to be referred to and followed.

---

[95] In contrast to the provision in the ECHR, the principle of *ne bis in idem* in Article 50 in the Charter 'applies not only within the jurisdiction of one State but also between the jurisdiction of several Member States'. This means that the articles in the Charter and in the ECHR on the principle of *ne bis in idem* correspond to each other when the principle is invoked in one single Member State and the interpretation of Article 50 in the Charter will accordingly be guided by the jurisprudence of the ECtHR. The situation in *Åkerberg* thus concerned the issue of interpreting the principle of *ne bis in idem* in an 'internal situation' since the Swedish courts alone imposed the penalties.

[96] Case C-17/10, *Toshiba Corporation and Others* [2012].

[97] See *contra* AG Kokott in *Toshiba Corporation and Others*, paras. 119–120.

In *Åkerberg*, the situation was different, since it concerned a purely internal application of the *ne bis in idem* principle; still, as in *Toshiba*, the ECJ did not mention Article 4 of Protocol no. 7 ECHR. It seems that the ECJ avoids tackling the relationship between Article 50 of the Charter and Article 4 of Protocol no. 7.[98] This decision also raised interesting and complex issues as to the interpretation of Article 52(3) of the Charter. Particularly, as discussed before, many States of the Council of Europe have not ratified the Protocol or have made specific reservations to the application of Article 4 of Protocol no. 7 in order to preclude its application to administrative penalties.[99] This situation leads to the legitimate question whether there is an obligation for the CJEU under Article 52(3) EUCFR to strictly follow the Strasbourg case law when it has to interpret such a type of 'corresponding right'. AG Cruz-Villalón in *Åkerberg* gave a negative answer. His reasoning, as discussed in Section 2 of this chapter, is founded on the divergences resorting from the

---

[98] J. A. E. Vervaele, 'The Application of the EU Charter of Fundamental Rights (CFR) and its *Ne bis in idem* Principle in the Member States of the EU', 134. In the *Fransson case* the CJEU has avoided tackling the relationship between article 4 ECHR-PR 7 and Article 50 CFR. Although the former has no transnational application, unlike Article 50 CFREU, it can lead to conflicting situations for Member States, as Article 50 CFREU also applies in domestic situations. What happens if Member States have not ratified ECHR-PR 7 or have formulated a reservation to its application and are not willing to accept the application of the *ne bis in idem* principle to the *bis* combination of punitive administrative and criminal penalties? In my opinion, Article 50 CFR de facto sets aside the non-ratification of declarations or reservations, in so far as the Charter applies in a domestic situation of the *ne bis in idem* right. Cited in note 3.

[99] *See* Opinion of AG Cruz Villalón in *Åkerberg*, cited in note 1, para. 83. According to the AG, 'the Member States of the Union all, to varying degrees, grant administrative authorities the power to impose penalties. In a large number of Member States, that power is compatible with the right to punish and can lead to the imposition of both administrative and criminal penalties for the same offence. However, that does not mean, under any circumstances, that Member States which allow double punishment do so with absolute discretion. On the contrary, in most cases, States which have measures for double punishment have provided for a formula which precludes an excessive punitive outcome. Thus, in France, the Constitutional Council has stipulated that the total amount of two penalties may not exceed the highest penalty laid down for each offence. The German courts apply a criterion of proportionality on a case-by-case basis, which is aimed at ensuring that the total amount of the penalties does not become excessive. Other States have established a rule of prior decisions in criminal cases pursuant to which administrative courts must stay the proceedings pending the final outcome of a criminal trial. Union law also provides for an approach of that kind, for example in Article 6 of the regulation on the protection of the Union's financial interests. In other legal systems, as appears to be the case of Sweden, a criminal court which is seised of the second set of proceedings is entitled to deduct the administrative penalty from the amount of the criminal penalty.'

ratification of Protocol no. 7 and the lack of consensus as to the inter-pretation of a specific ECHR right.[100] The AG draws, therefore, a dis-tinction between core principles (mandatory since all the States that are parties to the ECHR are bound) of the ECHR and the others (non-core principle) such as the *ne bis in idem* principle.[101] He believes, referring to Article 6(3) TEU, that 'the ECHR, as referred to in primary Union law, is the convention *as it stands*; in other words, the convention, with its combination of provisions which are mandatory and provisions which are, to a certain extent, conditional. The interpretation of the references to the ECHR contained in primary Union law cannot disregard that point.'[102]

Following this logic, it appears difficult to argue that there is always an obligation to respect the ECHR case law when an EUCFR right is corresponding with an ECHR right. Then a distinction should be drawn between core corresponding rights (mandatory interpretation in light of the ECHR case law) and peripheral corresponding rights (independent interpretation from the ECHR case law). On the other hand, the CJEU did not follow the interpretation proposed by the AG and went beyond Article 52(3) of the Charter in *Åkerberg*.[103] All in all, it appears difficult to establish the status of the jurisprudence of the ECtHR with regard to corresponding rights in the Charter and in the ECHR. The fact that a case before the CJEU involves the interpretation of a right in the Charter corresponding to an article in the ECHR does not seem to imply that the CJEU necessarily relies on the case law of ECtHR.

4.2 Beyond the Homogeneity Clause – The Plurality Clause, National Standards and Constitutional Purposive Interpretation

In this section, it is argued that the ECJ went beyond the 'homogeneity clause' of Article 52(3) of the Charter by interpreting this provision very restrictively and by giving, in turn, a 'pluralist' meaning to Article 53

---

[100] *Ibid.*, para. 86.   [101] *Ibid.*, para. 84.   [102] *Ibid.*

[103] *Åkerberg* elaborated on the scope of Article 50 in the Charter and specified the criteria used for determining whether the present situation was in violation with the article it did not refer to the case law of the ECtHR concerning the principle of *ne bis in idem*. Instead, the Court kept its reasoning in line with its previous jurisprudence. In contrast, when the Court was asked in the case of *Melloni* to interpret the corresponding rights to an effective remedy in and to a fair trial in Article 47 and the corresponding rights of the defence in Article 48(2) in the Charter, parallels to Articles 6(1) and (3) in the ECHR were made.

(level of protection) of the Charter which is certainly not in its wording. In other words and as we shall elaborate on later, Article 53 of the Charter does not mean what it says.[104] The *Åkerberg* case provides an excellent illustration of the minimalist stance of the ECJ regarding the interpretation of Article 52(3) of the Charter and of the rise of Article 53 of the Charter. It must be recalled that, in this decision, the national court asked in essence whether the *ne bis in idem* principle enshrined in Article 50 EUCFR should be interpreted as precluding criminal proceedings for tax evasion from being brought against a defendant where a tax penalty had already been imposed upon him for the same acts of providing false information. The Court considered that the application of the *ne bis in idem* principle under Article 50 EUCFR presupposes that the measures which have already been adopted against the defendant by means of a decision that has become final are of a criminal nature. In that sense, Article 50 EUCFR does not prevent, in principle, a Member State from imposing a combination of tax penalties and criminal penalties. For the sake of guaranteeing that all VAT revenue is collected and, in so doing, that the financial interests of the European Union are protected, the Member States have freedom to choose the applicable penalties. It is only if the tax penalty is criminal in nature for the purposes of Article 50 EUCFR and has become final that this provision precludes criminal proceedings related to the same acts from being brought against the same person.[105]

In its paragraph 35, the CJEU stated that three criteria are relevant for the purpose of assessing whether tax penalties are criminal in nature: 'The first criterion is the legal classification of the offence under national law, the second is the very nature of the offence, and the third is the nature and degree of severity of the penalty that the person concerned is liable to incur (Case C-489/10 *Bonda* [2012]).' Interestingly here, the Grand Chamber makes a single reference to its case law on the term 'criminal charge' (the *Bonda* case), referring neither to the ECHR case law (the *Engel* line of case law in which *the ECtHR* set these three criteria) nor to Article 52(3) of the Charter on corresponding rights – the so-called homogeneity clause. This is all the more surprising since the *Bonda* case makes an explicit reference to the ECHR case law.[106] By so ignoring

---

[104] *See* R. Barnett, 'The Ninth Amendment: It Means What It Says' (2006) 85 *Texas Law Review* 1.

[105] *Åkerberg*, cited in note 1, paras. 33–34.

[106] *See* Case C-489/10, *Bonda* [2012], para. 37.

the ECHR in *Åkerberg*, the Court gives us the impression to build an autonomous standard of protection whereas – arguably – it should have relied on Article 52(3) of the Charter and the relevant corresponding ECHR case law.[107] In the *Melloni* case, delivered on the same day as *Åkerberg*, the Court of Justice made a cryptic reference to the Article 6 ECHR case law but without any explicit mention of Article 52(3) EUCFR.[108] In *Åkerberg*, it took a step further by making no reference at all to the ECHR case law.[109] The overall sensation is that the Court wishes to give a limited meaning to the 'homogeneity clause' by relying instead on an autonomous interpretation of Article 50 of the Charter. This reasoning contrasts also with the position of the AG, who assessed in great detail, as discussed in the previous section, the relationship with the ECHR and the complex issue of corresponding rights. In his view, in order to accurately construe Article 50 of the Charter, it is essential to take into consideration the possible lack of consensus concerning a right in the ECHR system. This is not the position taken by the ECJ in *Åkerberg* in which it avoids making reference to Article 4 of Protocol no. 7 and to the issue of corresponding rights. Instead, it is made clear that the starting point of the interpretation in EU law of *ne bis in idem* is Article 50 EUCFR and the criteria given by the ECJ to the national courts for its interpretation are based on the EU case law. The consequence of which is to lead to the possible uniform application of the three *Engel* criteria in all the Member States of the EU.

---

[107] But after a quick look at the ECJ case law, it seems difficult to maintain that the Court follows 'scrupulously' the Strasbourg jurisprudence. *See* B. De Witte, 'The Use of the ECHR and Convention Case Law by the European Court of Justice', in P. Popelier, C. Van de Heyning and P. Van Nuffel (eds), *Human Rights Protection in the European Legal Order: The Interaction between the European and the National Courts* (Antwerp: Intersentia, 2011), p. 25. As demonstrated by de Witte, many examples can be found both in actions in annulment and preliminary rulings where the Court does not (but should have) analyze the ECtHR case law. His conclusion is that the ECJ jurisprudence reflects an eclectic and unsystematic use of Strasbourg case law. The analysis on *ne bis in idem* in light of *Toshiba* and *Åkerberg* confirms this line of reasoning.

[108] Case C-399/11, *Melloni* [2013]; para. 50.

[109] *See contra, Åkerberg* is given as an example of convergence between the ECJ and the ECtHR. K. Lenaerts and J. A. Gutiérrez-Fons, 'The Place of he Charter in the EU Constitutional Edifice', in S. Peers et al. (eds.), *The EU Charter of Fundamental Rights: A Commentary* (Oxford: Hart Publishing, 2014), p. 33. Unlike the Opinion of AG Cruz Villalón, the ECJ relied, albeit implicitly, on the interpretation of the *ne bis in idem* principle embraced by the ECtHR. Thus, *Åkerberg Fransson* confirms the converging trend between the case law of the two Courts.

Generally speaking, this minimalist interpretation of the 'homogeneity clause' differs not only from the broad interpretation of Article 51 of the Charter but also from the interpretation of Article 53 of the Charter in paragraph 36 of *Åkerberg*. This paragraph 36 is of utmost importance and – to be fully understood – must be read together with paragraph 29 of the same case and paragraph 60 in *Melloni*. According to the Court,

> 36 It is for the referring court to determine, in the light of those criteria, whether the combining of tax penalties and criminal penalties that is provided for by national law should be examined in relation to the national standards as referred to in paragraph 29 of the present judgment, which could lead it, as the case may be, to regard their combination as contrary to those standards, as long as the remaining penalties are effective, proportionate and dissuasive (see, to this effect, inter alia *Commission* v. *Greece*, paragraph 24; Case C-326/88 *Hansen* [1990] ECR I-2911, paragraph 17; Case C-167/01 *Inspire Art* [2003] ECR I-10155, paragraph 62; Case C-230/01 *Penycoed* [2004] ECR I-937, paragraph 36; and Joined Cases C-387/02, C-391/02 and C-403/02 *Berlusconi and Others* [2005] ECR I-3565 paragraph 65).

> 29 That said, where a court of a Member State is called upon to review whether fundamental rights are complied with by a national provision or measure which, in a situation where action of the Member States is not entirely determined by European Union law, implements the latter for the purposes of Article 51(1) of the Charter, national authorities and courts remain free to apply national standards of protection of fundamental rights, provided that the level of protection provided for by the Charter, as interpreted by the Court, and the primacy, unity and effectiveness of European Union law are not thereby compromised (see, in relation to the latter aspect, Case C-399/11 *Melloni* [2013] ECR I-0000, paragraph 60).

Paragraph 36 in *Åkerberg* gives the possibility for the referring court to examine the combining of tax penalties and criminal penalties in relation to the national standards referred to in paragraph 29, according to which in a situation where action of the Member States is not entirely determined by European Union law, national authorities and courts remain free to apply national standards of protection of fundamental rights, provided that the level of protection provided for by the Charter, as interpreted by the Court, and the primacy, unity and effectiveness of European Union law are not thereby compromised. This reasoning is new and its legal basis is surprisingly founded on Article 53 of the Charter.[110] It is worth underlining that

---

[110] *Melloni*, cited in note 108, para. 60. According to the ECJ, '[i]t is true that Article 53 of the Charter confirms that, where an EU legal act calls for national implementing

many in the doctrine have viewed Article 53 EUCFR as a mere 'non-regression clause', thus establishing the Charter as a minimum standard of protection (and establishing a conceptual link with Article 53 ECHR). Others have interpreted this provision more broadly as a 'fountain of law' or a 'co-existence' clause or even as a 'best protection clause'. One thing which is sure after *Åkerberg* and *Melloni* is that the ECJ has decided to give a meaning to Article 53 of the Charter different from a mere 'non-regression clause'.

Article 53 of the Charter is here used to allow the national courts to rely on their own national standards of protection of fundamental rights in a situation where action of the Member States is not entirely determined by European Union law (the so-called *Åkerberg* situation). By contrast, they cannot rely on national standards in a situation where action of the States is entirely determined by European Union law, for example in the context of the European Arrest Warrant (the so-called *Melloni* situation). In this last situation, Article 53 of the Charter cannot be used by the national court referring to a higher national standard of protection of fundamental rights, for example the Spanish constitutional tribunal in *Melloni* relied on the right not be tried in *abstentia*, a higher national standard. Therefore, in a *Melloni* situation, the minimum standard is at the same time the maximum standard, that is the CJEU's Union standard.

Importantly, to be at liberty to rely on the national standards in an *Åkerberg* situation, two cumulative conditions must be respected: first, the level of protection provided for by the Charter must not be compromised (the 'level of protection' condition). Second, the primacy, unity and effectiveness of European Union law must not be compromised (the 'uniformity' or 'effectiveness' condition). The meaning of the first condition is not entirely clear to us but we assume that it signifies that a national court may rely only on national standards that afford higher protection to the individual than the level of protection of the Charter. However, a national court cannot rely on a lower national standard of protection of fundamental rights that can compromise the level of protection of the Charter. The 'level of protection' condition as defined in *Åkerberg* is not easy to grasp and problems related to its interpretation are to be expected in our view from the national courts. Moreover, in

measures, national authorities and courts remain free to apply national standards of protection of fundamental rights, provided that the level of protection provided for by the Charter, as interpreted by the Court, and the primacy, unity and effectiveness of EU law are not thereby compromised'.

practice, it creates a complex system of protection of fundamental rights. The complexity will also undoubtedly increase in situations involving conflict of fundamental rights. As rightly put by Clemens Ladenburger in his EU institutional report during the XXV FIDE congress, 'a priori a cumulative application of several layers of fundamental rights binding Member States acts should be admitted . . . [however] the principle of co-existence of several layers of fundamental rights as arguably enshrined in Article 53 has a price: complexity'.[111]

The interpretation of Article 53 of the Charter in *Åkerberg* and *Melloni* provides a new test as to the application of fundamental rights to Member States' actions falling within the scope of EU law.[112] Also, this interpretation establishes a solid bridge between national standards of protection of fundamental rights and the Charter's standards. The ECJ has thus decided to give a meaning to Article 53 of the Charter which goes further than a simple 'non-regression' clause and has also given a mandate to itself to launch a dialogue with the national constitutional courts.[113] This provision can now be viewed as a 'pluralist' clause, or a 'co-existence' clause or, more precisely, as a limited or conditioned 'best protection' clause in cases not entirely governed by secondary EU law, meaning that a local maximum standard may apply depending on the circumstances, especially the regulatory context of the case, and having always the Charter and the uniformity (or effectiveness) of EU law as an interpretative backdrop. The interpretation of Article 53 of the Charter by the Court appears to us Janusian. On the one hand, it reflects the

---

[111] See C. Ladenburger, 'EU Institutional Report' of the XXV FIDE Congress, in J. Laffranque (ed.), The Protection of Fundamental Rights Post-Lisbon: The Interaction between the Charter of Fundamental Rights of the European Union, The European Convention on Human Rights and National Constitutions (Tartu, 2012), 141 at p. 173 and p. 175. Going further, Ladenburger provides us with the *clairvoyant* example of colliding rights or clash of fundamental rights. For him 'it can become a daunting task for a national administrator or judge to assess which margin if any, a norm of Union law may leave for applying rights other than those of the Charter, and then to identify the various applicable fundamental rights and their meaning pursuant to the case law of the Strasbourg, Luxembourg and the national constitutional courts', at p. 176.

[112] D. Sarmiento, 'Who's Afraid of the Charter? The Court of Justice, National Courts and the New Framework of Fundamental Rights Protection in Europe' (2013) 50 *CMLRev*, 5, 1267. As put by Sarmiento, in *Åkerberg* and *Melloni*, 'the ECJ has created a framework of "situations" with the purpose of allocating the respective scopes of application and protection of the Charter and of national fundamental rights. The new arrangement recognizes the strategic role of supreme constitutional courts, but it also assures the autonomy of Member States as well as the Charter's prominent role in fundamental rights protection.'

[113] *See* K. Lenaerts and J. Gutiérrez-Fons, 'The Place of the Charter in the EU Constitutional Edifice', p. 22. Cited in note 109.

pluralist nature of EU law by recognizing the cumulative application of several layers of fundamental rights binding Member States. On the other hand, it strongly protects the level of protection of the Charter and the effectiveness and uniformity of EU law.

But uniformity or effectiveness of EU law in respect of fundamental rights has a price. In *Melloni*, the CJEU applied the lower EU standard of fundamental rights and not the higher national standard as asked for by the Spanish Constitutional Court. Indeed, Article 53 of the Charter is not to be used in the context of the European Arrest Warrant as it is a fully EU-regulated area of law. The pluralist clause is, therefore, not a general 'best protection' clause as it is limited by the need to respect the uniformity and autonomy of EU law. The analysis of the CJEU case law on Article 50 of the Charter points towards the same conclusion. The Charter is used as the starting point of interpretation in fundamental rights cases and sits at the top of the normative pyramid as any Bill of Rights.[114] The Charter, in principle, appears to be used by the Luxembourg judges to provide for the unremitting protection of individual rights and liberties.[115] It is in this sense that the Charter can be viewed as a purposive document, its purpose being to guarantee and to protect within the limits of reason the enjoyment of the rights and freedoms it enshrines.[116] Arguably, the use of purposive constitutional interpretation may thus justify a ruling like *Åkerberg* in which an autonomous standard of protection was applied without taking into consideration the lack of consensus between the States of the Council of Europe in relation to Article 4 of Protocol no. 7. To put it differently, Article 50 EUCFR sets its own and uniform standard of protection of fundamental rights between

---

[114] A. Barak, *Purposive Interpretation in Law* (Princeton: Princeton University Press, 2005), p. 370. For Barak, 'a constitution is a legal text that grounds a legal norm. As such it should be interpreted like any legal text. However a constitution sits at the top of the normative pyramid. It shapes the character of society and its aspirations throughout history. It establishes a ... basic political points of view, It lays the foundation for social values, setting goals, obligations and trends.'

[115] *See* Chief Justice Dickson of the Canadian Supreme Court in one of the first decisions interpreting the Canadian Charter of Rights and Freedoms. *Hunter* v. *Southam Inc* [1984] 2 S.C.R. 145, 156. 'The task of expounding a constitution is crucially different from that of construing a statute. A statute defines present rights and obligations. It is easily enacted and as easily repealed. A constitution, by contrast, is drafted with an eye to the future. Its function is to provide a continuing framework for the legitimate exercise of governmental power and, when joined by a *Bill* or a *Charter of Rights*, for the unremitting protection of individual rights and liberties.'

[116] To be closer from the reality, it may be said that the ECJ uses in fact a dual purposive interpretation. The first purpose is to ensure the protection of the individual fundamental rights of the Charter. The second purpose is to ensure the effectiveness of EU law.

the twenty-eight Member States of the EU and the explicit reliance on the ECHR standards is, therefore, not compulsory.

4.3   The Constitutional Implications of Autonomous Interpretation

In the *Bonda* case, the ECJ fully applied, and this for the very first time, the *Engel* criteria to determine the criminal nature of the administrative penalty within the framework of a Charter right, an innovation in ECJ case law.[117] In *Åkerberg*, it took a step further by making no reference at all to the ECHR case law. The overall feeling is that the Court wishes to give a limited meaning to the 'homogeneity clause' by relying instead on an autonomous interpretation of Article 50 of the Charter. This reasoning contrasts also with the position of the AG, who assessed in great detail, as discussed in the previous section, the relationship with the ECHR and the complex issue of corresponding rights. In his opinion, in order to correctly interpret Article 50 of the Charter, it is important to take into consideration the possible lack of agreement concerning a right in the ECHR system. As discussed before, not all the Member Sates have ratified or signed Article 4 of Protocol no. 7 and many States have made reservations as to the application of Article 4 of Protocol no. 7. Nevertheless, it seems that the CJEU decided to elude this problem by simply not referring to Protocol no. 7 and to Article 52(3) of the Charter on corresponding rights and by referring the case back to the referring Swedish court. Therefore, it may be said that Article 52(3) EUCFR is given here a limited meaning by the CJEU. The minimalist interpretation of Article 52(3) of the Charter in this judgment has the effect of reinforcing the autonomous character of the Charter and its 'double jeopardy' clause. It is made clear that the starting point of the interpretation in EU law of *ne bis in idem* is Article 50 EUCFR, and the criteria given by the ECJ to the national courts for its interpretation are based on the EU case law.[118] However, it is difficult to deny that the starting point is clearly formed by the ECtHR's *Engel* criteria, as the CJEU clearly enumerates the

---

[117] J. A. E. Vervaele, 'The Application of the EU Charter of Fundamental Rights (CFR) and its *Ne bis in idem* Principle in the Member States of the EU', 132. Cited in note 3.

[118] *Ibid.*, at 133. According to Vervaele, 'it is quite clear from ECHR case law that this type of administrative fiscal penalties are punitive in Sweden and do have a criminal nature under the Engel-criteria and are thus a criminal charge under article 6 ECHR. In other words, there can only be one answer and there seems to be no room for other interpretations or for other national human rights standards, as suggested by the CJEU in paragraph 36 of the ruling.'

Engel criteria in *Åkerberg*, even if it does not explicitly refer to the *Engel* case. This situation reflects the 'relative autonomy' of the interpretation given by the CJEU.

Furthermore, this autonomous interpretation has the effect to 'nullify' the non-ratification of the Protocol no. 7 by many Member States (e.g. the United Kingdom) and the declarations of reservations of Article 4 of Protocol no. 7 by many others States (e.g. France).[119] In that sense, it could be argued that the ECJ has extended the competence of the Union and has thus acted in breach of Article 51(2) of the Charter. This is all the more true if we take into consideration the fact that the Union will not ratify Protocol no. 7 when it will accede to the ECHR. This effect has no direct consequence in *Åkerberg* since Sweden has ratified the Protocol no. 7. But it is not certain what will be the reactions in countries, such as the United Kingdom or France, which do not apply Article 4 of the Protocol no. 7. In the worst case scenario, *Åkerberg* might even legitimize the reactivation of Protocol 30 by the United Kingdom. That would be a serious drawback. Another consequence of this interpretation of Article 50 of the Charter in *Åkerberg* is that it leads to the uniform application of the three *Engel* criteria in all the Member States of the EU in areas outside the field of criminal law and having a cross-border dimension. As rightly put by Vervaele,

> [t]he consequences for the Member States are substantial when implementing and enforcing EU law. They can no longer limit the *ne bis in idem* principle to criminal law *sensu strictu* and will have to widen their scope of protection in order to include punitive administrative sanctioning. Moreover, the reach of article 50 CFR is not limited to one-jurisdictional situations, as it is the case with the reach of article 4 ECHR-PR 7. This means that article 50 CFR has also transnational effect in the integrated legal order of the EU and that Member States will have to face the transnational application of *ne bis in idem* for all punitive sanctioning in the EU when implementing and enforcing EU law, and also when they are not implementing or enforcing EU law, but the case nevertheless enters the scope of application of EU law, *e.g.* in cases concerning direct tax fraud in respect of emigration to another member State (such emigration activates the EU free movement rights, and with that, the Charter). The consequence is that there will be an increasing need for case allocation in the EU when it comes to investigations and punishment under administrative and criminal law.[120]

[119] *Ibid.*   [120] *Ibid.*

In the end and on a more negative note, the problem remains that the interpretation of Article 50 of the Charter is not uniform depending on whether the case concerns the area of Freedom Security and Justice or EU competition law. In a way, the *Åkerberg* decision, which uniformly applies the *Engel* criteria to the Member States, militates for applying them also within the context of EU competition law.[121] However, it is doubtful that the ECJ will uniformly apply the *Engel* criteria in all the fields of EU law. As discussed earlier, the full application of the *Engel* criteria might endanger the effectiveness of EU competition law. The autonomous interpretation of Article 50 of the Charter in *Åkerberg* legitimizes, in this sense, the dearth of uniform interpretation of *ne bis in idem* in EU law and also leads to a minimalist interpretation of Article 52(3) of the Charter. The ECJ has, on the other hand, chosen to give a significant, normative and pluralist meaning to Article 53 of the Charter.

5   Effects on National Interpretation of *Ne Bis in Idem* – Do Too Many Cooks Really Spoil the Broth?

The main stage for the concrete application of European human rights law being the national one, it is only natural that we also take a closer look at how the different expressions of *ne bis in idem* – the EU and the ECHR one – affect the national interpretation of this principle. Thus, the consequences of the plurality of European human rights law for the legal orders of the Member States will be assessed. In this regard, both the differences and the interplay between the Charter and the ECHR will be highlighted.

It is often said that the material scope of the rights enshrined in the Charter is broader than the material scope of the ECHR and that, in contrast, the personal scope of the ECHR is wider than the Charter since it is not limited to EU law situations but includes so-called purely internal situations (situation where EU law is not applicable due to the absence of an extraneity element). Such an assertion appears to be true at first blush. However, this is not the full picture. As rightly put by Garcia,

---

[121] *Ibid.* Finally, the CJEU's elaboration of a common *ne bis in idem* principle for all policy areas is long overdue, as there are still substantial differences between the *ne bis in idem* of the area of freedom, security and justice and the internal market/competition policy area. If Member States have to comply with the *Engel-Bonda* criteria, I do not see any reason why these criteria should not be applicable to the enforcement of the competition rules.

'the Charter is part of a context, the Union context which is constructed in conceptual terms as an autonomous legal order with an integrating vocation that tends to displace, by means of the principle of supremacy, the disparities between the Member States'.[122] In other words, the Charter's rights are rubbing shoulders with or can even be said, sometimes, to form an integral part of the EU policies fostering European integration. This has important consequences for how fundamental rights are protected, as the coupling of fundamental rights with the drive for European integration can greatly reinforce the legal impact of those rights at a national level. The existence of strong constitutional principles such as the principle of supremacy, which render the enforcement of EU law rights mandatory, and the duty of loyal cooperation which require Member States to disapply any national measure, including a national constitutional provision, where it conflicts with an EU law right, give these rights much greater 'traction' at a national level than ECHR rights.

Contrary to the position of EU law within the legal order of the EU Member States, the status of the ECHR within the legal orders of its contracting parties varies considerably. In some countries, such as the Netherlands, the judgments of the ECtHR enjoy primacy over all conflicting laws, and in Austria, the ECHR has the rank of directly applicable constitutional law. However, other countries have adopted a more cautious approach towards the ECHR. For example, in Germany, this convention has a legal value below that of the German Basic Law[123] and the courts in the United Kingdom are constitutionally restricted in disapplying Acts of Parliament where they conflict with the ECHR, being required merely to take the judgments of the ECtHR into account.[124] As will be exemplified further on in this section, the highest courts of Sweden have often been reluctant to use the methods of interpretation relied on in the ECHR legal order[125] and, at times, even refused to apply

---

[122] R. A. Garcia, 'The General Provisions of the Charter of Fundamental Rights of the European Union' (2012) 4 *Jean Monnet Working Paper* 02, 23.

[123] W. Weiss, 'Human Rights in the EU: Rethinking the Role of the European Convention on Human Rights After Lisbon' (2011) 7 *EuConst*, 1, 89.

[124] P. Craig, 'The Charter, the ECJ and National Courts' in D. Ashiagbor, N. Contouris and I. Lianos (eds.), *The European Union after the Treaty of Lisbon* (Cambridge: Cambridge University Press, 2012), p. 104.

[125] Even if the Swedish Supreme Court, in the *Pastor Green* case, did begin to show signs of constitutional pluralism by interpreting the constitutional provisions of freedom of expression and religion in light of the European human rights regime and thus has departed from the traditional methodology based on preparatory works. *See* J. Nergelius, '2005 – The Year When European Law and Its Supremacy Was Finally Acknowledged

ECtHR decisions. This situation would simply be impossible in the EU legal order, if a national legislation were to violate a Charter right. To put it differently, the national court would have a duty under Article 4(3) TEU to disapply the national legislation that conflicts with a Charter right. In the absence of a similar duty in relation to the ECHR, the application of its rights are dependent on national rules on the status of this particular international convention.

One should, however, keep in mind that the status of an international legal instrument, and the rights which are enshrined therein, is not necessarily static. A good example of such evolving status is the Belgian *Le ski* case.[126] In this influential judgment, the Belgian Cour de Cassation stated that in case of a conflict between domestic law and international law, which has direct effect in the domestic legal order, the rule established by the Treaty shall prevail. It added that such a pre-eminence stems from the very nature of conventional international law. This national judgment, with its reference to international law with direct effect in the domestic legal order, was heavily influenced by the – at the time, rather fresh – judgment of the ECJ in *Van Gend en Loos*,[127] and it was decisive in transforming the Belgian legal system into a so-called monistic one.

In light of the *Åkerberg* judgment, it appears pertinent to use the Swedish constitutional context to exemplify how national courts' approach to European human rights in general – and their interpretation of *Ne Bis in Idem* in particular – can be influenced. This will provide a more in-depth understanding of the causes and impacts of the particular case of *Åkerberg*, all the while allowing for a case-study illustrating the more general phenomenon of how the approach of national courts towards international human rights documents may evolve.

5.1   Swedish Interpretation of Ne Bis in Idem before Åkerberg

The case of *Åkerberg* is certainly not the first instance in which the question has been raised as to whether the Swedish system of tax sanctions is compatible with the principle of *ne bis in idem*. This system, allowing for both a tax surcharge and a penal sanction as cumulative

---

by Swedish Courts', in P. Cramer and T. Bull (eds.), *Swedish Studies in European Law* (Oxford: Hart Publishing, 2007), vol. 1, p. 145.

[126] Cass., 27 May 1971, Pas. 1971, p. 886.
[127] Case 26/62, *Van Gend en Loos* [1963] ECR 3.

penalties for the submission of wrongful information to the tax author-ities, has been questioned on multiple occasions in Swedish doctrine,[128] as well as before national courts and the ECtHR. Next, the most signifi-cant judicial challenges against this system will be presented to enable an understanding of the pre-Åkerberg situation in Sweden regarding the compatibility of the sanctions at hand with *ne bis in idem*.

First, the principle of *ne bis in idem* is reflected in the Swedish national law through chapter 30, paragraph 9 of the penal code (*Rättegångs-balken*). Second, Sweden has – unlike several other EU Member States – signed and ratified Protocol no. 7 to the ECHR. It did this already by 1985 and it did so unconditionally. Hence, Sweden has committed itself to respect the ECHR conception concerning *ne bis in idem*. Besides Sweden being bound by the ECHR as an international convention, it should be noted that this Convention, and consequently Article 4 of its seventh protocol, has been applicable as law in Sweden since the middle of the 1990s.[129] However, as the Convention has not been given a constitutional status within the national legal order, any conflicts between the ECHR and other Swedish laws will not necessarily result in such conflicting laws being set aside (see Section 5.3 for a more detailed discussion about the different modes of application of the ECHR in Sweden).

The most pertinent judgments of the ECtHR, directly concerning the Swedish system of tax sanctions, are *Janosevic*[130] and *Rosenquist*.[131] In *Janosevic*, the ECtHR declared the tax surcharge to be criminal in nature, due to its purpose and general nature. Hence, both of the sanctions liable to be imposed for submission of wrongful tax information should – contrary to what the Swedish legislator had initially predicted[132] – be regarded as criminal in nature. However, in *Rosenquist*, the ECtHR subsequently concluded that the Swedish system was still compatible

---

[128] *See* e.g. I. Cameron, 'Skattetillägg och Europakonventionen', SvJT 2001, pp. 745–769; P. Asp, 'Skattetilläggen och oskuldspresumtionen', Skattenytt 1999, pp. 702–714; P. Asp, 'Skatteregleringens förenlighet med Europakonventionen', Juridisk tidskrift 2000–2001, pp. 606–620; and K. Åman, 'Europakonventionen och förbudet mot dubbelbestraffning', SvSkT 2010:1, pp. 104–116.

[129] Law 1994:1219 on the European Convention for the Protection of Human Rights and Fundamental Freedoms.

[130] ECtHR, *Janosevic v. Sweden*, 23 July 2002 (Appl. No. 34619/97).

[131] EctHR, *Rosenquist v. Sweden*, 14 September 2004 (Appl. No. 69619/00).

[132] SOU:1996/96 (an Official Report of the Swedish Government, part of the preparatory works for the legislative acts concerning the tax surcharge).

with Article 4 of Protocol no. 7 to the ECHR, since the two sanctions did not concern the same offence. The reasoning of this judgment was based on the circumstance that the two offences (i.e. the administrative offence and the criminal offence) did not share the same 'essential elements', since they had different objectives and requirements concerning intent. Had the Strasbourg case law on the *'idem'* element not been overhauled in 2009, it would have remained clear that the Swedish system was indeed compatible with the rule on *ne bis in idem* in the ECHR.

Although not directly dealing with the Swedish tax sanctions, the *Zolothukin* judgment did, however, undeniably change the approach to be used when determining the *'idem'* element. This seminal judgment consequently cast a shadow of serious doubt as to whether the two Swedish sanctions would still be considered as connected to two different offences under the new approach. Such doubts intensified with the judgment in *Ruotsalainen*,[133] where the ECtHR ruled that a system with multiple sanctions, similar to the Swedish one, concerned the same offence. Shortly after the introduction of the ECtHR's new approach concerning the *'idem'* element, both of the highest courts in Sweden were faced with the question of whether the Swedish system could still be considered as compatible with the ECHR. In its judgment of September 2009 (the '2009 judgment')[134], *Högsta förvaltningsdomstolen* (the Supreme Administrative Court of Sweden) played down the importance of the *Zolothukin* judgment and considered that the two Swedish sanctions were still to be considered as compatible with the ECHR due to their specific characteristics, ensuring a fair and proportionate sanctioning of the offence at hand. Although eventually reaching the same conclusion of compatibility, *Högsta domstolen* (the Supreme Civil Court of Sweden) proved to be more hesitant on this point than its administrative counterpart.

To enable a better understanding of the change in jurisprudence eventually brought about by the *Åkerberg* judgment, it is useful to take a closer look at the judgment which *Högsta domstolen* handed down on 31 March 2010 ('the 2010 judgment').[135] This judgment acutely reflects the tensions surrounding the issue of the Swedish system's compatibility with the principle of *ne bis in idem*. Of the five judges deciding the case, only three supported the final outcome: upholding the validity of the Swedish system of tax sanctions, and one of these three judges even

---

[133] ECtHR, *Routsalainen* v. *Finland*, June 2009 (Appl. No. 13079/03).
[134] Judgment of 17 September 2009 in case RÅ, ref. 94.   [135] NJA 2010 p. 168.

presented a separate opinion justifying this outcome. As to the substance of the judgment, *Högsta domstolen* concluded that after the shift in approach concerning what is to be considered the same offence, introduced by *Zolothukin* and confirmed by subsequent judgments of the ECtHR, the two Swedish sanctions could no longer be considered as connected to different offences.[136] However, *Högsta domstolen* considered that it could not be excluded that the Swedish system may be deemed compatible with the ECHR as combined sanctions connected to the same offence – a construction that could be compatible with the principle of *ne bis in idem*, provided that there is a sufficiently close connection between the sanctions, in substance and in time, and that the sanctions are predictable.[137] Hence, despite considering that the Swedish system at hand constituted two sanctions of criminal nature concerning the same offence, *Högsta domstolen* concluded that there was still a possibility that this system would be deemed to be compatible with the ECHR, noting that the jurisprudence of the ECtHR concerning permissible coordinated sanctions was meagre and open to different interpretations.[138] After having recalled that Swedish law can only be set aside on the basis of an incompatibility with the ECHR if there is 'clear support' in either the Convention text or the jurisprudence of the ECtHR, *Högsta domstolen* concluded that no such clear support could be found, given the aforementioned vague jurisprudence concerning combined sanctions.[139]

In this regard, it is interesting to note that *Högsta domstolen* did not actually take a positive stand on whether the Swedish system should be deemed compatible with the ECHR or whether the ECHR case law on combined sanctions for the same offence was effectively applicable to the Swedish system. It merely asserted that it could not be excluded that the system would classify as permissible combined sanctions and would, thereby, be compatible with the ECHR. According to the majority, there was consequently not the required 'clear support' to generally disqualify the Swedish system.[140] The two authors of the dissenting opinion, however, did look into the question of whether the national sanctions could

---

[136] *Ibid.*, points 18 and 19.
[137] *Ibid.*, points 20 to 24. The reasoning of the *Högsta domstolen* in this regard is largely based on an admittedly meager jurisprudence about combined sanctions for traffic offences, concerning the combination of a criminal laws and the administrative sanction of the driver's license being revoked.
[138] *Ibid.*, point 24.   [139] *Ibid.*, points 32 and 33.   [140] *Ibid.*, point 38.

be classified as a permissible combined sanction and concluded that they could in fact not.[141] These judges, hence, advocated that there was clear support of the incompatibility of the Swedish system with the Article 4 of Protocol no. 7 to the ECHR.[142]

Another national judgment worth mentioning is the one *Högsta domstolen* handed down on 29 June 2011 ('the 2011 judgment'),[143] in which this court confirmed its stance on the validity of the Swedish system with regard to the ECHR and – more importantly – concluded that this system did in no way constitute implementation of EU law. *Högsta domstolen* asserted that the EU directives on VAT did not prescribe any administrative or criminal sanctions, nor were the national rules shaped in line with any solution designated through EU law.[144] With regard to these circumstances, *Högsta domstolen* concluded that Article 50 of the Charter could not be applicable to a case involving the Swedish system of tax sanctions and there was consequently no need to refer a question for preliminary ruling to the ECJ. It should be noted that two of the five judges involved were dissenting, in so far as they advocated the referral of a question to the ECJ. According to the dissenting judges, it was not clear at that point in time how Article 51 of the Charter, concerning its applicability, should be interpreted and the CILFIT criteria were consequently not fulfilled in regard to sanctions related to the common VAT system.[145]

The rather controversial and less than unanimous stance of *Högsta domstolen* sparked a minor rebellion among lower courts.[146] One appeal court openly defied the 2010 judgment, shortly after it had been pronounced, and considered the Swedish system incompatible with the ECHR. Moreover, in what has now become part of EU law legend, a first instance court in the far north jurisdiction of *Haparanda* disregarded the statements made concerning the applicability of EU law in the 2011 judgment and made a reference to the ECJ concerning the

---

[141] See The dissenting opinion of Marianne Lundius and Stefan Lindskog in the 2010 judgment, points 35 to 42. Their main argument was that the two Swedish sanctions clearly constituted two separate proceedings with separate assessments of responsibility, something that would not be permissible if the sanctions were to qualify as combined sanctions for the same offence.

[142] *Ibid.*, point 51.   [143] NJA 2011, p. 444.   [144] *Ibid.*, points 13 and 14.

[145] See The dissenting opinion of Kerstin Calissendorff and Johnny Herre in the 2011 judgment, point 3.

[146] *See* A.S. Lind, Ett par kommentarer rörande mål C-617/10, *Åklagaren mot Åkerberg Fransson*, dom av den 26 februari 2013, *ERT* 2013, p. 389.

compatibility of the Swedish combination of sanctions with the principle of *ne bis in idem*, as enshrined in Article 50 of the Charter.

5.2   Swedish Interpretation of Ne Bis in Idem after Åkerberg

As elaborated upon previously in this chapter, the judgment in the *Åkerberg* case established that the Swedish regulation involving parallel sanctions did in fact, as far as it concerned sanctioning infringements connected to the levying of VAT, imply an implementation of EU law within the meaning of Article 51(1) of the Charter.[147] As to the substantive interpretation of the Charter rule on *ne bis in idem* and its consequences for the Swedish regulation, the ECJ held that Article 50 of the Charter precluded a criminal proceeding in relation to acts of noncompliance with declaration obligations if it followed a sanction of criminal nature in respects of the same acts and that sanction had become final. As has already been discussed, the ECJ did not make any reference to the case law of ECtHR in this regard, nor did it discuss the possibility under EU law to maintain combined criminal sanctions for the same offence. This latter issue was, in fact, raised in the order for reference but never included in the concrete questions referred.

Before *Haparanda tingsrätt* even got the chance to apply the response given by the ECJ in the *Åkerberg* case, *Högsta domstolen* granted leave to appeal in another national dispute concerning the Swedish system of parallel sanctions. It was clear that the judgment from Luxembourg had the potency for overturning the earlier jurisprudence of *Högsta domstolen* and this court most likely wanted to regain control of how *ne bis in idem* was to be interpreted in relation to the applicability of the national sanctions, to avoid diverging interpretations by various lower courts. Consequently, *Högsta domstolen* hurriedly retried the question of the compatibility of the Swedish system with *ne bis in idem*. It did so in its plenary formation, handing down a unanimous judgment on 11 June 2013 ('the 2013 judgment').[148] First of all, *Högsta domstolen* had to

---

[147] For further discussion about the implications connected to this interpretation of the meaning of the term 'implementing', *see* K. Lenaerts and J. A. Gutiérrez-Fons, 'The Place of the Charter in the EU Constitutional Edifice', in S. Peers et al. (eds.), *The EU Charter of Fundamental Rights: A Commentary* (Oxford: Hart Publishing, 2014), and V. Skouris, 'Développements récents de la protection des droits fondamentaux dans l'Union européenne: les arrêts *Melloni* et *Åkerberg Fransson*' (2013) *Il Diritto dell'Unione Europea*, 13, 233–235.

[148] Case nr. B 4946-12.

concede that, in light of the *Åkerberg* judgment, the assertions made in the 2011 judgment needed to be reconsidered.[149] Without much further ado, the Swedish court thereby accepted that it had to apply EU law and the Charter when it assessed the validity of parallel sanctions concerning incorrect information submitted with regards to VAT. It also emphasized that the rights enshrined in the Charter had to be given full effect and that it was not permissible for Swedish courts to require a 'clear support' in this regard. Although the ECJ did not itself refer to the *Engel* or *Zolothukin* cases when it set out the criteria for assessing whether certain sanctions violate the EU rule on *ne bis in idem*, *Högsta domstolen* took for granted that these cases were relevant and applicable to the assessment that was to be carried out on the national level.[150] When carrying out this assessment, it comes as no surprise that *Högsta domstolen* found the tax penalty to have a criminal nature.[151] As previously mentioned, this was already taken for a fact in the 2010 judgment. In this regard, *Högsta domstolen* promotes unity in the European human right law by expressly stating that the conclusion about the criminal nature of a sanction has to be the same, whether the assessment is made in the light of Article 4 of Protocol no. 7 to the ECHR or Article 50 of the EU Charter.[152] The possibility mentioned in the *Åkerberg* judgment to apply national stand-ards, and the conditions imposed on such an application, were briefly discussed in the 2013 judgment, but no additional substantive standards were in fact applied. As to substance, the Swedish court simply stated that it follows from what has been held by the ECJ that a person who has already been subjected to a tax penalty concerning VAT could not be tried in criminal proceedings in respect of the same acts.[153] On a procedural note, however, *Högsta domstolen* did extend the protection against double jeopardy in so far as it stated that the mere initiation of a proceeding of criminal nature would suffice to block another proceeding, without requiring that the person concerned be convicted and that conviction have become final.[154]

Furthermore, the Swedish system with two different sanctions for tax offences was a general one and did not only apply to infringements concerning VAT. *Högsta domstolen* therefore proceeded to examine whether it should change its holding in the 2010 judgment also with regard to infringements concerning income tax, employers' contributions and similar levies (the sanctioning of which escapes the scope of EU law).

---

[149] *Ibid.*, point 25.   [150] *Ibid.*, points 28 and 29.   [151] *Ibid.*, point 34.
[152] *Ibid.*, points 36 and 37.   [153] *Ibid.*, point 48.   [154] *Ibid.*, points 69 and 70.

In doing so, *Högsta domstolen* elaborated on the degree of prudence that had to be adopted when assessing the validity of national legislation in the light of the ECHR. It stated that the use of the requirement of 'clear support' in the 2010 judgment was justified at the time of that judgment, bearing in mind that the game-changing *Zolothukin* judgment was still very fresh and that the practical consequences of disqualifying the Swedish system would have been great. At that time, it was preferable to give the Swedish legislator time to react to the new approach outlined in the *Zolothukin* judgment.[155] However, *Högsta domstolen* then asserted that the situation had changed significantly since the 2010 judgment. By referring to the fact that the '"damage had already been done' to the Swedish system, in so far as it had been put out of play with regard to VAT infringements, and that fundamental principles of foreseeability and equal treatment militated for a uniform application of *ne bis in idem*, *Högsta domstolen* concluded that there was now 'sufficient support' to disqualify the system of parallel sanctions as a whole, due to its incompatibility with both EU and ECHR law.[156]

Shortly after the 2013 judgment, *Högsta domstolen* announced its intention to clarify whether and in what circumstances earlier convictions for tax offences, that had become final, would be subject to revision. Indeed, on the 16 July of that same year, *Högsta domstolen* handed down a judgment determining the retroactive consequences of the 2013 judgment.[157] After establishing that the case at hand could not be subject to revision on the basis of the restricted possibilities to grant such extraordinary judicial remedy under established Swedish law,[158] *Högsta domstolen* set out to assess whether revision could be granted on the basis of ECHR law.[159] On the basis of an analysis covering both the provisions of the ECHR and the jurisprudence of the ECtHR, the Swedish court then concluded that a revision was indeed merited – considering that *ne bis in idem* is a fundamental rule connected to the rule of law, that a revision

---

[155] *Ibid.*, point 57.   [156] *Ibid.*, point 60.   [157] Case Ö 1526-13.
[158] *Ibid.*, points 13 to 15.
[159] *Ibid.*, point 17, which states that: 'The assessment should primarily be carried out in accordance with the ECHR. The judicial application of the ECJ, in this regard, only targets VAT, while [Protocol no. 7 to the ECHR] has a wider scope of application as regards double jeopardy concerning tax infringements. The assessment shall be based upon the circumstance that it is contrary to the protocol to persecute and convict a person for a tax offence if he or she has already been ordered to pay a tax surcharge, as a consequence to the same false information that is concerned by the criminal prosecution' [our translation and emphasis].

would provide a remedy that would be more appropriate than other alternative remedies, and that the Swedish system of parallel sanctions had been set aside as a whole by the 2013 judgment.[160] An interesting last point to note about this judgment is that *Högsta domstolen* determined the date from which convictions that had become final can be revised on as 10 February 2009, the date of the ECtHR's *Zolothukin* judgment. The Swedish court expressly stated that the ECJ's judgment in *Åkerberg* did not entail a change of ECHR law, even if this judgment changed the view of the content of the ECHR law.[161] One might of course ponder on whether the latter does not effectively imply the former. In any case, this reasoning concerning the period from which revision is warranted does imply that *Högsta domstolen* acted *ultra vires* in the 2010 judgment, the validity of which the plenary chamber of this court was so careful to defend in the 2013 judgment.

As for the stance taken by *Högsta förvaltningsdomstolen*, having been even more protective of the Swedish system, the *Åkerberg* judgment did not spark any immediate reaction. However, after the firm stance taken by *Högsta domstolen* in the two aforementioned judgments, its administrative counterpart eventually followed suit. On 29 November 2013, *Högsta förvaltningsdomstolen* handed down a clear (even if sparsely reasoned) judgment, reiterating the same conclusions reached by *Högsta domstolen*. It should be noted that the taxpayer concerned by the 2009 judgment of *Högsta förvaltningsdomstolen*, a man named Björn Henriksson, has lodged a complaint against Sweden with the ECtHR.[162] The approach taken by the *Högsta förvaltningsdomstolen* would, hence, have been directly and concretely scrutinized by the Strasbourg court in light of the ECHR rule about 'double jeopardy' in due time. This might explain why the CJEU in *Åkerberg* did not, as it did in *Bonda*, decide itself on the criminal nature of the sanction, but left that matter to the national Court (and with that, to the ECtHR).

5.3   Appetizing Consequences of the Plurality of European Human Rights Law

Through this case-study in how the approach of national courts towards European human rights law may evolve, we learn that a plurality of human rights standards – in themselves restricted in one way or an

---

[160] *Ibid.*, point 25.   [161] *Ibid.*, point 32.
[162] ECtHR, *Björn Henriksson*, 19 January 2010 (Appl. No. 7396/10).

other – may together contribute to a national legal development towards both higher standards and their wider scope of application. In fact, it lies in the nature of a human right standard to be a minimum standard of protection. A small change in one minimum standard may then spark a development in another set of standards, as the latter one must 'catch-up' with the former. All this cross-fertilization is particularly felt on the national level, where the national judge must manage the interplay between the domestic, the EU and the ECHR standards.

As regards this managing act, it follows from the new rule introduced by *Åkerberg* and *Melloni* that, when EU law is applicable, national standards (i.e. standards other than the uniform EU standard) can be used in a complementary fashion only if they fulfil both the conditions mentioned earlier in Section 4.2 (the 'level of protection' condition and the 'uniformity' or 'effectiveness' condition'). This seems to give a quite narrow possibility for effectively applying a national human rights standard different from the EU one. Even if the national standard is compatible with the Charter, in the sense that it promotes at least the same level of human rights protection, it could still not be applied in a way which would compromise the effectiveness of other (i.e. not human rights related) EU law. This possibility of using a national standard will, as the case in *Melloni* shows, be particularly slim when the EU rule whose *effet utile* is at stake restricts rather than promotes fundamental rights. In those cases, the hands of the national judge will be tied to the specific human rights compromise struck at EU level. That having been said, commentators claiming that the recent case law in this field is still a step towards more leeway for plurality[163] are not necessarily wrong in their observations. In fact, one might argue that the possibility for using national standards has long been firmly restricted by the effectiveness of EU law (it follows from constant case law since *Internationale Handelsgesellschaft*[164] that even a constitutional national provision must be waived, if its application would endanger the effectiveness and supremacy of EU law). Hence, it could be argued that in this respect, the ECJ has merely maintained the status quo. Also the second limitation seems to resonate with pre-Charter case law; in as far as national measures falling within the scope of EU law may not restrict the level

---

[163] E.g. V. Skouris, 'Développements récents de la protection des droits fondamentaux dans l'Union européenne: les arrêts *Melloni* et *Åkerberg Fransson*', p. 237 et seq. Cited in note 147.

[164] Case 11/70, *Internationale Handelsgesellschaft mbH* [1970] ECR 1125.

of human rights protection which the ECJ has vowed to uphold. One might argue that the only novelty brought about by *Åkerberg* and *Melloni* is that this limitation, where the EU level of human rights must not be substituted by a lower national one, is recast in terms relating to the Charter rather than general principles of EU law.

After the judgment in *Åkerberg*, the use of a test requiring a 'clear support' in relation to constitutional review of national legislation is excluded in relation to EU law. That much is certainly sufficiently clear. However, in view of the functional differences between EU and ECHR law, it is questionable if such a test would ever have been applicable in an EU law context. Even if it had been applied, such a requirement wouldn't necessarily have posed a practical problem in relation to EU law. In fact, if it is not clear whether a national system is compatible with EU law, the national court faced with this uncertainty will always have the option (or, in certain circumstances, the obligation) to send a preliminary reference to the ECJ on the basis of Article 267 TFEU. As such a mechanism of preliminary rulings is foreign to the ECHR system, a national court risks being trapped in a guessing game with regard to the compatibility of a national standard with a Convention standard. In view of the far-reaching consequences of a court invalidating national legislation, it is, hence, understandable that the Swedish courts developed a test which would ensure that national legislation would not be thrown aside on the basis of a guess that could subsequently turn out to be unfounded.

It should be recalled that, except from the aforementioned functional differences between ECHR and EU law, the important difference between the two legal orders is their way of being absorbed into the national legal order; EU law imposing itself on its own merits, and ECHR law taking a more subsidiary role, being dependent on the particular status afforded to it by the constitutional idiosyncrasies of each individual Contracting Party. As regards the status of the ECHR in Sweden, the key can be found in the reasoning of *Högsta domstolen* in point 53 in the 2013 judgment, where this court re-elaborates on the requirement of clear support. It should be noted that this requirement does not concern the application of the ECHR, as incorporated into Swedish national law, in individual cases.[165] The requirement of clear support has only become relevant when a question arises about the validity of a provision of Swedish law and the judiciary would be disqualifying an act of national parliament on

---

[165] *See* e.g. Case RH 2006:79, where Article 4 of Protocol no. 7 to the ECHR was interpreted and applied without any considerations in regards to a clear support.

the basis of the ECHR as an international convention. This is something it has proved very unwilling to do, and maybe understandably so.

Moving on the actual interplay between EU and ECHR human rights law, as exemplified by the Swedish legal developments surrounding the *Åkerberg* case, the development of the requirement for 'clear support' is particularly interesting. In point 60 of the 2013 judgment, *Högsta domstolen* seemed to abandon the requirement of 'clear support' hitherto applied in the Swedish constitutional review of the national rules in relation the ECHR. Instead, the use of the considerably more flexible requirement of 'sufficient support' was justified by a time element and the effects of EU law. However, none of these factors has anything to do with the clarity of support for the constitutional review. From this, we can draw the conclusion that the *Åkerberg* judgment did not only influence how the content of ECHR law is perceived substantially, but also how easily it can penetrate the national legal order and be used as a basis for constitutional review. In other words, not only did the Swedish court equate the meaning of *ne bis in idem* in the ECHR with that of the Charter, but the new test developed for the non-VAT sanctions' compatibility with the ECHR is also affected by the consequences of EU law and the Charter.[166]

The aftermath of the *Åkerberg* judgment does indeed provide a good example of when the interplay between the EU and ECHR legal orders results in a raised level of human rights protection, not envisaged or attainable without the input of each strand of standards. Of course, *Högsta domstolen* was correct when it said that the ECJ's interpretation of Article 50 of the Charter does not change the meaning of Protocol 7 to the ECHR. *Per se*, it does not. But since the national court does not want to risk falling below any of the minimum standards set up by the EU and the ECHR, and thereby chooses to use a homogenous standard across the board, the protection given by the ECHR principle of *ne bis in idem* in Sweden will, in practical terms, have increased. And rightly so, given the existing ECtHR judgments in *Jussila* and *Zolothukin*. Moreover, due to this EU-induced increase in ECHR protection, the ECJ's interpretation of *ne bis in idem* will now spill over and affect purely internal situations of direct taxation. In fact, since tax surcharges for wrongful information concerning VAT are most frequently imposed on companies (which are

---

[166] See U. Bernitz, 'The Åkerberg Fransson Case: Ne bis in idem: Double Procedures for Tax Surcharge and Tax Offences not Possible' in J. Nergelius and E. Kristoffersson, *Human Rights in Contemporary European Law* (Oxford: Hart Publishing, 2015), p. 191.

not themselves liable to be charged with a criminal offence, only their executives are), the *Åkerberg* judgment will most likely have more effects on purely internal situations involving direct taxation) than situations covered by EU law.[167]

6   Conclusion

From what we have observed in this chapter, we can conclude that there are certainly major differences in how *ne bis in idem* is perceived in the various states of Europe. And although the ECJ cannot be accused of being in open rebellion against the ECtHR when it comes to defining and applying the principle of *ne bis in idem*, enshrined in both the ECHR and the Charter, the EU court has certainly been very careful in its rhetoric, as to preserve its interpretative autonomy of this principle. This independent attitude can certainly be questioned on the basis of the 'homogeneity clause' of Article 52(3) in the EU Charter. Yet, as has been exemplified by the consequences of the ECJ's judgment in the *Åkerberg* case on the Swedish interpretation of *ne bis in idem*, the preservation of a certain plurality of human rights standards may actually foster a positive development in the national application of particular right at hand towards a higher standard of human rights protection. One may even argue that if all European human rights law would be completely uniform, there would not be different standards of minimum protection providing a dynamic application of human rights law. Put differently, if each applicable standard is exactly the same, there is no need to adapt and improve the level of protection to be applied. There would simply be no more constitutional competition.

---

[167] See the new law on tax surcharge entered into force on the 1st of January 2016 (Lag om talan om skattetillgägg i visa fall, 2015:632).

3

Ne Bis in Idem in the Case Law
of the European Court of Justice

DANIEL SARMIENTO

1 Introduction

Ne bis in idem has become a multifaceted principle of considerable relevance in EU law. The principle has been given a prominent place in the Charter of Fundamental Rights of the European Union, whilst several instruments of secondary law, such as the Framework Decision on the European Arrest Warrant or the Schengen Agreement, to name a few, openly refer to the prohibition of double criminal procedures and punishment. At the same time, the practice of EU law, both at the level of EU institutions and of national authorities, has given plenty of occasions to develop the principle in areas such as competition, agriculture, taxation or the statute of the EU's civil servants. *Ne bis in idem* is everywhere in EU law, its influence touches every area of EU policy, but the definition of its precise contours is still open to considerable discussion.[1]

The case law of the European Court of Justice (hereinafter, CJEU) lies at the heart of *ne bis in idem* in EU Law. The relevance of the EU's ultimate interpreter of the law is not only due to the fact that it provides the authoritative interpretation of EU rules, including the principle of *ne*

---

[1] For an overall view on the scope of the principle of *ne bis in idem* in EU Law, see, *inter alia*, B. van Bockel, *The Ne Bis In Idem Principle in EU Law* (Alphen aan de Rijn: Kluwer Law International, 2010); M. Fletcher, 'Some Developments to the Ne Bis in Idem Principles in the EU' (2003) 66 *Modern Law Review*, 5, 769; J. da Cunha Rodrigues, 'A propos du principe 'ne bis in idem' – Un regard sur la jurisprudence de la Cour de Justice des Communautés Européennes' *Une Communauté de Droit. Festschrift für Gil Carlos Rodriguez Iglesias* (Berlin, 2005); S. Peers, 'Mutual Recognition and Criminal Law in the European Union: Has the Council Got It Wrong?' (2004) 41 *CMLrev*, 1, 5; H. van der Wilt, 'The European Arrest Warrant and the Principle Ne Bis In Idem', in R. Blekxtoon and W. van Ballegooij (eds.), *Handbook on the European Arreset Warrant* (The Hague: T.M.C. Asser Press, 2005); J. Vervaele, 'The Transnational *Ne Bis in Idem Principle* in the EU: Mutual Recognition and Equivalent Protection of Human Rights' (2005) 1 *Utrecht Law Review*, 2 and, by the same author, 'Ne Bis In Idem: Towards a Transnational Constitutional Principle in the EU?' (2013) 9 *Utrecht Law Review*, 4, 211.

bis idem. It is also significant because, despite its apparent lack of overall coherence, a general vision of the principle can be deduced from the sum of the CJEU's individual judgments. This codifying role of the CJEU's case law has become even more relevant after the entry into force of the Charter of Fundamental Rights of the European Union, whose Article 50 serves as a general statement of *ne bis in idem* touching all areas of EU law. The CJEU has now begun to interpret this rule and in its first decisions it has given relevant insights into its scope, its relationship with the European Convention of Human Rights (ECHR) and with general principles of EU Law. The purpose of this chapter is to portray the said case law and to shed some light into the CJEU's approach to *ne bis in idem* as an overarching principle of EU law.

To begin with, Section 2 will approach the case law on the sources of primary law of *ne bis in idem*. These concern Article 50 of the Charter and the unwritten general principle of law of *ne bis in idem*. In Section 3, the role of the ECHR and national constitutional traditions will be analysed, since Article 6 TEU states their role as sources of interpretation of EU law, particularly when it comes to fundamental rights and general principles. Ultimately, Section 4 will deal with the interpretation the CJEU has provided of instruments of secondary law concerning *ne bis in idem*, such as Justice and Home Affairs, competition or staff cases. The result of this three-part study will clarify the CJEU's overall conception of *ne bis in idem*, although it will also show that, at least for now, some differences still remain depending on the area of policy. Although a potentially universal vision of *ne bis in idem* is in the making in the case law of the CJEU, it appears that there is still some room for differentiation between different areas of law.

2   *Ne Bis in Idem* as a Principle of EU Primary Law

2.1   Ne Bis in Idem *and the Charter*

After its entry into force on 1 December 2009, the Charter has become a basic reference amongst the EU's constitutional rules. The explanations of the Charter are of valuable use when interpreting Article 50, as the Charter itself provides that the explanations should be taken into account.[2] In two brief but heavily charged paragraphs, the Presidium of

---

[2] See Article 52, para. 7, of the Charter.

the Convention in charge of drafting the Charter (as amended in 2007), stated the following:

> The non bis in idem rule applies in Union law (see, among the many precedents, the judgment of 5 May 1966, Joined Cases 18/65 and 35/65 Gutmann v Commission [1966] ECR 149 and a recent case, the decision of the Court of First Instance of 20 April 1999, Joined Cases T-305/94 and others Limburgse Vinyl Maatschappij NV v Commission [1999] ECR II-931). The rule prohibiting cumulation refers to cumulation of two penalties of the same kind, that is to say criminal-law penalties.
>
> In accordance with Article 50, the non bis in idem rule applies not only within the jurisdiction of one State but also between the jurisdictions of several Member States. That corresponds to the acquis in Union law; see Articles 54 to 58 of the Schengen Convention and the judgment of the Court of Justice of 11 February 2003, C-187/01 Gözütok [2003] ECR I-1345, Article 7 of the Convention on the Protection of the European Communities' Financial Interests and Article 10 of the Convention on the fight against corruption. The very limited exceptions in those Conventions permitting the Member States to derogate from the non bis in idem rule are covered by the horizontal clause in Article 52 (1) of the Charter concerning limitations. As regards the situations referred to by Article 4 of Protocol No 7, namely the application of the principle within the same Member State, the guaranteed right has the same meaning and the same scope as the corresponding right in the ECHR.

From both the literal terms of Article 50 of the Charter and its explanations, some conclusions may be deduced. Also the case law of the CJEU, both prior and posterior to 2009, will provide further insight into the scope of Article 50. For the sake of clarity, the contents of the provision will be arranged distinguishing its objective, subjective and territorial scope of application. The first refers to the protected subject matter (criminal proceedings, administrative proceedings, final judgments, etc.), whilst the second concerns the individuals protected by the rule. The third refers to the scope of the rule in national and transnational contexts.

2.1.1 Subjective Scope of Application

The individuals protected by Article 50 of the Charter are those who have been previously and finally acquitted or convicted. The Charter does not extend the protection of Article 50 to legal or natural persons intricately linked to the person or persons previously judged, or to the facts of the previous case. This issue was considered by the CJEU in the case of

Gasparini,[3] a preliminary reference on the interpretation of Article 54 of the Schengen Agreement in which a Spanish court questioned if the *ne bis in idem* also applied to two defendants who had not been judged in Portugal on the grounds that their prosecution had been time-barred under Portuguese law. According to the CJEU, and referring to the wording of Article 54 of the Schengen Agreement, 'it is clear . . . that only persons who have already had a trial finally disposed of once may derive advantage from the ne bis in idem principle'.[4]

2.1.2   Territorial Scope of Application

As also discussed in Chapter 1, Section 3.1, although Article 50 of the Charter keeps silent as to the territorial dimension of the right, both the explanations of the provision and the CJEU's case law confirm that its territorial scope encompasses both internal and inter-State situations alike. The explanations could not be clearer on this point: 'in accordance with Article 50, the non bis in idem rule applies not only within the jurisdiction of one State but also between the jurisdictions of several Member States. That corresponds to the *acquis* in Union law'.[5] This last sentence recognizes the fact that Article 50 is ambiguous as to its application in proceedings between two Member States, but its applicability to the said situations has been confirmed, as the explanations state,

---

[3] Case C-467/04, *Gasparini and Others*, EU:C:2006:610.

[4] *Gasparini*, at para. 35. The CJ carried on its reasoning and justified its decision on the following grounds: 'This interpretation is borne out by the purpose of the provisions of Title VI of the EU Treaty, as set out in the fourth indent of the first para. of Article 2 EU, namely "to maintain and develop the Union as an area of freedom, security and justice, in which the free movement of persons is assured in conjunction with appropriate measures with respect to . . . the prevention and combating of crime"'.

Consequently, the answer to the second question must be that the *ne bis in idem* principle, enshrined in Article 54 of the Convention Implementing the Schengen Agreement (CISA), does not apply to persons other than those whose trial has been finally disposed of in a Contracting State' (paras. 36 and 37).

The CJEU was following here the Opinion of Advocate General Sharpston (15 June 2006), where she proposed the same outcome, with additional arguments, particularly at point 123 of her Opinion, where she highlighted: 'Article 54 of the CISA explicitly states that "a person whose trial has been finally disposed of in one Contracting Party may not be prosecuted in another Contracting Party for the same acts". It follows from a literal reading of that provision that it benefits only the specific individual or individuals who have been finally acquitted or convicted. On its face, that provision does not therefore cover other individuals who may have been involved in the same acts but who have not yet been tried'.

[5] See Explanations of Article 50, quoted earlier in Section 2.

in the *acquis*, that is, in the CJEU's previous case law and in several instruments of secondary law, such as the Schengen Agreement.

When it comes to proceedings taking place entirely within one Member State, Article 50 will apply only if the circumstances of the case are within 'the scope of application of Union law', in the sense of Article 51.1 of the Charter. This means, as the CJEU has had the chance to confirm in several judgments after the entry into force of the Charter, that either the first or the second proceeding must be the result of an application of a rule of EU law.[6] If the first or the second proceeding concerned the breach of tax rules as harmonized by EU law, then Article 50 applies.[7] Also, in areas not fully determined by EU law, it is important to note that, since the decisions in the seminal cases of *Melloni* and *Åkerberg Fransson*, the national judge will be able to chose whether to apply Article 50 or its internal standard of protection in case the latter is more protective.[8]

A different scenario appears when the first proceedings take place in a third State, whilst the second proceedings are initiated in a Member State. The presence of EU law in these cases is more questionable. First, the case will require some connection with EU law, in contrast with cases concerning two Member States, now regulated by Article 54 of the Schengen Agreement. No such rule applies to a situation in which the first judgment has been rendered by a third country court. Second, even if the case concerns an area of Union competence, as in the case of, for example, competition, the CJEU has been reluctant to recognize any role for EU law, including its *ne bis in idem* principle. The issue was first addressed in the *Boehringer* case, where the CJEU left open the possibility for the Commission to take into account anti-trust sanctions imposed by the US authorities.[9] However, in its latest case law, both the CJEU and the

---

[6] See the Opinion of Advocate General Kokott (15 December 2011) in Case C-489/10, *Bonda*, EU:C:2012:319 at points 13 et seq.

[7] Case C-617/10, *Åklagaren v. Åkerberg Fransson*, EU:C:2013:105 and Case C-399/11, *Melloni*, EU:C:2013:107.

[8] *Åkerberg Fransson*, quoted, and, *Melloni*, quoted: 'Article 53 of the Charter confirms that, where an EU legal act calls for national implementing measures, national authorities and courts remain free to apply national standards of protection of fundamental rights, provided that the level of protection provided for by the Charter, as interpreted by the Court, and the primacy, unity and effectiveness of EU law are not thereby compromised' (*Melloni*, at para. 60). On this criteria, see D. Sarmiento, 'Who's Afraid of the Charter? The Court of Justice, national courts and the new framework of fundamental rights protection in Europe,' (2013) 50 *Common Market Law Review*, 1256 et seq.

[9] Case 7/72, *Boehringer v. Commission*, EU:C:1972:125.

General Court (hereinafter GC) have finally confirmed that the principle of *ne bis in idem* does not apply 'to situations in which the legal systems and competition authorities of non-member States intervene within their own jurisdiction'.[10] The CJEU has reached this conclusion based on several arguments, but mostly on the fact that the elements forming the basis of other States' legal systems in the field of competition not only include specific aims and objectives, 'but also result in the adoption of specific substantive rules and a wide variety of legal consequences, whether administrative, criminal or civil, when the authorities of those States have established that there have been infringements of the applicable competition rules.'[11]

2.2   Ne Bis in Idem *as a General Principle*

So far we have dealt with Article 50 of the Charter, but this does not exclude that the principle of *ne bis in idem* might appear in other sources of EU primary law. Whilst written primary law makes no further references to *ne bis in idem*, it is open to question if *ne bis in idem* is a general principle of EU law and, if so, in what ways it overlaps with Article 50 of the Charter. It is unclear at present whether general principles of EU law retain such status once codified by the Charter, or whether they have been neutralized as a result of the entry into force of the Charter. These issues will be addressed at this point.

2.2.1   Status of *Ne Bis in Idem* as a General Principle

In its first decisions on *ne bis in idem*, delivered in the late sixties, the CJEU referred to '*the rule* of non bis in idem'[12] and to 'a general requirement of natural justice'.[13] No mention whatsoever was made of the status of *ne bis in idem* as a general principle of EU Law. In the mid-eighties the CJEU moved forward and began to differentiate between double prosecution (*Erledigungsprinzip*) and double punishment (*Anrechnungsprinzip*), a distinction that would later be confirmed in the CJEU's case law. However, at this early point the CJEU stated in some judgments that the prohibition of double punishment would be

---

[10] Case C-289/04 P, *Showa Denko v. Commission*, EU:C:2006:431, para. 56.

[11] *Showa Denko v. Commission*, quoted, para. 53.

[12] Joined Cases 18/65 and 35/65, *Gutmann v. Commission*, EU:C:1967:6, paras. 79, 81 and 82.

[13] Case 14/68, *Wilhelm and Others*, EU:C:1969:4, para. 11.

considered to be part of the principle of proportionality,[14] but in other decisions it would categorize that prohibition under 'the principle of non bis in idem'. Although double punishment would eventually be treated independently from *ne bis in idem* (with the exception of competition, as it will be later explained), it is in this context that the CJEU, in its judgment in the case of *Salzgitter*, began to refer to the principle of *ne bis in idem* as such.[15]

Shortly after the judgment in *Salzgitter*, the CJEU cleared the ground in the case of *Limburgse Vinyl*[16] and stated that EU law's *ne bis in idem* referred to double prosecution, and not just to double penalties.[17] Furthermore, in this judgment, and for the first time, *ne bis in idem* was declared 'a fundamental principle of [European Union] Law',[18] thus confirming the status of *ne bis in idem* as a general principle of EU Law. In subsequent case law and in line with the judgment in *Limburgse Vinyl*, the CJEU has repeatedly referred to *ne bis in idem* as a 'principle'.

Although the CJEU has not explained in detail why *ne bis in idem* is a general principle of EU law, there are sufficient arguments in favour of such a recognition.[19] First, *ne bis in idem* is currently proclaimed in the ECHR, a fact that has been outlined by the CJEU on several occasions. Second, the principle is also a part of all national legal orders. There may be nuances between the Member States' conception of the principle, but it is unquestionable that it is part of the constitutional traditions common to the Member States. Lastly, *ne bis in idem* has a general scope that transcends specific areas of the law, a requirement that the CJEU

---

[14] Case 137/85, *Maizena and Others*, EU:C:1987:493, para. 21.

[15] Case C-182/99 P, *Salzgitter v. Commission*, EU:C:2003:526, paras. 99 and 104.

[16] Joined Cases C-238/99 P, C-244/99 P, C-245/99 P, C-247/99 P, C-250/99 P to C-252/99 P and C-254/99 P, *Limburgse Vinyl Maatschappij and Others v. Commission*, EU:C:2002:582.

[17] *Ibid.*, paras 59 and 60.   [18] *Ibid.*, para. 59.

[19] In this vein, see the Opinion of Adovcate General Sharpston in *Gasparini*, quoted, at point 80: 'For the purposes of EU law, it seems to me almost inevitable that, in consequence, the concept of ne bis in idem (which, as the Court noted in Vinyl Maatschappij, is a fundamental principle of Community law) is to be understood as a free-standing, or propriae naturae, principle. In the absence of further initiatives by way of Treaty amendment or secondary Community legislation, it is therefore to be refined and developed by the Court in the exercise of its "hermeneutic monopoly" on such key concepts of EU law. (69) The specific application of the principle in particular areas (be these competition law or through Article 54 of the CISA) should form part of a core understanding of what that fundamental principle means (or ought to mean) within the Community legal order.'

insisted on in its judgment in *Audiolux*.[20] All areas of law in which public authorities exercise punitive powers are covered by the principle of *ne bis in idem*. It is thus, in the language of the CJEU, a 'constitutional principle' and not a sectorial or specialized maxim applicable only to a specific area of law.

2.2.2 The Non-Resolved Relationship between General Principles and Charter Rights

Whether *ne bis in idem* is a general principle or not has important practical consequences. First and foremost, if it is a principle, it transforms into a norm of primary law, a parameter of validity of all EU acts and all Member State acts under the scope of application of EU Law. Second, it gives an enormous power to the CJEU, since it will be its task to determine the scope and content of the principle, with no interference from the Union's legislature or executive. And third and most importantly, the status of general principles remains autonomous *vis-à-vis* the Charter. This last consequence raises specific issues that deserve particular attention.

Indeed, once a fundamental right has the status of general principle, it is, in theory, an autonomous legal rule non-dependent from other rules of the legal system, including the Charter. In theory, the general principle of *ne bis in idem* acts independently from Article 50 of the Charter, as so do many other fundamental rights holding the dual status of general principles and Charter rights. This situation is now under question as a result of the CJEU's case law on the scope of application of the Charter. In its judgment in the case of *Åkerberg Fransson*,[21] the CJEU stated that the fundamental rights guaranteed by the Charter must be respected where national legislation falls within the scope of EU law. In other words, 'the applicability of EU law entails the applicability of the fundamental rights guaranteed by the Charter'.[22] Until then, some doubts remained as to the precise scope of application of Charter rights in Member States, some authors defending that such rights would only be applicable when Member States 'implement' EU law. Since this is a strict criterion, it would leave many areas within the scope of application of EU law unprotected by

---

[20] Case C-101/08, *Audiolux SA and Others* v. *Groupe Bruxelles Lambert SA and Others and Bertelsmann AG and Others*, EU:C:2009:626.

[21] Quoted in footnote 7.   [22] *Ibid.*, paras. 20 and 21.

Charter rights, and only protected by national fundamental rights and the ECHR.[23] This interpretation has been discarded by the CJEU in the case of *Åkerberg Fransson*, in which it adhered to what some authors have called the 'mirror' criterion: all situations in which Member States are within the scope of application of EU law are also within the scope of the Charter.[24]

This solution leaves the relationship between general principles and Charter rights in a difficult position. Under a strict interpretation of the scope of application of the Charter, it makes sense to keep general principles as a safety net for those situations that are within the scope of EU law, but which are not considered to be 'implementation' of EU law by the Member States in the narrow sense. But now, having rejected this narrow approach, the omnipresent Charter leaves scarcely any field of application to fundamental rights recognized as general principles and also contained in the Charter. Why would a fundamental right such as *ne bis in idem* hold a dual status, a duality that has no practical consequences since it has been settled that the Charter applies to all situations within the scope of EU Law? The position of scholars is divided, and the

---

[23] Taking a strict stance, see P. Huber 'The Unitary Effect of the Community's Fundamental Rights: the ERT-Doctrine Needs to be Reviewed', (2008) 14 *European Public Law*, 3, 323. In similar terms, see P. Cruz Villalón, 'All the Guidance,' ERT and Wachauf' in M. Poiares Maduro and L. Azoulaï (eds.), *The Past and Future of EU Law. The Classics of EU Law Revisited on the 50th Anniversary of the Rome Treaty* (Oxford: Hart Publishers, 2010). Taking a moderate stance, but inviting the CJEU to undertake a self-restrained approach to Article 51(1) contrasting with previous case law, C. Ladenburger, 'EU Institutional Report' of the XXV FIDE Congress Tallinn, vol. 1. 2012, at p. 14 et seq.; T. von Danwitz and K. Paraschas, 'A Fresh Start for the Charter: Fundamental Questions on the Application of the European Charter of Fundamental Rights' (2012) 35 *Fordham International Law Journal*, 1399 et seq., and M. Nusser, *Die Bindung der Mitgliedstaaten an die Unionsgrundrechte* (Tübingen: Mohr Siebeck, 2011). Taking a broader view, see L. Besselink, 'The Member States, the National Constitutions and the Scope of the Charter', (2001) 8 *Maastricht Journal of European and Comparative Law*, 1, 79; P. Craig, *EU Administrative Law*, 2nd edition (Oxford: Oxford University Press, 2012), p. 446 et seq.; J. Kokott and C. Sobotta, 'The Charter of Fundamental Rights of the European Union after Lisbon' (2010) 6 *EUI Working Papers*, Academy of European Law, 6 et seq., and X. Groussot, L. Pech and G. Petursson, 'The Scope of Application of Fundamental Rights on Member States' Action: In Search of Certainty in EU Adjunction' (2011) 1 *Eric Stein Working paper*. For an overall vision of the debate, see the ECJ's Special Edition of its *Bulletin Reflet* 2013/1, devoted to the Charter, and in particular p. 43 et seq.

[24] The Charter thus becomes the 'shadow' of substantive EU rules, in the expressive terms of K. Lenaerts and J. Gutiérrez-Fons, 'The Place of the Charter in the EU Constitutional Edifice', in S. Peers, T. Hervey, J. Kenner and A. Ward (eds.), *The EU Charter of Fundamental Rights; A Commentary* (Oxford: Hart Publishers, 2013).

CJEU is not helping to clear the doubts.[25] So far, the formal distinction between coincidental general principles and Charter rights remains untouched and the CJEU, when interpreting a Charter right, keeps referring to the equivalent principle. However, it is open to discussion whether such duality makes any sense, and whether it is consistent with the Charter's insistence on the need to respect Member State competence in the field of fundamental rights.

This doubt is perfectly illustrated by the *ne bis in idem* right/principle. As it has been explained, Article 50 of the Charter is mostly in line with the CJEU's previous case law on the principle. In fact, those aspects of the provision that seem to depart from the said case law will be, or are in the process of being, rectified as a result of the European Court of Human Right's case law on Article 4 of Protocol no. 7: 'criminal proceedings' are to be interpreted as *materially* criminal proceedings in the sense of the Engel criteria, and the term 'offence', must, despite its literal meaning, be reconsidered in light of *Zolotukhin* v. *Russia*, in which the Strasbourg Court embraced the criterium of the 'same facts'. Overall, the nuanced differences between Article 50 and the CJEU's case law on the general principle of *ne bis in idem* have been neutralized as a result of Strasbourg case law, and the CJEU is recently confirming such effect (except in competition cases). Thus, it is questionable up to what point it makes sense to maintain a distinction between general principles and Charter rights when they concern the same fundamental right. For the time being, the CJEU is keeping the distinction untouched.

3   *Ne Bis in Idem* and External Sources of Interpretation: the ECHR and National Constitutional Traditions

In both its forms as a Charter right and as a general principle, *ne bis in idem* benefits from two significant and *living* sources of interpretation, expressly mentioned by Articles 52 of the Charter and 6(3) TEU, respectively. According to Article 52(2) and (3) of the Charter, the meaning and scope of the rights therein contained 'shall be the same as those laid down by the [ECHR]', *and* they shall be interpreted 'in harmony' with 'the constitutional traditions common to the Member States'. When it comes to Article 6(3) TEU, this provision states that general principles are

---

[25] See, in general, an overall view of the debate in H. Hofmann and C. Mihaescu, 'The Relation between the Charter's Fundamental Rights and the Unwritten General Principles of EU Law: Good Administration as the Test Case' (2013) 9 *EUConst*. 1, 73.

'constituted' as a result of the fundamental rights guaranteed by the ECHR and of the constitutional traditions common to the Member States.

The CJEU has struggled in the past to develop a coherent relationship between fundamental rights, the ECHR and national constitutional traditions. The entry into force of the Charter, the enlargement of the Union to twenty-eight Member States and the possibility of a future accession of the Union to the ECHR have made things even more complex, as it will now be explained. Because of the differences in approach of *ne bis in idem* in the legal orders of the Member States, but also as a result of the asymmetrical effects of the principle in the ECHR, this triangular relationship presents specific difficulties that will be now addressed.

3.1   The ECHR

3.1.1   Autonomy of Charter Rights *vis-à-vis* ECHR Rights

Before the entry into force of the Charter, the ECHR was a prominent point of reference in the interpretation and construction of EU fundamental rights as general principles. The existence, since 2009, of a fully-fledged bill of rights for the EU with its own scope and content, leaves unclear the exact role to be played by the ECHR. Of course once the Union becomes a party to the ECHR its status will be settled, for its rights and the interpretation given to them by the Strasbourg Court will bind the Union and will thus condition the minimal standard of protection by the Charter's rights.[26] However, whilst the Union still negotiates its accession to the Convention system, the position of the ECHR regarding the Charter has become somewhat puzzling.

---

[26] P. Gragl, 'A giant leap for European Human Rights? The Final Agreement on the European Union's accession to the European Convention on Human Rights' (2014) 51 *CMLrev*, 1, 13; C. Eckes, 'EU Accession to the ECHR: Between autonomy and adaptation' (2013) 76 *MLR*, 2, 254; P. Gragl, *The Accession of the European Union to the European Convention on Human Rights* (Oxford: Hart Publishers, 2013); O. de Schutter, 'L'adhésion de l'Union européenne à la Convention européenne des droits de l'homme: Feuille de route de la negotiation' (2010) 21 *Revue Trimestrielle des droits de l'homme*', 83, 533; T. Lock, 'Walking on a Tightrope: The draft ECHR accession agreement and the autonomy of the EU legal order' (2011) 48 *CMLrev*, 1025 and J. Králová, 'Comments on the draft agreement on the accession of the European Union to the Convention for the Protection of Human Rights and Fundamental Freedoms' (2012) 2 *Czech Yearbook of Public & Private International Law*, 127.

In a first line of case law, the CJEU has made a rather standardized use of the Charter, highlighting its role as a source of interpretation and as a standard of minimal protection of fundamental rights. Whenever the European Court of Human Rights has changed its case law, the CJEU has reacted accordingly, proving that the ECHR is not just a distinguished piece of soft law, but a relevant source of law to be closely followed. This can be clearly seen in the case of *N.S.*,[27] a Grand Chamber judgment of the CJEU in which the EU's asylum regulations were reinterpreted in order to accommodate Strasbourg's recent decision in the cases of *M.S.S. v. Belgium and Greece*.[28]

However, in another line of case law the CJEU has rejected to make use of Strasbourg's case law by omitting all references to it, even though the ECHR could have been a valuable inspiration when interpreting the Charter.[29] Some Advocates General have highlighted that the Charter deserves an autonomous status, using the ECHR as a point of reference in case of doubt, but not as a binding instrument that forcefully conditions the scope and meaning of the Charter in all cases.[30] The CJEU seemed to agree in cases such as *Sky Österreich*[31] or *Åkerberg Fransson*, where fundamental rights issues were raised and the Luxembourg Court decided not to refer to the ECHR nor to its case law.

Both lines of case law have been applied to *ne bis in idem*. In *Bonda*,[32] the CJEU faced the issue of double prosecution in the case of a Polish

---

[27] Joined Cases C-411/10 and C-493/10, *N. S. and Others*, EU:C:2011:865.

[28] ECtHR, *M.S.S.* v. *Belgium and Greece*, 21 January 2011, (Appl. No. 30696/09).

[29] See, *inter alia*, Case C-383/13, *PPU G. and R*, EU:C:2013:533, on the right to be heard in proceedings entailing deprivation of liberty, or Cases C-378/12, *Onuekwere*, EU: C:2014:13 and C-400/12, *M.G.*, EU:C:2014:9, on the status of prisoners in a host Member State prison.

[30] See, for example, the Opinion of Advocate General Cruz Villalón in Case C-69/10, *Samba Diouf*, EU:C:2011:524 at point 39: 'the right to effective judicial protection, as expressed in Article 47 of the CFREU, has, through being recognized as part of European Union law by virtue of Article 47, acquired a separate identity and substance under that article which are not the mere sum of the provisions of Articles 6 and 13 of the ECHR. In other words, once it is recognized and guaranteed by the European Union, that fundamental right goes on to acquire a content of its own, the definition of which is certainly shaped by the international instruments on which that right is based, including, first and foremost, the ECHR, but also by the constitutional traditions from which the right in question stems and, together with them, the conceptual universe within which the defining principles of a State governed by the rule of law operate. This is in no way to disregard the very tradition represented by the *acquis* of over half a century of European Union law, which, as a system of law, has given rise to the development of its own set of defining principles.'

[31] Case C-283/11, *Sky Österreich GmbH* v. *Österreichischer Rundfunk*, EU:C:2013:28.

[32] Case C-489/10, *Bonda*, EU:C:2012:319.

farmer who had been subject to an administrative measure consisting in the loss of entitlement to the single area payment for a period of three years, followed later by criminal proceedings based on the same facts. The CJEU considered that the administrative measure was not 'criminal' in light of the European Court of Human Right's case law, and thus it did not come under Article 4 of Protocol no. 7 of the ECHR. It is surprising to see how the CJEU ignores Article 50 of the Charter and relies exclusively on the ECHR and on previous pre-Charter case law on the non-criminal nature of agricultural policy measures.[33] Advocate General Kokott was more willing to bring Article 50 of the Charter into her analysis of the case, but after confirming the applicability of the Charter to the circumstances of Mr Bonda, she simply referred to 'the EU principle of ne bis in idem' and interpreted it in light of the ECHR, with no further mention of Article 50 of the Charter.[34] In conclusion, *Bonda* confirms the CJEU's willingness to keep the ECHR as a crucial parameter of interpretation of EU fundamental rights, but at the same time it leaves many questions unresolved as to the exact relationship between both instruments.

The second line of case law sheds more light on this relationship and seems, at least in this author's opinion, more conclusive. In the case of *Åkerberg Fransson* the CJEU faced once again the delicate issue of administrative penalties and criminal sanctions, but with the added complication that the Swedish criminal courts would deduct the administrative (fiscal) penalty from the criminal sentence. Both dimensions of *ne bis in idem* came into play, double prosecution and double punishment. The CJEU stated that the imposition of an administrative and criminal penalty was not contrary to Article 50 of the Charter as long as the Engel criteria were not met. In the CJEU's opinion, the provision would come into play, thus precluding criminal proceedings in respect of the same acts, 'only if the tax penalty is criminal in nature for the purposes of Article 50 of the Charter and has become final'.[35] In this statement the CJEU stays closely in line with the ECHR, but it makes no mention whatsoever to the case law of the Strasbourg Court.[36] It is obvious that

---

[33] Case 137/85, *Maizena* quoted in footnote 14, para. 13; Case C-240/90, *Germany* v. *Commission*, EU:C:1992:408, para. 25; and Case C-210/00, *Käserei Champignon Hofmeister*, EU:C:2002:440, para. 43.

[34] Ibid., Opinion of Advocate Generak Kokott, quoted, point 32 *et seq.*

[35] *Åkerberg Fransson*, quoted in footnote 7, para. 34.

[36] At the most, the reference comes indirectly, for the CJ relies here in the previous judgment in *Bonda*, where it did indeed make a direct reference to the Engel criteria of the ECHR.

the CJEU is interpreting Article 50 of the Charter in line with *Zolotukhin* v. *Russia*, for it refers to 'the same acts' and not to the same 'offence' (the latter being the term used by the Charter). Also, the CJEU states that the definition of what constitutes a 'criminal' penalty is based on three criteria, the same criteria enunciated in the *Engel* case,[37] but omitted a direct reference to Strasbourg's decision in the said case.[38]

This autonomous interpretation of Article 50 of the Charter appears even more reinforced as a result of the complex status of Article 4 of Protocol no.7. As Advocate General Cruz Villalón pointed out in his Opinion in *Åkerberg Fransson*, the application of the ECHR to double administrative and criminal penalties is subject to an asymmetrical protection among the signatories of the ECHR.[39] Several Member States have not ratified or have submitted reservations to this provision of the ECHR, pointing out that *ne bis in idem* does not apply when the first penalty is of an administrative nature.[40] Other Member States have submitted identical statements by way of a declaration.[41] To make things even more complex, in *Gradinger* v. *Austria*, the ECHR ruled Austria's declaration on this point as invalid for lack of motivation.[42] The Advocate General proposed the CJEU to develop a *partly* autonomous interpretation of Article 50 of the Charter, because Article 4 of Protocol no. 7, at least on the point of dual administrative and criminal penalties, could not be considered to be a consensual provision constitutive of a constitutional tradition common to the Member States.[43] The CJEU seemed to disagree with its Advocate General on the specific solution, but not on the partly autonomous approach to Article 50 of the Charter. It is unclear whether this autonomy is the result of the complex context of Article 4 of Protocol no. 7 or not, but on this point both the CJEU and its Advocate General seemed to be well aware of the consequences of closely following what the Strasbourg Court had

---

[37] *Åkerberg Fransson*, quoted in footnote 7, para. 35.

[38] For a detailed analysis of this aspect of the *Åkerberg Fransson* case, see Peter Wattel's contribution (Chapter 5) in this book.

[39] Opinion of Advocate General Cruz Villalón, at points 72 to 74.

[40] Germany, Belgium, the Netherlands and the United Kingdom have not ratified Protocol no. 7, whilst France has introduced a reservation to Article 4 on the specific issue of dual criminal and administrative penalties.

[41] Germany, Austria, Italy and Portugal have lodged a number of declaration with the same purpose as the French reservation. Series A no. 328-C.

[42] ECtHR, *Gradinger* v. *Austria*, 23 October 1995, (Appl. No. 15963/90).

[43] Opinion of Advocate General Cruz Villalón, quoted, points 81 *et seq.*

stated to date for member States which had *not* ratified Article 4 of Protocol no. 7.

Overall, it seems that the CJEU has decided to grant the Charter a relative autonomy *vis-à-vis* the ECHR. It is relative because the principal source of interpretation is the Charter itself, a text that can be self-sufficient when giving meaning to its provisions. The ECHR will thus become a relevant source of law in two circumstances: first, when there are doubts as to the appropriate standard applicable to the case (Art. 52.3), and second, when the provision subject to interpretation requires complex balancing tests and, at the same time, the European Court of Human Rights has already ruled on the same point of law. If none of these situations arise, the CJEU will be comfortably in a position to rule without relying on the authority of the ECHR nor its case law.

3.1.2   Autonomy of General Principles *vis-à-vis* ECHR Rights

The position of general principles *vis-à-vis* the ECHR is radically different to that of the Charter. General principles lack a written source of law and are the product of the judge's mind, not the legislator's. In the history of EU law, general principles have been a creature of the CJEU's case law, deduced from sources as varied and heterogeneous as comparative law, maxims of Roman law or standards of protection in international law.[44] Therefore, the ECHR has been a particularly valuable source of interpretation when it came to fundamental rights in the form of general principles, as all member States acceded to the ECHR, making it a common legal tradition. In the case of *ne bis in idem*, the influence has been also relevant, but problematic at times.

The CJEU's *ne bis in idem* case law in competition cases reflects a typical development of a general principle, in contrast to other areas, such as Schengen, where Article 54 of the Schengen Agreement enunciates in writing the content of the principle: it is written law, not an *ex novo* jurisprudential construction, as in the case of competition. It is therefore here, in competition cases, where the CJEU has made use of the ECHR in ways that prove the importance of this treaty, but also the autonomy of the CJEU and of EU law in the development of general principles.

---

[44] See T. Tridimas, *The General Principles of EU Law* (Oxford: Oxford University Press, 2006), p. 591 *et seq.*

3.2   National Constitutional Traditions

Whilst the ECHR is a relatively manageable source of interpretation, national constitutional traditions are a considerably more difficult source to rely on. The CJEU has been prone to make use of such traditions when solving points of law open to discretion and when needed to fill a gap, or to find a balance between two conflicting values.[45] Also, the CJEU has used comparative law as a source of interpretation, not always with the purpose to find out whether a 'constitutional tradition' exists among the Member States, but to spot the best solution among the many present in national legal orders ('best practice'). This shows how 'constitutional traditions' play an ambiguous role in the CJEU's case law, an ambiguity that is also present in its case law on *ne bis in idem*.[46]

Although the role of constitutional traditions is not always evident in the CJEU's judgments, it is clearly present in the Opinions of the Advocates General. For example, in *Gözütok and Brügge*,[47] Advocate General Ruiz-Jarabo Colomer made an extensive use of national domestic law in order to determine if a penal settlement constitutes a 'final decision' pursuant to *ne bis in idem*. After scrutinizing the law of the (then) fifteen Member States, the Advocate General came to the conclusion that settlements between the prosecutor and the accused, confirmed by the judge competent to rule on the case, were an exercise of criminal jurisdiction and thus could trigger the *ne bis in idem* rule in Article 54 of the Schengen Agreement.[48] In *Gasparini*, Advocate General Sharpston undertook a detailed analysis of the role of time-limits in criminal law amongst the different domestic legal systems in order to determine if criminal liability can be subject to a temporal time-frame under EU law.[49] In *Kretzinger*,[50] Advocate General Sharpston referred to

---

[45] See K. Lenaerts and J. Gutiérrez-Fons, 'To say what the law of the EU is: methods of interpretation and the European Court of Justice' (2013) 09 *EUI Working Papers*, p. 31 *et seq.*

[46] See T. Tridimas, *The General Principles of EU Law*, quoted; G. Schermers and D. Waelbroeck, *Judicial Protection in the European Union* (Alphen aan de Rijn: Kluwer, 2000), p. 132 *et seq.* and K. Lenaerts, 'Le droit compare et le travail du juge communautaire' (2001) 37 *Revue Trimestrielle de Droit de l'Union Européenne*, 3, 487 and K. Lenaerts, 'Interlocking Legal Orders in the European Union and Comparative Law' (2003) 52 *International Comparative Law Quarterly*, 04, 873.

[47] Joined Cases C-187/01 and C-385/01, *Gözütok and Brügge*, EU:C:2003:87.

[48] Opinion of Advocate General Ruiz-Jarabo Colomer, points 64–77.

[49] Opinion of Advocate General Sharpston in the case of *Gasparini*, quoted, points 66–71.

[50] Case C-288/05, *Kretzinger*, EU:C:2007:441.

constitutional traditions when opining on whether a suspended custodial sentence amounts to a penalty that has either 'been enforced' or is 'actually in the process of being enforced'.[51]

The case law shows that the CJEU does not require that there is unanimity or a clear majority among domestic legal orders in order to discern a 'constitutional tradition common to the Member States'. As Advocate General Poiares Maduro stated in his Opinion in the case of *FIAMM*,[52] although the Court of Justice must certainly be guided by the most characteristic provisions of the systems of domestic law,

> it must above all ensure that it adopts a solution appropriate to the needs and specific features of the Community legal system. In other words, the Court has the task of drawing on the legal traditions of the Member States in order to find an answer to similar legal questions arising under Community law that both respects those traditions and is appropriate to the context of the Community legal order. From that point of view, even a solution adopted by a minority may be preferred if it best meets the requirements of the Community system.[53]

This has been the case of *ne bis in idem*, where the CJEU has made use of national experience in a very pragmatic way, depending on the best fit of each solution in light of the goals of each policy area. This will be seen in the upcoming section, where the CJEU's case law in the said policy areas will be explored.

4 *Ne Bis in Idem* and the Interpretation of EU Secondary Law

4.1 *Justice and Home Affairs*

It is in the area of Justice and Home Affairs where *ne bis in idem* has witnessed its most relevant development. Both the applicable rules of EU secondary law as well as the case law of the CJEU have also been addressed in Chapter 1 of this book. The purpose of this section is to explore the CJEU's case law and determine how it has contributed to flesh the general principle of *ne bis in idem* as well as Article 50 of the Charter.

---

[51] Opinion of Advocate General Sharpston in the case of *Kretzinger*, point 43.
[52] Joined Cases C-120/06 P and C-121/06 P, *FIAMM and Others* v. *Council and Commission*, EU:C:2008:476.
[53] Opinion of Advocate General Poiares Maduro in the case of *FIAMM*, quoted, point 55.

The case law is conditioned by the scope of application of Article 54 of the Schengen Agreement, as well as by other instruments of secondary law in the area of Justice and Home Affairs.[54] Therefore, *ne bis in idem* in this domain is confined to criminal proceedings, leaving administrative penalties in a secondary role. It is still open to discussion whether the said instruments might apply when the first proceedings concern an administrative penalty. The CJEU has not addressed this question yet, but in principle it should not be excluded, given the Engel doctrine, previously commented on. If an administrative penalty complies with the conditions to determine that it is 'criminal' in nature, there should be no obstacle to invoke the principle of *ne bis in idem* as expressed in provisions such as Article 54 of the Schengen Agreement. The recent entry into force of Framework Decision 2005/214/JHA on the application of the principle of mutual recognition to financial penalties,[55] reinforces this view, although the CJEU's case law on this text is still too scarce to be conclusive.[56]

Also, it must be highlighted that both the written rules in this area of the law, as well as the CJEU's case law, only concern the prohibition of double proceedings, and not double punishment. In this regard, *ne bis in idem* in the area of Justice and Home Affairs is mostly a *procedural* principle affecting the initiation of proceedings before a criminal court. This is probably related to the fact that *ne bis in idem* here applies to transnational situations involving moving individuals. Contrary to what happens in most Member States, where *ne bis in idem* is the expression of legal certainty, in the area of Justice and Home Affairs it is also the result of the rationale of mutual recognition and mutual trust among legal orders, driven by the requirements of free movement of persons. Therefore, *ne bis in idem* appears here as the corollary of free movement rules, confined to a procedural dimension more concerned with the ability of

---

[54] For an overall picture of the role of the principle in this area of the law, see inter alia J. Lelieur-Fischer, 'La règle ne bis in idem. Du principe de l'autorité de la chose jugée au principe d'unicité d'action répressive', PhD, Université Panthéon-Sorbonne (Paris I), Paris, 2005; J. Vervaele, 'Ne Bis In Idem: Towards a Transnational Constitutional Principle in the EU?', quoted in footnote 1; A. Weyembergh, 'Le principe ne bis in idem: pierre d'achoppement de l'espace pénal européen?', (2004) 40 *Cahiers de Droit Européen*, 3, 337; M. Luchtman, 'Transnational Law Enforcement in the European Union and the ne bis in idem principle', (2011) 4 *Review of European Administrative Law*, 2, 5.

[55] Council Framework Decision 2005/214/JHA of 24 February 2005 on the application of the principle of mutual recognition to financial penalties, OJ 2005 No. L76, p. 16, as amended by Council Framework Decision 2009/299/JHA of 26 February 2009 (OJ 2009 No. L81, p. 24).

[56] See Case C-60/12, *Baláž*, EU:C:2013:733.

individuals to move within the Union than with the punitive dimension of the principle.

The first decisions of the CJEU in this terrain were due to Article 54 of the Schengen Agreement, a provision intended to promote free movement of persons by precluding the continuation or initiation of criminal proceedings in one Member State once the main proceedings concerning the same facts have been terminated in another Member State.[57] One of the first issues the CJEU had to face concerned the status of *ne bis in idem*: whether it was a new rule of written law, as it then appeared in Article 54 of the Schengen Agreement, or whether such written rule was the expression of a more general principle. At first, in the case of *Gözütok and Brügge*, Advocate General Ruiz-Jarabo Colomer stated that 'article 54 is the expression of that safeguard for persons who are subject to the exercise of the *ius puniendi*',[58] thus implying that the provision was the reflection of a general rule of law. Although the CJEU did not address this issue in its judgment in the said case, Advocate General Sharpston, in *Gasparini*, was more explicit. In her Opinion,

> For the purposes of EU law, it seems to me almost inevitable that, in consequence, the concept of ne bis in idem (which, as the Court noted in Vinyl Maatschappij, is a fundamental principle of Community law) is to be understood as a free-standing, or propriae naturae, principle. In the absence of further initiatives by way of Treaty amendment or secondary Community legislation, it is therefore to be refined and developed by the Court in the exercise of its 'hermeneutic monopoly' on such key concepts of EU law. (69) The specific application of the principle in particular areas (be these competition law or through Article 54 of the CISA) should form part of a core understanding of what that fundamental principle means (or ought to mean) within the Community legal order.[59]

This reasoning has been tacitly accepted by the CJEU. The case law on *ne bis in idem* in the area of Justice and Home Affairs, although developed on very autonomous grounds in its first stages, has proved to rely on

---

[57] Article 54 of the Schengen Agreement reads as follows: 'A person whose trial has been finally disposed of in one Contracting Party may not be prosecuted in another Contracting Party for the same acts provided that, if a penalty has been imposed, it has been enforced, is actually in the process of being enforced or can no longer be enforced under the laws of the sentencing Contracting Party.'

[58] Opinion of Advocate General Ruiz-Jarabo Colomer in the case of *Gözütok and Brügge*, quoted in footnote 49, point 46.

[59] Opinion of Advocate General Sharpston in the case of *Gasparini*, quoted above in footnote 3, point 80.

more general sources, such as national constitutional traditions and, above all, the ECHR.[60] This confirms that, just as the Advocate General points out, *ne bis in idem* in the area of Justice and Home Affairs is the concrete expression of a more general principle, but also the reflection of the specific needs of this area of policy. As it will now be shown, the specificity of the principle here suggests that its contents and standards of protection will not necessarily be the same as in other areas of policy, such as competition or staff cases.

The CJEU's case law in the area of Justice and Home Affairs is mostly characterized by its concern to promote free movement of persons and, at the same time, to guarantee fundamental rights of the accused. Thus, the CJEU has developed a pragmatic definition of what constitutes a 'judgment' in the first proceedings. In *Gözütok and Brügge*, settlements between the Prosecution and the accused, as confirmed by a court, amounted to a 'judgment' and thus triggered the application of Article 54 of the Schengen Agreement. However, in *Miraglia*[61] the CJEU came to the conclusion that a judicial decision taken after the public prosecutor has decided not to pursue the prosecution on the sole ground that criminal proceedings have been initiated in another Member State, but where no determination has been made as to the merits of the case, did not constitute a decision finally disposing of the case within the meaning of the said Article 54. The same solution applies, as results from the judgment in *Turansky*,[62] when an authority of a Member State, after examining the merits of the case brought before it, makes an order, at a stage before the charging of a person suspected of a crime, suspending the criminal proceedings, where the suspension decision does not definitively bar further prosecution and therefore does not preclude new criminal proceedings, in respect of the same acts, in that State. However, as the CJEU determined in the case of *Bourquain*,[63] Article 54 applies even though, under the law of the State in which the accused was convicted, the sentence which was imposed on him could never, on account of specific features of procedure such as those referred to in the main proceedings, have been directly enforced. In the case of *Mantello*,[64] this case law was later extended to the interpretation

---

[60] See, *inter alia*, Case C-436/04, *Van Esbroeck*, EU:C:2006:165, para. 28.
[61] Case C-469/03, *Miraglia*, EU:C:2005:156.
[62] Case C-491/07, *Turanský*, EU:C:2008:768.
[63] Case C-297/07, *Bourquain*, EU:C:2008:708.
[64] Case C-261/09, *Mantello*, EU:C:2010:683.

of Framework Decision 2002/584/JHA, on the European Arrest Warrant and the surrender procedures between Member States. However, the CJEU used a different approach in *Spasic*, and considered that there was no breach of Article 54 if there has been a mere payment of a fine by a person sentenced also to a custodial sentence in the same proceedings and judgment.[65]

The CJEU also departed from previous case law and developed a specific notion of 'same acts' for the law of Justice and Home Affairs. In *Van Esbroeck*,[66] the CJEU was asked about the *idem* as applied to Article 54 of the Schengen Agreement, and it came to the conclusion, in line with the Advocate General, that 'the criterion of the identity of the protected legal interest cannot be applicable since that criterion is likely to vary from one Contracting State to another'.[67] Therefore, in the opinion of the CJEU, 'the only relevant criterion for the application of Article 54 is *the identity of the material acts*, understood in the sense of the existence of a set of concrete circumstances which are inextricably linked together'.[68] This determination was later confirmed and refined in the case of *Van Straaten*,[69] *Kretzinger*[70] and *Kraaijenbrink*,[71] and was also extended to Framework Decision 2002/584/JHA, on the European arrest warrant and the surrender procedures between Member States, in the case of *Mantello*.[72]

In line with the principle of subjective liability in criminal law, the CJEU has also highlighted that the guarantee in Article 54 applies only to individuals whose liability has been previously determined by a court in a final decision. This conclusion applies also when its application benefits the accused. In *Gasparini* the CJEU faced a case in which a national jurisdiction questioned if persons being tried in another Member State on the basis of the same facts could also benefit from a limitation period applied to other individuals in different proceedings and in a different Member State, but based on the same facts. However, the CJEU was categorical on this point and stated, in light of the wording of Article 54 of the Schengen Agreement, that only persons who have already had a trial finally disposed of once may derive advantage from the *ne bis in idem* principle.[73] It is important to note how the CJEU puts an emphasis

---

[65] Case C-129/14 PPU, *Spasic*, EU:C:2014:586.
[66] Case C-436/04, *Van Esbroeck*, EU:C:2006:165.   [67] *Ibid.*, paragragh 32.   [68] *Ibid.*, 36.
[69] Case C-150/05, *Van Straaten*, EU:C:2006:614.
[70] Case C-288/05, *Kretzinger*, EU:C:2007:441.
[71] Case C-367/05, *Kraaijenbrink*, EU:C:2007:444.   [72] Case C-261/09, *Mantello*, quoted.
[73] *Gasparini*, quoted in footnote 3, paras. 34–37.

on the wording of said Article 54.[74] If the literal enunciation of the rule had been more ambiguous, maybe the CJEU's solution would not have been so stringent.

4.2   Competition Law

The development of the *ne bis in idem* principle in competition cases is analysed in more depth in Chapter 4. It is nevertheless useful to briefly address a few points raised by that case law here. In contrast with the legal framework in the area of Justice and Home Affairs, the written rules of EU competition law lack any reference to *ne bis in idem*, which was developed in this area only in the CJEU's case law. Even after the major legislative reform of 2003, the EU's legislator refrained from determining precise conditions concerning the limits of double proceedings and punishment, despite the fact that the issue had been raised on plenty of occasions in the past.

Before turning to the CJEU's case law in this domain, it is important to portray the context in which the *ne bis in idem* principle is applied. First, it must be noted that competition is an exclusive area of competence of the Commission, whose authority in the enforcement of the EU's anti-trust legal framework is particularly enhanced in comparison with other areas of policy. In contrast to the situations ruled by the transnational *ne bis in idem* in Justice and Home Affairs, the issues in the domain of competition involve EU authorities exercising exclusive competence and implementing a common legal framework. Second, despite the pre-eminence of the EU authorities and, in particular, the EU Commission in this domain, it is also important to highlight that national competition authorities, particularly after the 2003 reform, have assumed growing powers in the enforcement of EU competition law. This has forced national competition authorities to coordinate their actions with Commission authorities, a feature that has obviously contributed to efforts to avoid *bis in idem*, but that has not completely exempted the risk of violations of the principle. And third, this context is strongly conditioned by a growing debate on the compliance of the Commission with fundamental rights standards, an issue that raises concerns as a result of the EU's peculiar system of enforcement and its non-accession (yet) to the ECHR. A considerable

---

[74] *Ibid.*, para. 35.

number of writers question whether the Commission and, above all, the CJEU, have been side-lining fundamental rights protection for too long already.[75]

These three issues are crucial in understanding the current position of the CJEU regarding *ne bis in idem* in EU competition law. It could be argued that, as a result of the said features, EU competition law, including its variant of *ne bis in idem*, is strongly insulated from other areas of EU law. The peculiar blend of exclusive competence, highly technical expertise, and growing need of coordination with national competition authorities, have probably contributed to create a self-sufficient system of supranational rules strongly in need of a robust central authority to manage it. This does not only show in the development of *ne bis in idem*, but also in other aspects in which EU competition law has proved to be an autonomous and self-sufficient area of law.

However, the peculiarity of EU competition law should not be over-emphasized. It is true that there is a tendency towards autonomy in EU competition, but this is not by any means an absolute autonomy. EU competition law has been permeable to other areas of EU law, among other reasons because it shares common rules with other policy areas. This can be clearly seen in the case of access to documents, where Regulation 1049/2001 applies to all EU Institutions, its caveats putting EU competition policy under no special status.[76] Also, the concerns over fundamental rights must be seen with some caution. The European Court of Human Rights has recently green-lighted an enforcement system similar to the Commission's in the case of *Menarini* v. *Italy*.[77] Also, the CJEU has continued to develop its fundamental rights case law in competition cases, fleshing the rules of the Charter in ways that should

---

[75] See *inter alia* K. Lenaerts, 'Due Process in Competition Cases' (2013) 1 *Neue Zeitschrift für Kartellrecht*, 1, 175; W. Wils, 'Antitrust Enforcement Powers and Procedural Rights and Guarantees: The Interplay between EU Law, National Law, The Charter of Fundamental Rights of the EU and the European Convention on Human Rights' (2011) 34 *World Competition: Law and Economics Review*, 2 and H. Lidgard, 'Due Process in European Competition Procedure: a Fundamental Concept or a Mere Formality' in P. Cordonel, A. Rosas and N. Wahl (eds.) *Constitutionalising the EU judicial system: essays in honor of Pernilla Lindh* (Oxford: Hart Publishers, 2012).

[76] Compare Case C-477/10 P, *Commission* v. *Agrofert Holding*, EU:C:2012:394 or Case C-404/10 P, *Commission* v. *Éditions Odile Jacob*, EU:C:2012:393. with Joined Cases C-514/07 P, C-528/07 P and C-532/07 P, *Sweden and Others* v. *API and Commission*, EU:C:2010:541.

[77] ECtHR, *Menarini Diagnostics* v. *Italy,* 27 September 2011 (Appl. No. 43509/08).

not raise peculiar concerns over the standards applied.[78] Of course there will still be areas of concern in which the Commission and the CJEU will have to reconsider their stance, but it would be unfair to say that the EU has a serious fundamental rights problem in the area of competition. However, as far as our subject is concerned, it is true that *ne bis in idem* is currently the source of well-founded criticisms that will now be addressed.

The main source of discussions concerns the understanding of the *bis* in competition law. Since its early decisions on the matter, the CJEU has emphasized that in order to trigger the guarantee of *ne bis in idem* in competition cases, three requirements must be met: identity of the facts, unity of offender and unity of the legal interest protected. As a result of this triple requirement, in competition law the same person cannot be sanctioned more than once for a single unlawful course of conduct *designed to protect the same legal asset*. Whilst this approach was accepted by the European Court of Human Rights until its decision in *Zolutukhin* v. *Russia*, it has not even been accepted by the CJEU itself in other areas of EU law previously depicted, as the Area of Justice and Home Affairs.

The fact that competition law still holds a minor level of *ne bis in idem* protection in contrast to other areas of EU law has thus been a source of concern. In the case of *Toshiba*,[79] Advocate General Kokott openly addressed the issue and made a strong critique of the CJEU's stance. In her own words:

> To interpret and apply the ne bis in idem principle so differently depending on the area of law concerned is detrimental to the unity of the EU legal order. The crucial importance of the ne bis in idem principle as a founding principle of EU law which enjoys the status of a fundamental right means that its content must not be substantially different depending on which area of law is concerned. For the purposes of determining the scope of the guarantee provided by the ne bis in idem principle, as now codified in Article 50 of the Charter of Fundamental Rights, the same criteria should apply in all areas of EU law. This point has rightly been made by the EFTA Surveillance Authority.

---

[78] See *inter alia* Case C-272/09 P, *KME and Others* v. *Commission*, EU:C:2011:810, para. 106; Case C-386/10, *P Chalkor* v. *Commission*, EU:C:2011:815, para. 67; Case C-389/10 P, *KME Germany and Others* v. *Commission*, EU:C:2011:816, para. 133, and Case C-199/11, *Otis and Others*, EU:C:2012:684, para. 47.

[79] Case C-17/10, *Toshiba Corporation and Others*, EU:C:2012:72.

> There is no objective reason why the conditions to which the ne bis in idem principle is subject in competition matters should be any different from those applicable to it elsewhere. For, in the same way as, within the context of Article 54 of the CISA, that principle serves to guarantee the free movement of EU citizens in EU territory as a 'single area of freedom, security and justice', so, in the field of competition law, it helps to improve and facilitate the business activities of undertakings in the internal market and, ultimately, to create uniform conditions of competition (a 'level playing field') throughout the EEA [European Economic Area].[80]

However, the CJEU has not been receptive to the critique. In its judgment in *Toshiba*, the Grand Chamber decided to reaffirm its position and maintain the threefold requirements of *ne bis in idem* in competition law.[81] It is unclear why the CJEU is resolved to maintain the status quo on this point, for the judgment's reasoning is very cryptic. The reason might be related to the traditional margin of manoeuvre that the CJEU has granted to the Commission in competition cases, a margin that in this case would extend to the Commission's faculty to determine the scope of its sanctioning powers.

A second issue resulting from *ne bis in idem* in competition law concerns its objective scope. As it was previously stated, it is common ground that *ne bis in idem* in EU law applies to double prosecution (*Erledigungsprinzip*), whilst double punishment (*Anrechnungsprinzip*) has been traditionally conceived as a component of the principle of proportionality. However, in competition law the CJEU has expressly refused this approach and has declared on several occasions that *ne bis in idem* only applies to situations of double punishment. This question becomes even more complex as a result of the different scenarios in which double punishments may arise in EU competition cases. Thus, a double sanction may be the result of a Commission decision and a national decision that concern the same agreement, but in breach of two different legal orders. It could also be the case that the dual punishment arises as a result of two different proceedings before the

---

[80] Opinion of Advocate General Kokott in the case of *Toshiba Corporation*, points 117 and 118.

[81] Judgment in the case of *Toshiba Corporation*, quoted, paras. 97 and 98. On this decision, see A. Lacresse, 'La CJUE ne renonce pas au critère de l'unité de l'intérêt juridique protégé pour l'application du principe ne bis in idem en matière de concurrence', *Concurrences*, (2012) 2; R. Werdnik, 'Aktuelle Entwicklungen im europäischen Kartellrecht zu ne bis in idem', *Österreichisches Recht der Wirtschaft* (2012); G. Monti, 'Managing decentralized antitrust enforcement: Toshiba', (2014) 51 *Common Market Law Review*, 1, 261.

Commission, or of two national authorities deciding over the same agreement. It becomes even more complex when the Commission or a national authority faces a previous decision from a third country authority concerning the same agreement.

So far, the CJEU's stance is ambiguous to say the least. As it has already been stated, the case law admits that *ne bis in idem* in competition law includes both double prosecution and double punishment. However, when it comes to the latter the CJEU has maintained its restrictive approach towards the *idem*, that is, towards the defining criteria of what constitutes a same offence. Thus, even though one or two authorities may consider the imposition of two distinct sanctions as a result of the same agreement, the second decision will not be considered to result from the same 'offence'. According to the CJEU, when the first decision originates from another legal system, such decision 'not only includes specific aims and objectives, but also results in the adoption of specific substantive rules and a wide variety of legal consequences', sufficiently distinct to differentiate it from an ulterior proceeding in another legal system.

4.3   Civil Service Law

Article 9.3 of the Staff Regulations states that 'a single case of misconduct shall not give rise to more than one disciplinary penalty'. Although this rule applies to staff subject to the said Regulations, the CJEU has declared that *ne bis in idem* applies to all personnel subject to disciplinary measures. Therefore, *ne bis in idem* is not considered to be a rule of EU civil service law, but a general principle applied to all staff cases.

In *X* v. *ECB*,[82] the GC agreed with the defendant (the European Central Bank) and declared that *ne bis in idem* did not apply to the ECB's decision to provisionally suspend an employee and later formally dismiss him. The two decisions were considered to be different in aims and nature. The same reasoning was followed by the Civil Service Tribunal in *BM* v. *ECB*[83], where the position was rejected that the termination of a contract following a disciplinary measure might breach *ne bis in idem*. However, the Tribunal was careful to distinguish the principle of *ne bis in idem* from the principle of

---

[82] Case T-333/99, *X* v. *ECB*, EU:T:2001:251, paras. 151–153.
[83] Case F-106/11, *BM* v. *ECB*, EU:F:2013:91.

proportionality, although it is not clear what is the exact scope of application of each of these principles.[84]

5 Conclusion

This overview of the CJEU's case law on *ne bis in idem* provides some useful insights into this multifaceted principle of EU law. The development over the years poses several questions over the role of this principle, but also on the way in which EU law adapts its rules to each context and area of policy. *Ne bis in idem* first emerged as a rule of 'natural justice' destined to introduce moderation in areas where disciplinary measures were the rule, such as staff cases or competition. The complexity of European integration forced the CJEU to explore the principle's contents in transnational contexts, where several legal orders interact and produce solutions that might clash with *ne bis in idem*. To make things more complex, the EU has also had to adapt to the international and national legal context, particularly to the ECHR and to national constitutional traditions. At this point, *ne bis in idem* has a solid unitary content, but it also has aspects that depart from the general rule depending on the area of policy concerned. This is not in any way exceptional and it is a feature that can be found in domestic legal orders when dealing with general principles of law.

The tensions facing the principle have multiple sources and depend on different institutions. The evolution of *ne bis in idem* has proved to be rather minimalist in the area of competition, where the CJEU has traditionally recognized the Commission's margin of discretion in handling this area of EU competence. However, when the EU began to gradually develop its own Justice and Home Affairs policy, an area always in need of special safeguards for the protection of fundamental rights, *ne bis in idem* assumed a different visage. The fact that competition is an area of reinforced Union competence, whilst the Area of Freedom, Security and Justice has traditionally been a terrain of shared competence with the Member States, is a feature that has contributed to this tension in the case law.

However, the tensions underlying the CJEU's case law are now intensified as a result of a claim of coherence. This raises the question of how a principle of law can assume one-size-fits-all criteria when applicable to

---

[84] Case F-40/05, *Andreasen* v. *Commission*, EU:F:2007:189, paras. 181–183.

heterogeneous areas of law. The main demand of coherence comes from the ECHR, particularly in the definition of the *idem* as interpreted by the Strasbourg Court in *Zolotukhin* v. *Russia*. The CJEU is refusing so far to adjust its competition case law on this point to Strasbourg's criterion. It is not clear whether this stance is fully justified; at least the CJEU has refrained from providing powerful arguments to date. And as the date of the EU's accession to the ECHR approaches, it is even more doubtful if it is all really worth a fight.

Parallel Proceedings in EU Competition Law

Ne Bis in Idem as a Limiting Principle

RENATO NAZZINI

1   The Problem and the Structure of the Enquiry

Articles 101 and 102 TFEU prohibit, under certain conditions, agreements, concerted practices and decisions of associations of undertakings and abuses of a dominant position, respectively. The effectiveness of these provisions rests on two pillars: public enforcement by the European Commission ('Commission') and national competition authorities and private enforcement by claimants who consider themselves harmed by a breach of Article 101 or 102 TFEU. The focus of this chapter is on public enforcement, where the application of the *ne bis in idem* principle more frequently arises.[1]

Public enforcement of EU competition law is governed by Regulation 1/2003,[2] which gives the Commission and national competition authorities (NCAs) the power to order that infringements of Articles 101 and 102 TFEU be brought to an end and to impose fines on undertakings that committed an infringement. One of the objectives of the regime enacted by Regulation 1/2003 is to enhance the effectiveness of the enforcement of EU competition law by empowering the national competition

---

I am grateful to Alice Galbusera, Silvia Massaro and Valerio Torti for their research assistance. A version of this paper will appear in Phi Lowe, M. Marquis and G. Monti (eds.), *Effective and Legitimate Enforcement of Competition Law*, (Oxford: Hart Publishing, forthcoming).

[1] The application of the *ne bis in idem* principle in private enforcement is rare but may be triggered, for example, by private law rules that allow the award of punitive damages when the defendant has already been punished for the same infringement by the Commission or an NCA: see *Devenish Nutrition Ltd* v. *Sanofi-Aventis SA (France)* [2009] 3 All ER 27, [2008] EWCA Civ 1086, [2009] 3 WLR 198.

[2] Council Regulation (EC) No. 1/2003 of 16 December 2002 on the implementation of the rules on competition laid down in Articles 81 and 82 of the Treaty OJ 2003 No. L1/1 ('Regulation 1/2003').

authorities to apply Articles 101 and 102 alongside the Commission. Such a regime, however, gives rise to an acute risk of multiple proceedings against the same undertakings for the same infringement. This is for the following reasons:

1. Under Regulation 1/2003, national competition authorities and the Commission all have concurrent jurisdiction to apply Articles 101 and 102 TFEU;[3]
2. The powers of the national competition authorities and the Commission to impose fines are criminal in nature for the purpose of the *ne bis in idem* rules;[4]
3. There are no territorial limitations to the enforcement powers of the Commission or the national competition authorities in Regulation 1/2003. This means that, in principle, EU competition authorities have the power, under Regulation 1/20013, to investigate cases and impose fines for effects beyond their national markets;[5]

[3] See Art. 5 of Regulation 1/2003.

[4] The European Court of Human Rights (EctHR) adopted a substantive test for the definition of the autonomous meaning of 'criminal charge' under Art. 6 of the European Human Rights Convention in ECtHR, *Engel* v. *Netherlands*, 8 June 1976 (1979/80) 1 EHRR 647. Administrative proceedings under Community law are considered criminal for the purposes of Art. 6 of the European Human Rights Convention: Case C-235/92 P, *Montecatini Spa* v. *Commission* [1999] ECR I-4539, paras. 175–176. In principle, the same applies to proceedings in the Member States: see, e.g., in the United Kingdom *Napp Pharmaceutical Holdings Ltd* v *Director General of Fair Trading (Napp No 3)* [2001] Comp AR 33, [2002] ECC 3, paras. 68–76; *Napp Pharmaceutical Holdings Ltd* v. *Director General of Fair Trading (Napp No 4)* [2002] ECC 13, paras. 98–103, and, in Italy, ECtHR, *Menarini Diagnostics srl* v. *Italy*, 27 September 2011 (Appl. No. 43509/08).

[5] This results from a number of considerations, including the following: a) there is nothing in Regulation 1/2003 that limits in any way the territorial scope of the infringements that may be investigated and punished by national competition authorities; b) the Commission Notice on cooperation within the Network of Competition Authorities [2004] OJ C101/43 envisages instances in which a single national competition authority is well placed to act in relation to infringements the effects of which are not limited to its own territory (see para. 11 in particular); c) certain national competition authorities consider that they have the power to impose fines taking into account effects outside their own territory (see OFT Guidance as to the appropriate amount of a penalty, OFT423, September 2012, para. 2.10, where the OFT states that it will take account of such effects through the its assessment of relevant turnover but when the relevant turnover includes foreign turnover and the market is wider than the United Kingdom, the OFT will take such foreign turnover into account only with the express consent of the relevant Member State or national competition authority, as appropriate). There may, of course, be limitations on the jurisdiction of national competition authorities resulting from their own national law and, possibly, from general principles of EU law or public international law. A study of these limitations and their implications under EU law is outside the scope of this chapter. What matters for

4. National competition authorities do not have the power to make a final non-infringement decision;[6]

5. National competition authorities retain the power to apply national law alongside EU law;[7]

6. In competition law, the EU courts apply a three-fold test to the definition of the same offence for the purposes of the *ne bis in idem* principle, requiring the identity of the facts, the identity of the offender and the identity of the legal interest protected.[8] The requirement of the identity of the legal interest protected rules out the application of the *ne bis in idem* principle whenever the first and the second offence protect different legal interests. Since no other offences in EU or national law arguably protect the same interest as Articles 101 and 102 TFEU, the result is that the *ne bis in idem* principle only applies when the same undertaking is prosecuted or punished again for the same violation of EU competition law which is already the subject-matter of a final decision on the merits by the Commission or an NCA concerning the same undertaking;

7. Regulation 1/2003 does not prohibit parallel proceedings by the Commission under EU law and national competition authorities under national law. Article 3 of Regulation 1/2003 provides for a duty of national competition authorities to apply Articles 101 and 102 TFEU whenever they apply national competition law to conduct that has an effect on trade between Member States. Furthermore, save for the application of stricter unilateral conduct rules under national law, any conflict between EU and national law is expressly prohibited. This provision must be read against the background of the case law of the Court of Justice, which, since 1969, has allowed parallel proceedings by the Commission under EU law and by national competition authorities under national law provided that the primacy of EU law is respected and, if multiple sanctions are imposed on the same person

---

present purposes is that national competition authorities have the power, in principle, to investigate and punish infringements of EU competition law that have effects beyond their national territory and may take such effects into account when imposing fines on undertakings.

[6] Case C-375/09, *Prezes Urzędu Ochrony Konkurencji i Konsumentów* v. *Tele2 Polska sp. z o. o., now Netia SA* [2011] ECR I-3055.

[7] Case 14/68, *Walt Wilhelm* v. *Bundeskartellamt* [1969]; Case C-17/10, *Toshiba Corporation v. Úřad pro ochranu hospodářské soutěže* [2012] OJ C98/3.

[8] Joined Cases C-204/00 P, C-205/00 P, C-211/00 P, C-213/00 P, C-217/00 P and C-219/00 P, *Aalborg Portland A/S* v. *Commission* [2004] ECR I-123, para. 338.

under EU and national laws, the previous punishment is taken into account in determining the second sanction;[9]

8. When a competition authority has established an infringement and imposed fines on an undertaking, further proceedings are not barred if the previous decision is annulled by a court on procedural grounds. The case law concerning decisions of the Commission is clear: when a decision has been set aside by the EU courts because of a procedural defect, there is no final conviction any more. No decision on the merits exists because the original decision has been annulled on procedural, rather than substantive, grounds and such an annulment is, therefore, not an acquittal.[10] Thus, competition authorities can make serious procedural mistakes affecting the validity of an infringement decision without losing the power to resume the proceedings after the decision has been set aside by the courts.[11] Furthermore, it may not always be clear when a decision has been set aside on procedural grounds and when there has been a decision on the merits instead. In a pending case, the applicant is challenging the Commission's decision to reopen cartel proceedings after its previous decision has been partially set aside by the General Court. The applicant does so on the ground that the reopening of the proceedings infringes the *ne bis in idem* principle;[12]

9. As regards decisions in non-EU Member States, the *ne bis in idem* principle would appear not to apply at all and the EU authorities are not required to take into account the penalties imposed in non-EU Member States.[13] As a result, the protection of undertakings against multiple sanctions for the same conduct is entirely left to the exercise of self-restraint by competition authorities and courts around the

---

[9] Case 14/68, *Walt Wilhelm* v. *Bundeskartellamt*, para. 11.

[10] Joined Cases C-238/99 P, C-244/99 P, C-245/99 P, C-247/99 P, C-250/99 P to C-252/99 P and C-254/99 P, *Limburgse Vinyl Maatschappij NV (LVM)* v. *Commission (PVC No 2)* [2002] ECR I-8375, paras. 59–62; Case T-24/07, *ThyssenKrupp Stainless AG* v. *Commission* [2009] ECR II-2309, para. 190.

[11] The Commission normally re-adopts cartel decisions that have been annulled by the EU courts on procedural grounds: *Gas insulated switchgear* (summary decision) [2013] OJ C70/12; *Alloy surcharge* (summary decision) [2007] OJ L182/31; *Steel beams* (summary decision) [2008] OJ C235/4; *PVC* [1994] OJ L239/14.

[12] Case T-240/12, *Eni* v. *Commission* [2012] OJ C217/27.

[13] Case C-289/04 P, *Showa Denko KK* v. *Commission* [2006] ECR I-5859; Case C-308/04 P, *SGL Carbon AG* v. *Commission* [2006] ECR I-5977; Case C-328/05 P, *SGL Carbon AG* v. *Commission* [2007] ECR I-3921.

world ensuring that fines imposed in each given jurisdiction reflect only the harm caused by a global cartel in that jurisdiction.

This system of EU and international concurrent jurisdictions finds a limit in the *ne bis in idem* principle, which, at the general level, may be described as prohibiting further prosecution or punishment of a person who has already been finally acquitted or convicted of the same offence. In EU competition law, the principle of *ne bis in idem* is a fundamental right recognized in Article 50 of the EU Charter of Fundamental Rights (the 'EU Charter'),[14] which applies to EU institutions as well as to the Member States when they are implementing Union law.[15] Even before the EU Charter was given the same legal value as the Treaties by the Treaty of Lisbon,[16] the principle of *ne bis in idem* was a general principle of EU law[17] and, as such, continues to apply alongside Article 50 EU Charter[18] even if it has probably lost most of its autonomous significance.[19] The EU fundamental right not to be tried or punished twice must be interpreted in the light of the principle of *ne bis in idem* in Article 4 of Protocol no. 7 to the European Convention on Human Rights and Fundamental Freedoms (ECHR).[20] Well before the EU Charter came into force, the EU courts have referred to the ECHR right not to be tried

---

[14] Art. 50 EU Charter forbids a second criminal prosecution or punishment if a person has already been finally convicted or acquitted of the same offence within the Union in accordance with the law.

[15] Art. 51(1) EU Charter. The scope of application of the EU Charter is given a broad interpretation: see Case C-617/10, *Åklagaren* v. *Hans Åkerberg Fransson* [2013] OJ C114/7, paras. 16–31.

[16] Art. 6(1) of the Treaty on the European Union [2012] OJ C326/01.

[17] The principle was expressed as precluding a person from being subject to proceedings or punished a second time for unlawful conduct in respect of which he has already been punished or exonerated by a previous decision that is no longer amendable to challenge: Case T-224/00, *Archer Daniels Midland* v. *Commission* [2003] ECR II-2597, paras. 85–86; Joined Cases T-271/03 and T-245/03, *Fédération nationale des syndicats d'exploitants agricoles (FNSEA)* v. *Commission* [2004] ECR II-271, para. 340; Case T-39/06, *Transcatab SpA* v. *Commission* [2011] ECR II-6831, para. 254; Case C-17/10 *Toshiba Corporation* v. *Úřad pro ochranu hospodářské soutěže*, para. 94.

[18] W. P. J. Wils, 'EU Antitrust Enforcement Powers and Procedural Rights and Guarantees: The Interplay between EU Law, National Law, the Charter of Fundamental Rights of the EU and the European Convention on Human Rights' (2011) 34 *World Competition*, 189, 207.

[19] On this issue, see Chapter 3 by Sarmiento in this volume.

[20] Convention for the Protection of Human Rights and Fundamental Freedoms, Rome, 4 November 1950, Protocol no. 7, Art. 4. Article 4 of Protocol no. 7 to the ECHR provides in the first paragraph for the right of a person not 'to be tried or punished again in criminal proceedings under the jurisdiction of the same State for an offence for which he

or prosecuted twice as reflecting a fundamental principle of EU law.[21] Furthermore, there are other *ne bis in idem* rules in EU law, including, in particular, Chapter 3 of the Convention implementing the Schengen Agreement (CISA)[22] and Article 3(2) of the Council Framework Decision of 13 June 2002 on the European arrest warrant and the surrender procedures between Member States, as amended ('Framework Decision on the EAW').[23] The case law of the Court of Justice on these provisions may be of persuasive authority in interpreting Article 50 EU Charter and

has already been finally acquitted or convicted in accordance with the law and penal procedure of that State', thus limiting the geographical application of the principle to a single jurisdiction. Furthermore, paragraph 2 of Art. 4 sets out the circumstances in which further proceedings and a second punishment are admissible, namely if, 'in accordance with the law and penal procedure of the State concerned', there is evidence of new or newly discovered facts or there has been a fundamental defect in the previous proceedings, which could affect the outcome of the case. Not all Member States have ratified Protocol no. 7 but this has not prevented the EU courts from referring to it as a 'reference point' or a source of inspiration of the general principle of EU law of *ne bis in idem*: see, e.g., Now, Art. 52(2) EU Charter expressly provides that: 'In so far as this Charter contains rights which correspond to rights guaranteed by the Convention for the Protection of Human Rights and Fundamental Freedoms, the meaning and scope of those rights shall be the same as those laid down by the said Convention. This provision shall not prevent Union law providing more extensive protection'.

[21] Joined Cases C-238/99 P, C-244/99 P, C-245/99 P, C-247/99 P, C-250/99 P to C-252/99P and C-254/99P, *Limburgse Vinyl Maatschappij NV (LVM)* v. *Commission (PVC No 2)*, para. 59; see also W. P. J. Wils, 'The Principle of Ne Bis in Idem in EC Antitrust Enforcement: A Legal and Economic Analysis' (2003) 26 *World Competition* 131, 133. For a general overview of the problems arising from the application of the European Human Rights Convention to administrative proceedings by the Commission, see A. Riley, 'The ECHR Implications of the Investigation Provisions of the Draft Competition Regulation' (2002) 51 *International and Comparative Law Quarterly*, 1, 55 and R. Wainwright, 'Human Rights: What Have They to Do with Competition Law?' M. Andenas, M. Hutchings, Ph. Marsden (eds.), *Current Competition Law*, vol. III (London: British Institute of International and Comparative Law, 2005), pp. 473– 480.

[22] Convention implementing the Schengen Agreement of 14 June 1985 [2000] OJ L239/19.

[23] Council Framework Decision of 13 June 2002 on the European arrest warrant and the surrender procedures between Member States, OJ 2002 L190/1, amended by Council Framework Decision 2009/299/JHA of 26 February 2009 amending Framework Decisions 2002/584/JHA, 2005/214/JHA, 2006/783/JHA, 2008/909/JHA and 2008/947/JHA, thereby enhancing the procedural rights of persons and fostering the application of the principle of mutual recognition to decisions rendered in the absence of the person concerned at the trial OJ 2009 L81/24, Art. 3(2), which provides for a mandatory ground of non-execution of a European arrest warrant 'if the executing judicial authority is informed that the requested person has been finally judged by a Member State in respect of the same acts provided that, where there has been sentence, the sentence has been served or is currently being served or may no longer be executed under the law of the sentencing Member State'.

the general principle of *ne bis in idem*. Finally, the principle of *ne bis in idem* is also recognized in public international law but, unless an international convention provides otherwise, its application is limited to a second prosecution or punishment within the same State.[24]

Against the background of the risk of multiple proceedings and decisions against the same undertakings for the same competition law infringements, the thesis in this chapter is that discretionary prosecutorial restraint is not a sufficient safeguard against such a risk whereas the principle of *ne bis in idem* can effectively perform the function of limiting vexatious and inefficient exercise of concurrent jurisdiction in competition matters within the Union. This limiting function of the *ne bis in idem* principle is analysed by focusing on the six elements by which the *ne bis in idem* principle is capable of regulating the exercise of concurrent jurisdiction within the EU: a) what constitutes the same offence for the purpose of the principle of *ne bis in idem* in competition law; b) whether a prosecuting authority is allowed to bring separate proceedings concerning different elements of the same offence, for example by considering the same conduct as constituting separate offences depending on the Member State where the anti-competitive effects occur; c) what types of decision bar a second prosecution or punishment; d) the consequences of the first acquittal or conviction being set aside on appeal or judicial review for the application of the principle of *ne bis in idem*; e) the application of the EU principle of *ne bis in idem* in the relationship between EU law and national law proceedings within the Union; f) the application of the EU principle of *ne bis in idem* in an international context, namely when the first decision was made in a non-EU State.

2 Inadequacy of Discretionary Prosecutorial Restraint as a Limiting Principle

As explained in the previous section, the basic features of the EU competition enforcement system are, almost by design, conducive to multiple proceedings and multiple decisions. Any abuse may, of course, be avoided as a matter of prosecutorial restraint. Thus, within the Union, widespread abuse of the system has been avoided by a sensible administrative allocation of cases within the European Competition Network

---

[24] Opinion of AG Tizzano in Case C-397/03 P, *Archer Daniels Midland Co* v. *Commission* [2006] ECR I-4429.

(ECN),[25] whereby the national competition authorities and the Commission aim at identifying the authority best placed to act on each given case, thus avoiding multiple proceedings and, by necessary implication, multiple fining decisions for the same conduct.[26] However, prosecutorial restraint cannot be the answer to the problem of multiple prosecutions and decisions, particularly because the Commission and national competition authorities enjoy wide and largely uncontrollable discretion in allocating cases, defining the scope of the investigations, and launching a second investigation even if the same or another authority has already investigated the same conduct.

Firstly, instead of using the ECN case allocation mechanism to avoid duplication of proceedings, the Commission and national competition authorities may find it expedient, on efficiency grounds, to allocate different aspects of what may constitute a single infringing conduct to different authorities. One example of this practice may be the consumer textile detergents cartel where it appears that the Commission and the French competition authority may have brought proceedings against the same parties concerning closely connected behaviours that could have amounted to a single overall infringement. The issue came to light because, in the French proceedings, Henkel applied to the Commission for permission to use certain documents obtained in the Commission investigation in order to prove that the two sets of proceedings were closely connected but its application was rejected and the decision upheld by the General Court.[27] It appears that a similar issue could arise in the Commission's second probe into the LCD market. The second investigation would appear to relate to LCD screens for mobile devices whereas the first decision concerns LCD screens for television sets and computer monitors. However, the meetings in which the alleged cartel conduct took place were possibly the same as regards both types of LCD screens.[28] Finally, in July 2013, Orange made an application to the

---

[25] The ECN is a network of public authorities formed by the Commission and the national competition authorities for the purposes, *inter alia*, of coordinating the enforcement of Articles 101 and 102 TFEU under Regulation 1/2003. The structure and functioning of the ECN is set out in the Commission Notice on cooperation within the Network of Competition Authorities OJ 2004 C101/43.

[26] Commission Notice on cooperation within the Network of Competition Authorities, paras. 5–42.

[27] Case T-64/12, *Henkel AG & Co KGaA* v. *Commission* [2013] OJ C129/20.

[28] Case T-128/11, *LG Display* v. *Commission* [2011] OJ C130/10, pending. The issue of double jeopardy is raised under the fourth plea.

General Court challenging the validity of a decision by the Commission ordering Orange to submit to an inspection under Article 20(4) of Regulation 1/2003 claiming, *inter alia*, that the practices investigated by the Commission were very similar to conduct investigated by the French competition authority only nine months earlier and in respect of which the latter authority found no evidence of infringement.[29] While the Commission and the national competition authorities enjoy wide discretion at case allocation stage, with the power to consolidate or subdivide investigations as they find most expedient, parties have no or very limited scope to challenge case allocation decisions.[30] As a result, a challenge can be made only *ex post* on *ne bis in idem* grounds. Indeed, the absence of the parties' involvement in the case allocation procedure and of a right to challenge case allocation decisions calls for stronger *ne bis in idem* rules to regulate multiple proceedings and fines *ex post*.

Furthermore, case allocation and decisions as to the scope of a case occur when an investigation commences and a case is notified to the ECN. There is no mechanism within the ECN to bar a second investigation once the first case has been closed. This problem has been exacerbated by the ruling of the Court of Justice in *Tele2Polska* that national competition authorities do not have the power to 'acquit' an undertaking by way of a final non-infringement decision.[31] Similarly, Regulation 1/2003 does not impose a duty on the Commission to make a non-infringement decision if an investigation has not established sufficient evidence to prove an infringement. Article 10 of Regulation 1/2003 provides for the discretionary power of the Commission to make a finding of inapplicability when the Union public interest so requires but no such finding has been made so far and, in any event, the decision whether to do so is highly discretionary. On the other hand, Article 7 of Commission Regulation 773/2004 provides for the power of the Commission to reject a complaint but such a decision is not a finding that there has been no infringement[32]

---

[29] Case T-402/13, *Orange v. Commission* [2013] OJ C313/28.

[30] N. Khan and C. Kerse, *Kerse & Khan on EU Antitrust Procedure* (London, Sweet & Maxwell 2012), pp. 50–51.

[31] Case C-375/09, *Prezes Urzędu Ochrony Konkurencji i Konsumentów v. Tele2 Polska sp. z o.o., now Netia SA.*

[32] Commission Regulation 773/2004/EC of 7 April 2004 relating to the conduct of proceedings by the Commission pursuant to Articles 81 and 82 of the EC Treaty OJ 2004 L23/18.

and, on the basis of a purely formalistic application of what constitutes a previous conviction, it would appear that it does not necessarily bar further proceedings.[33] Therefore, the same undertaking can be investigated time and again in the Union by national competition authorities and the Commission and, as long as no sufficient evidence is found or the authority decides not to make an infringement decision, further proceedings are not barred.

It is clear, therefore, that even in an integrated system such as the ECN, prosecutorial restraint cannot be the answer to the problem of multiple investigations and convictions. Even less so in the international context, where there is no formal mechanism for allocating cases and coordinating investigations and no rule of public international law that imposes on the Commission or a national competition authority a duty not to punish or investigate an undertaking that has already been finally acquitted or convicted for the same infringement in a non-EU country[34] or even to take into account previously imposed penalties.[35]

The only justiciable and, at least in principle, predictable way of limiting the proliferation of proceedings and decisions concerning the same competition infringements against the same undertakings is a robust and coherent application of the *ne bis in idem* principle. This function of the *ne bis in idem* principle is, however, currently impaired by its overly restrictive judicial interpretation in competition matters.

---

[33] On this general proposition, see N. Khan, *Kerse & Khan on EU Antitrust Procedure*, p. 86. The case law appears to be of more limited scope: see Case C-279/95 P, *Langnese-Iglo GmbH* v. *Commission* [1998] ECR1-5609, para. 30 (in relation to a comfort letter) and Case T-241/97, *Stork Amsterdam* v. *Commission* [2000] ECR II-309, para. 80 (in relation to a complaint rejected for lack of sufficient Union interest).

[34] Opinion of AG Geelhoed in Case C-301/04 P, *Tokai Carbon* v. *Commission* [2006] ECR I-5915, paras. 46–52; Opinion of AG Mazak in Case C-328/05 P, *SGL Carbon* v. *Commission* [2007] ECR I-3921, paras. 39–41; Opinion of AG Geelhoed in Case C-289/04 P, *Showa Denko* v. *Commission* [2006] ECR I-5859, paras. 74–75; Opinion of AG Geelhoed in Case C-308/04 P, *SGL Carbon* v. *Commission* [2006] ECR I-5977, paras. 46–52; Opinion of AG Tizzano in Case C-397/03 P, *Archer Daniels Midland* v. *Commission*, paras. 86–115.

[35] Opinion of AG Geelhoed in Case C-301/04 P, *Tokai Carbon* v. *Commission*, paras. 46–52; Opinion of AG Mazak in Case C-328/05 P, *SGL Carbon* v. *Commission*, paras. 39–41; Opinion of AG Geelhoed in Case C-289/04, P *Showa Denko* v. *Commission*, paras. 74–75; Opinion of AG Geelhoed in Case C-308/04 P *SGL Carbon* v. *Commission*, paras. 46–52; Opinion of AG Tizzano in Case C-397/03 P *Archer Daniels Midland* v. *Commission*, paras. 86–115.

3 *Ne Bis in Idem* as a Limit to Parallel Proceedings

3.1 *Definition of the Same Offence*

The key governing concept for the application of the *ne bis in idem* rules is the definition of what constitutes the same offence. In competition law, the EU courts apply a three-fold test to the definition of the same offence, requiring the identity of the facts, the identity of the offender and the identity of the legal interest protected.[36] The requirement of the identity of the legal interest protected comes into play to rule out the application of the *ne bis in idem* principle to offences committed by the same person and arising out of the same facts in different legal systems, as different legal systems are assumed to protect competition within their own national markets,[37] or in violation of rules aimed at achieving different regulatory or policy objectives, such as, for example, competition rules, on the one hand, and rules in the areas of telecommunications regulation[38] or patent law,[39] on the other. The Grand Chamber of the Court of Justice confirmed the requirement of the identity of the legal interest protected in *Toshiba*[40] even though Advocate General Kokott forcefully invited the Court to adopt a criterion based only on the identity of the facts, which the Court itself applies in other areas of EU law[41] and which the European Court of Human Rights applies under Article 4 of Protocol

---

[36] Joined Cases C-204/00 P, C-205/00 P, C-211/00 P, C-213/00 P, C-217/00 P and C-219/00 P, *Aalborg Portland A/S v. Commission*, [2004] ECR I-0123, para. 338.

[37] Case C-150/05, *Jean Leon Van Straaten v. Staat der Nederlanden* [2006] ECR I-9327.

[38] Undertakings may be subject to telecommunications regulation as well as competition law: see, e.g., Case C-280/08 P, *Deutsche Telekom AG v. Commission* [2010] ECR I-9555, paras. 56–110, where the applicant argued that the relevant telecommunications regulation did not leave it any scope for determining its competitive conduct autonomously and that its compliance with telecommunications regulation gave rise to a legitimate expectation that there was no breach of Art. 102 TFEU in the circumstances. Conversely, if national telecommunications regulatory authorities had sanctioned the applicant for conduct that also amounted to margin squeeze, a *ne bis in idem* issue could have arisen.

[39] See, e.g., Case C-457/10, *AstraZeneca AB v. Commission* [2013] OJ C26/2, paras. 74–100, where the dominant undertaking could in theory have been exposed to fines under national law for providing false or misleading information to patent offices, a conduct that was also found to be an infringement of Art. 102 TFEU.

[40] Case C-17/10, *Toshiba Corporation v. Úřad pro ochranu hospodářské soutěže*, para. 97, even if the Court then decided the case on the ground that the facts were not identical: see paras. 98–103.

[41] Case C-150/05, *Jean Leon Van Straaten v. Staat der Nederlanden and Republiek Italië*, paras. 48 and 53; Case C-436/04, *Criminal proceedings against Leopold Henri Van Esbroeck* [2006] ECR I-2333; Case C-288/05 P, *Criminal proceedings against Jürgen*

no. 7 to the ECHR.[42] The Advocate General relied strongly, albeit implicitly, on the identity of the rationales for the *ne bis in idem* principle in different areas of EU law and in Article 4 of Protocol no. 7 to the ECHR. First, the Advocate General emphasized the shared free movement rationale between the *ne bis in idem* principle in EU competition law and the same principle in Article 54 CISA and under the Framework decision on the EAW.[43] Then, she pointed to the need to ensure that the protection under EU law did not fall short of the minimum standard of protection under Article 4 of Protocol no. 7 to the ECHR.[44] Thus, it is the protection of the fundamental right of the undertakings concerned that requires homogeneity of results under EU law and Article 4 of Protocol no. 7 to the ECHR. Such a protection cannot be lower under EU law than it is under the ECHR system.

The Opinion of the Advocate General in *Toshiba* sets out the correct approach and it is to be regretted that the Court of Justice refused to follow it and even confirmed the requirement of the identity of the legal interest although it was not required to do so to decide the case. Indeed, the requirement of the identity of the legal interest protected reduces significantly the scope of protection enjoyed by the defendant and runs counter to the rights-based foundation of the *ne bis in idem* principle. It is for this reason that the European Court of Human Rights rejected this requirement under Article 4 of Protocol no. 7 to the ECHR.[45] The European Court of Human Rights reached this conclusion notwithstanding the use of the word 'offence' in Article 4 of Protocol no. 7,[46] emphasizing that the approach based on the legal characterisation of the offence 'is too restrictive of the rights of the individual' and 'risks undermining' the principle of *ne bis in idem*.[47] These considerations apply with equal force to the principle of *ne bis in idem* under EU competition law.

Kretzinger [2007] ECR I-06441, paras. 29–31; Case C-367/05, *Criminal proceedings against Norma Kraaijenbrink* [2007] ECR I-06619, paras. 23–26.

[42] ECtHR, *Zolotukhin* v. *Russia,* 7 June 2007 (Appl. No. 14939/03).

[43] Opinion of AG Kokott in Case C-17/10, *Toshiba Corporation* v. *Úřad pro ochranu hospodářské soutěže,* paras. 116–118.

[44] Opinion of AG Kokott in Case C-17/10, *Toshiba Corporation* v. *Úřad pro ochranu hospodářské soutěže,* paras. 119–123.

[45] ECtHR, *Zolotukhin* v. *Russia,* 7 June 2007 (Appl. No. 14939/03). R. Nazzini, 'Fundamental Rights beyond Legal Positivism: Rethinking the Ne Bis in Idem Principle in EU Competition Law' (2014) *Journal of Antitrust Enforcement* 1, 16.

[46] *Zolotukhin* v. *Russia,* para. 80.   [47] *Zolotukhin* v. *Russia,* para. 81.

The EU courts, of course, are not bound by the case law of the Strasbourg Court. They could depart from it if there was a good reason to do so. It is difficult to see, however, why the protection of the *ne bis in idem* principle should be lower under EU competition law than under the ECHR system. On the contrary, because of the internal market rationale for the EU principle of *ne bis in idem*, the need for a conduct-based interpretation of the concept of 'offence' is even stronger. The reason is clear: the characterization of an offence is, by definition, different in different legal systems as the legal interest protected changes when considered from the perspective of different sovereign States.[48] This is why international definitions of the *ne bis in idem* principle such as the one in Article 4 of Protocol no. 7 to the ECHR or in Article 14(7) of the International Covenant on Civil and Political Rights prohibit multiple prosecutions and convictions within one and the same State: it is inconceivable that one sovereign state could forgo its right to prosecute and punish offences under its own law because they are an infringement of its own legal order and, therefore, *different* in nature from offences under the law of other states that protect a *different* legal interest. But to extend this approach to the EU-wide principle of *ne bis in idem* would be to deprive it of most if its effectiveness in a cross-border context. The Court of Justice's approach to competition cases thus results in a market fragmentation which in other areas the Court itself has consistently held to be incompatible with one single internal market. As Advocate General Ruiz-Jarabo said in his opinion in *Van Esbroeck*, 'if, instead of the acts alone, account were taken of the offences or of the rights protected by the prohibition of the said acts, the *ne bis in idem* principle would never function at international level'.[49] This is the reason why, in *Van Esbroeck*, the Court of Justice decided that Article 54 CISA applies regardless of the legal classification of the offence.[50] The only requirement is the identity of material facts, understood as 'a set of facts which are inextricably linked together in time, in space and by their

---

[48] A point rightly made by the Court of Justice in Case C-288/05 P, *Criminal proceedings against Jürgen Kretzinger* [2007] ECR I-6441, para. 31.

[49] Opinion of AG Ruiz-Jarabo Colomer in Case C-436/04, *Criminal proceedings against Leopold Henri Van Esbroeck* [2006] ECR I-2333, para. 47.

[50] Case C-436/04, *Criminal proceedings against Leopold Henri Van Esbroeck* [2006] ECR-2333, para. 38; Case C-467/04, *Criminal proceedings against Giuseppe Francesco Gasparini* [2006] ECR I-9199, para. 56; Case C-150/05, *Jean Leon Van Straaten* v. *Staat der Nederlanden and Republiek Italië* [2006] ECR I-9327, para. 52.

subject-matter'.[51] As the Court rightly held, following the Advocate General, 'a criterion based on the legal classification of the acts or on the protected legal interest might create as many barriers to freedom of movement within the Schengen territory as there are penal systems in the Contracting States'. This conduct-based definition is also consistent with the Framework Decision on the European Arrest Warrant (EAW),[52] which provides that, for offences other than those listed in Article 2, paragraph 2 (essentially, a list of serious offences where dual criminality is presumed), 'surrender may be subject to the condition that the acts for which the European arrest warrant has been issued constitute an offence under the law of the executing Member State, whatever the constituent elements or however it is described'. Clearly, the EAW adopts a conduct-based definition of same offence. The express exclusion from what constitutes an offence under the law of the executing Member States of the 'constituent elements' of the offence or its description demonstrate the precise, unequivocal intention to avoid an approach based on the legal characterization of the offence and, even less, on the legal interest protected. Why this reasoning should not apply to *ne bis in idem* as a general principle of EU law or to Article 50 EU Charter is difficult to understand. The only principled argument that could be made in this respect is that Article 50 EU Charter refers to the 'offence' rather than to 'same acts' as Article 54 CISA. The Court of Justice in *Van Esbroeck* did rely on this literal argument.[53] However, the arguments based on ensuring that the principle of *ne bis in idem* is given its full effect as a fundamental right and on the freedom of movement rationale are much more powerful and should be capable of overcoming the literal argument. This is even more so given that the use of the term 'offence' is in itself not conclusive: it is a neutral term that begs the question of its meaning in designing the boundaries of the *ne bis in idem* principle rather than answering it. The European Court of Human Rights in *Zolotukhin* had no difficulty in interpreting the term 'offence' under

---

[51] Case C-367/05, *Criminal proceedings against Norma Kraaijenbrink* [2007] ECR I-6619, paras. 23–26; Case C-288/05 P, *Criminal proceedings against Jürgen Kretzinger* [2007] ECR I-6441, paras. 29–31.

[52] Council Framework Decision 2002/584/JHA of 13 June 2002 on the European arrest warrant and the surrender procedures between Member States, OJ L190/1, 13 June 2002.

[53] Case C-436/04, *Criminal proceedings against Leopold Henri Van Esbroeck* [2006] ECR I-2333, paras. 27–28.

Article 4 of Protocol no. 7 to the ECHR as a set of facts rather than a legal construct.

In conclusion, the correct position under Article 50 EU Charter and the general EU law principle of *ne bis in idem* is that two infringements are the same offence when they are constituted by the same or inextricably linked facts. The case law of the EU courts on the principle of *ne bis in idem*, which still requires the identity of the legal interest protected, should be reviewed and brought in line with the case law of the Court of Justice on Article 54 CISA and the jurisprudence of the European Court of Human Rights on Article 4 of Protocol no. 7 to the ECHR.

3.2   Fragmentation of the Same Offence

A question related to the definition of what constitutes the same offence is whether competition authorities can subdivide a set of facts which are inextricably linked together in time, in space and by their subject-matter into several infringements of competition law which can be separately prosecuted and punished. If the separate violations arise from facts which are inextricably linked together in time, in space and by their subject-matter, the *ne bis in idem* principle could bar a second prosecution or punishment even if the facts that were the subject-matter of the previous decision clearly and unequivocally did not include the facts that are the subject-matter of the new investigation. The classic example in which this could occur is a EU-wide cartel where the conduct, while consisting of individual agreements or concerted practices, has the same anti-competitive object and amounts, therefore, to a single overall infringement,[54] but which the Commission and the national competition authorities choose to prosecute as a set of separate infringements based on the countries where the effects of the conduct took place or the different products involved. Reasons of efficiency may favour this approach to prosecuting complex cartels but the question is whether an undertaking is entitled to the protection of the *ne bis in idem* principle whenever the offence is a single one, concerning inextricably linked facts.

---

[54] Case C-441/11 P, *Commission v. Verhuizingen Coppens NV* [2013] OJ C26/14; Case T-15/89, *Chemie Linz v. Commission* [1992] ECR II-1275, para. 308; Case C-49/92 P, *Commission v. Anic* [1999] ECR I-4125, para. 113; Joined Cases T-25/95 to 39/95, T-42/95 to T-46/95, T-48/95, T-50/95 to T-65/95, T-68/95 to T-71/95, T-87/95, T-88/95, T-103/95, T-104/95, *Cimenteries CBR v. Commission* [2000] ECR II-491, paras. 4025 *et seq*.

The right-based foundation of the *ne bis in idem* principle appears to require a strict application of this safeguard whenever a person is prosecuted again for the same offence. The same offence is defined as the same sets of facts or inextricably linked facts. This test is an objective one: the Court of Justice ruled that it does not depend on the subjective intention of the perpetrator.[55] But equally, the test cannot depend on the discretion of the prosecuting authorities. If the prosecuting authorities were free to decide, in the definition of an offence, which facts are inextricably linked together and which are not, the guarantee of *ne bis in idem* would become totally ineffective. The argument follows, *a fortiori*, from the reasoning of the Court of Justice in relation to Article 54 CISA[56] and the European Court of Human Rights[57] in relation to Article 4 of Protocol no. 7 to the ECHR. The definition of what constitutes the same offence cannot depend on the legal classification of the offence, otherwise the national legislature would be free to limit the effectiveness of the principle as he sees fit. But if this applies to the legislature, the same applies with even more force to the prosecuting authorities, who have a strong incentive in prosecuting cases and would not be bound, in the definition of the offence, by anything other than their own discretion.

The freedom of movement foundation of the *ne bis in idem* principle in EU law also suggests that fragmentation of the same offence should not allowed. If a person must be free to exercise his right of freedom of movement without the fear of being prosecuted or punished again for the same offence in different Member States, the principle should apply to all offences across all Member States that arise from the same or inextricably linked facts. Different legal characterizations or the possibility of dividing a single offence depending, for instance, on where the effects of the conduct are felt, would make the *ne bis in idem* principle devoid of purpose and run directly counter to the freedom of movement rationale.

Nor does it appear that the effective enforcement of EU competition law requires that competition authorities be given such a high degree of discretion to conduct multiple prosecutions and take multiple decisions concerning inextricably linked facts. The Commission and national

---

[55] Case C-367/05, *Criminal proceedings against Norma Kraaijenbrink*, para. 29.
[56] Case C-150/05, *Jean Leon Van Straaten v. Staat der Nederlanden and Republiek Italië*, paras. 48 and 53; Case C-436/04, *Criminal proceedings against Leopold Henri Van Esbroeck*; Case C-288/05 P, *Criminal proceedings against Jürgen Kretzinger*, paras. 29–31; Case C-367/05, *Criminal proceedings against Norma Kraaijenbrink*, paras. 23–26.
[57] *Zolotukhin* v. *Russia*, para. 16.

competition authorities are well equipped to pursue single continuous infringements or infringements that have effects in several Member States. Indeed, Regulation 1/2003 and the Notice on cooperation within the network of EU competition authorities ('ECN Notice') provide for specific mechanisms of case allocation, coordination and investigation designed to facilitate a single prosecution of multi-jurisdictional[58] or complex infringements.[59] Mere reasons of expediency and efficient resource allocation within the ECN could never result in the practical obliteration of an undertaking's right not to be prosecuted or punished twice, which would be the inescapable consequence if competition authorities were permitted to define the factual scope of the offence at their discretion.

The test for when the facts are the same or inextricably linked must be applied in the circumstances of each individual case. However, two areas are probably sufficiently typified in the case law. First, whenever a set of facts gives rise to a single overall infringement, there is a single offence under Article 101 TFEU. The very test for the establishment of a single continuous infringement requires that the facts are closely connected and, therefore, inextricably linked for the purposes of the *ne bis in idem* principle.[60] Second, whenever the effects of anti-competitive conduct are caused by the same behaviour or are dependent on each other, the facts are inextricably linked and there is, therefore, a single offence even if the effects in question are felt in different Member States. This is the case, for example, when the parties agree at the same meetings to raise the price of their products in several Member States or when the parties agree to raise the price of an input sold in one Member State, which has the further effect of significantly raising the price of an output which is sold in several Member States.

Finally, the application of the test presupposes that the first prosecuting authority had jurisdiction in relation to all the elements of the conduct in question. No preclusion can arise if there was no jurisdiction to decide a matter and no issue of the application of the *ne bis in idem* principle can be even conceivable if a person has never been in jeopardy

---

[58] See Art. 22(1) of Regulation 1/2003.

[59] See Arts. 17–21 and 22(2) of Regulation 1/2003.

[60] Case C-441/11 P, *Commission v. Verhuizingen Coppens NV*, nyr.; Case T-15/89, *Chemie Linz v. Commission*, para. 308; Case C-49/92 P, *Commission v. Anic*, para. 113; Joined Cases T-25/95 to 39/95, T-42/95 to T-46/95, T-48/95, T-50/95 to T-65/95, T-68/95 to T-71/95, T-87/95, T-88/95, T-103/95, T-104/95, *Cimenteries CBR v. Commission*, paras. 4025 *et seq.*

of been convicted. Therefore, single continuous infringements affecting new Member States can be prosecuted under national law for the period of time when Article 101 TFEU did not apply to them even if the Commission has adopted a decision on the same cartel.[61]

3.3 The Nature of the Decision Giving Rise to a Preclusion of Further Prosecution or Punishment

Only a final acquittal or conviction within the Union gives rise to a preclusion of further proceedings.[62] The case law requires that, for the *ne bis in idem* principle to apply, there must have been a first decision that exonerated or penalized an undertaking and that is no longer amenable to challenge.[63] Therefore, the principle of *ne bis in idem* applies not only when there has been a conviction or a penalty but also when an undertaking has been acquitted or exonerated. But what constitutes an acquittal for the purposes of the *ne bis in idem* principle? It is clear that if the legislature or a prosecuting authority has complete freedom in deciding what an acquittal means or when an acquittal decision can be made, the *ne bis in idem* rule protecting a person from further proceedings after acquittal would be abolished and the right would be reduced to the right not to be prosecuted again or punished only after conviction but not after acquittal. To achieve this, it would suffice for legislation to prohibit acquittal decisions and provide for mere case closures on *non liquet* grounds whenever the defendant's guilt cannot be proved to the required standard or to give the prosecution or court complete freedom to bring a case to an end without an acquittal whenever they think fit. It seems obvious that this runs counter to right not to be prosecuted again or punished after acquittal. And yet, it appears that this is the current position in EU competition law. This results from three sets of rules:

1. Under Article 10 of Regulation 1/2003, the Commission has the power to make a finding of inapplicability of Article 101 or 102 TFEU in its discretion when the Union public interest so requires. It is never required to do so and the wording of Article 10 suggests that the finding of inapplicability is an exception rather than the norm;

---

[61] Case C-17/10, *Toshiba Corporation v. Úřad pro ochranu hospodářské soutěže.*
[62] Art. 50 EU Charter.
[63] Case T-39/06, *Transcatab SpA v. Commission*, para. 254; Case T-224/00, *Archer Daniels Midland v. Commission*, paras. 85–86; Case C-17/10, *Toshiba Corporation v. Úřad pro ochranu hospodářské soutěže*, para. 94.

2. When the Commission considers that, on the basis of the information in its possession, there are insufficient grounds for acting on a complaint, it shall reject the complaint according to Article 7 of Commission Regulation 773/2004.[64] The decision is not defined as a final acquittal but simply as a complaint rejection as it does not establish that no infringement has been committed. As a result, at least *prima facie*, further proceedings can be opened without necessarily engaging the *ne bis in idem* rules;[65]

3. In *Tele2 Polska*, the Court of Justice ruled that, under Article 5 of Regulation 1/2003, national competition authorities do not have the power to make non-infringement decisions.[66] Therefore, an undertaking is exposed to multiple investigations in the Member States as long as no national competition authority establishes sufficient evidence of an infringement. If no or insufficient evidence of infringement is found, a national competition authority is only allowed to decide that there are no grounds for action. Again, *prima facie*, it would appear that the *ne bis in idem* principle does not apply in these circumstances.

The EU competition enforcement system appears to have been designed so that only the Commission, in exceptional circumstances, can make acquittal decisions giving rise to a preclusion of further proceedings. In all other cases, if there is no proof of an infringement, the proceedings will be closed by a *non liquet* decision, which allows for further proceedings against the same parties in relation to the same or inextricably linked facts. And this is so even if the substance of the case has been fully explored in the first set of proceedings and the competition authority came to the conclusion that there is no infringement. The problem is well illustrated by *Tele2 Polska* itself. The Polish competition authority in that case had come to the conclusion that there was no infringement of Article 102 TFEU and the equivalent national provision. However, it had decided that there were 'no grounds for action' under EU law and that there was no infringement under national law. Indeed, in *Tele2 Polska*, the Polish competition authority was convinced that there was no infringement of Article 102 TFEU. However, it issued a *non liquet* decision instead of a decision on the merits.[67] The question is whether a

---

[64] See Art. 7 of Commission Regulation 773/2004/EC.   [65] See footnote 30.

[66] Case C-375/09, *Prezes Urzędu Ochrony Konkurencji i Konsumentów* v. *Tele2 Polska sp. z o.o., now Netia SA, nyr.*

[67] Case C-375/09, *Prezes Urzędu Ochrony Konkurencji i Konsumentów* v. *Tele2 Polska sp. z o.o., now Netia SA, nyr.*

non liquet decision in such circumstances bars a second prosecution whatever its legal label under secondary EU legislation or, in a national context, under national law. The same question arises as regards decisions by the Commission rejecting a complaint under Article 7 of Commission Regulation 773/2004.

Currently, both the Court of Justice and the European Court of Human Rights essentially defer to national law to determine whether a decision is final so as to bar a second prosecution.

Under Article 54 CISA, the Court of Justice held in *Vladimir Turanský* that in order to assess whether a decision is final for the purpose of the application of the *ne bis in idem* principle, it must be ascertained whether the decision is final and binding in the Member State concerned and whether it leads, in that Member State, to the protection granted by the *ne bis in idem* principle. A decision which does not definitively bar a second prosecution in the Member State in which it was adopted cannot prevent further proceedings or punishment in another Member State.[68] This approach is consistent with the previous case law and, in particular, with *Gözütok and Brügge*, where the Court of Justice, while giving a wide interpretation of Article 54 CISA as applying also to decisions of the prosecutor to discontinue the proceedings based on the defendant performing certain obligations, clearly emphasized that it was material to this conclusion that the decision in question barred further prosecution under German law.[69] This outcome, however, is justified in the light of the special features of the CISA, which recognizes the preclusive effects of national criminal decisions and is in no way conditional on the harmonization or approximation of the criminal laws of the Member States.[70] Article 54 CISA is, therefore, based on the mutual trust of the Contracting States in their criminal justice systems.[71] As a consequence, it is entirely logical, and indeed unavoidable, that the finality of a decision is assessed under the relevant national law. However, under Regulation 1/2003, the decisional powers of the Commission and the national competition authorities are directly governed by EU law. Secondary

---

[68] Case C-491/07, *Criminal proceedings against Vladimir Turanský* [2008] ECR I-11039, paras. 35–36.

[69] Joined Cases C-187/01 and C-385/01, *Criminal proceedings against Hüseyin Gözütok and Klaus Brügge* [2003] ECR I-1345, paras. 25, 27, 29–31, and 34.

[70] Case C-297/07, *Klaus Bourquain* [2008] ECR I-9425, para. 36; Joined Cases C-187/01 and C-385/01, *Criminal proceedings against Hüseyin Gözütok and Klaus Brügge*, para. 32.

[71] Case C-297/07, *Klaus Bourquain*, para. 37; Joined Cases C-187/01 and C-385/01, *Criminal proceedings against Hüseyin Gözütok and Klaus Brügge*, para. 33.

legislation must be interpreted in a way which is consistent with the *ne bis in idem* principle, which is a hierarchically superior norm. There is no issue of mutual trust in, or deference to, national legal systems. Quite the contrary, following the approach of the Court of Justice in *Tele2 Polska*, the area of the types of decision that national competition authorities must and are allowed to make has been fully harmonized under EU law.

The European Court of Human Rights has not ruled on whether Article 4 of Protocol no. 7 to the ECHR imposes a constraint on the Contracting States as to the circumstances in which criminal proceedings can be discontinued without giving rise to a preclusion of further proceedings or punishment for the same offence. The jurisprudence of the Court generally holds that a decision is final 'when no further ordinary remedies are available or when the parties have exhausted such remedies or have permitted the time-limit to expire without availing themselves of them'.[72] Thus, the question as to whether a decision is final must be answered under national law.[73] However, this concept of finality is procedural as it merely denotes that the decision is no longer amenable to ordinary challenges. The test does not relate to the content of the decision, which is what matters to determine whether a decision constitutes an acquittal or is a mere case closure. Therefore, this case law is not relevant to the problem at hand.

A further strand of the Court's case law holds that there is no right to a formal acquittal under Article 6 ECHR. Proceedings can be discontinued without any decision on the merits.[74] However, the question as to whether there is an infringement of the presumption of innocence if proceedings are discontinued without a decision on the merits is different from the question as to whether such a practice offends against the *ne bis in idem* principle. The rule that a prosecution may be discontinued without a formal acquittal would be fully compatible with the rule that, in certain circumstances, a prosecution discontinued without formal acquittal bars further proceedings.

It appears, therefore, that the case law of the European Court of Human Rights does not provide any specific guidance on whether *non*

---

[72] ECtHR, *Zolotukhin v. Russia*, 7 June 2007 (Appl. No. 14939/03), para. 107; ECtHR, *Nikitin v. Russia*, 20 July 2004 (Appl. No. 50178/99), para. 37; ECtHR, *Horciag v. Romania*, 15 March 2005 (Appl. No. 70982/01).

[73] ECtHR, *Sundqvist v. Finland*, 22 November 2005 (Appl. No. 75602/01); ECtHR, *Müller v. Austria (No 2)*, 18 September 2008 (Appl. No. 28034/04).

[74] ECtHR, *Niedermeier v. Germany*, 3 February 2009 (Appl. No. 70982/01); ECtHR, *Withey v. United Kingdom*, 26 August 2003 (Appl. No. 59493/00).

liquet decisions may bar further proceedings under the *ne bis in idem* principle. Therefore, the question must be answered on first principles. And as the Court said in *Zolotukhin*, the Convention must be interpreted so as to give effect to the rights it aims to protect.[75] To allow the Contracting States *carte blanche* to adopt *non liquet* decisions would be tantamount to cancelling the *ne bis in idem* right from Protocol no. 7. The dissenting opinion of Judge Zupančič in *Sievert* v. *Germany*[76] appears to go in this direction when he said that, in deciding whether the protection against double jeopardy applies, the question is 'what is *the real nature of the decision* taken by the prosecutor'[77] and that '*any* decision based on *any* lack of evidence . . . is . . . of necessity a *final* decision'.[78]

It follows from the above analysis that, under the EU general principle of *ne bis in idem* and Article 50 EU Charter, it would be wrong to accept that 'no grounds for action' decisions by national competition authorities and complaint rejections by the Commission do not bar subsequent proceedings as, formally, they do not constitute acquittals on the merits.

First, from a right-based perspective, there is no point in recognizing a right not to be tried or punished twice while at the same time giving the legislature a free hand to permit proceedings to be discontinued by issuing *non liquet* decisions even if there has been a significant appraisal of the merits of the case.

Second, from an internal market perspective, it seems that allowing EU national competition authorities and the Commission to conduct as many investigations against the same undertakings in relation to the same facts as they think fit in their discretion is precisely what the *ne bis in idem* principle should prohibit. Indeed, the problem that occurs

---

[75] *Zolotukhin* v. *Russia*, para. 16.
[76] ECtHR, *Sievert* v. *Germany*, 19 July 2012 (Appl. No. 29881/07). The case concerned the principle of *ne bis in idem* only indirectly. The applicant complained that he had been unable to examine two witnesses because they availed themselves of the privilege against self-incrimination and refused to answer questions. There was an issue as to whether the decisions to discontinue the prosecutions of the two witnesses in question would bar a new prosecution. If it did, then the privilege against self-incrimination would not have been available. The majority did not address this point and decided the case without asking whether the privilege against self-incrimination had been rightly invoked: ibid., paras. 58–69.
[77] Ibid., para. 19 (emphasis in the original).
[78] Ibid., para. 29 (emphasis in the original). R. Nazzini, 'Fundamental Rights beyond Legal Positivism: Rethinking the Ne Bis in Idem Principle in EU Competition Law' (2014) *Journal of Antitrust Enforcement* 1, 23–24.

because of the absolute freedom of the legislature to permit *non liquet* decisions in a national context becomes even more acute across the Union because the risk of multiple investigations increases considerably for undertakings engaging more actively in the provision of goods and services in different Member States.

Third, to allow, without constraints, repeated fishing expeditions against the same undertaking in connection with the same facts is also inefficient as repeated investigations into the same alleged infringements result in a waste of public and private resources and lower the incentives of competition authorities to investigate and prosecute cases diligently and effectively.

The only argument that can be made in favour of repeated investigations is based on the effective enforcement of EU competition law: the detection and punishment of competition infringements requires that competition authorities be allowed to test allegations and close an investigation without this precluding further proceedings. There may be good reasons to do so: new evidence could come to light or new resources could mean that a case which previously could not be pursued as a priority can now be investigated. However, the correct approach would be to balance these considerations against the need to protect undertakings against multiple investigations. Thus, a distinction should be made between decisions to close a case that are based on a preliminary and summary investigation, which should not bar further proceedings, and decisions to close a case that follow a significant consideration of the merits of the case and are adopted in a procedure where the defendant has had a full opportunity to exercise his rights of defence, which should bar further proceedings whatever the formal classification of the final decision. This test is close to that proposed by Advocate General Sharpston in her opinion in *Gasparini*, where she argued that a defendant should be entitled to the protection of the *ne bis in idem* principle when 'he has *de facto* been placed in jeopardy' and the 'criminal proceedings have involved any significant consideration of the merits of the case'.[79] The case law of the Court of Justice does lend some support to this test. In *Miraglia*, the Court had to rule on whether a judicial decision to close the case following the public prosecutor's determination to discontinue the prosecution on the sole ground that proceedings had been commenced in another Member State gave rise to a preclusion under

---

[79] Opinion of AG Sharpston in Case C-467/04, *Criminal proceedings against Giuseppe Francesco Gasparini* [2006] ECR I-9199, para. 96.

Article 54 CISA.[80] Not surprisingly, the answer was that further proceedings were not precluded because 'no determination has been made as to the merits of the case'[81] and 'there had been no assessment whatsoever of the unlawful conduct with which the defendant was charged'.[82] The Court then went on to consider the EU objective of ensuring free movement of persons in conjunction with appropriate measures to prevent and combat crime.[83] But arguably, this objective would not have prevailed over the right of the individual if the case closure decision had involved a substantive assessment of the case. In *Van Straaten*, the Court had no hesitation in ruling that a final decision acquitting the defendant for lack of evidence precludes further proceedings because, unlike in *Miraglia*, such a decision is based on 'a determination as to the merits of the case'.[84] The objective of protecting the right to freedom of movement played a key role in the reasoning of the Court.[85] The same strong freedom of movement rationale led the Court in *Gasparini* to hold that decisions acquitting the defendant because the prosecution is time barred give rise to a preclusion of further proceedings.[86] For the same reasons, in *Gözütok and Brügge*, the Court held that a decision of the prosecution giving effect to a plea agreement barred a second prosecution.[87] This case law on Article 54 CISA is relevant under Article 50 of the EU Carter and for the development of *ne bis in idem* as a general principle of EU law because all these provisions and principles share the same foundations: safeguarding individual rights and ensuring free movement. Its logical development is that, at least when EU legislation is concerned, provisions allowing proceedings to be closed without a formal acquittal must be interpreted as precluding further proceedings if there has been a substantive appraisal of the case and the defendant has had the opportunity of exercising his rights of defence in full.

---

[80] Case C-469/03, *Criminal proceedings against Filomeno Mario Miraglia* [2005] ECR I-2009, para. 30.

[81] Case C-469/03, *Criminal proceedings against Filomeno Mario Miraglia*, para. 30.

[82] Case C-469/03, *Criminal proceedings against Filomeno Mario Miraglia*, para. 34.

[83] Case C-469/03, *Criminal proceedings against Filomeno Mario Miraglia*, para. 34.

[84] Case C-150/05, *Jean Leon Van Straaten v. Staat der Nederlanden and Republiek Italië*, paras. 56–60.

[85] Case C-150/05, *Jean Leon Van Straaten v. Staat der Nederlanden and Republiek Italië*, para. 58.

[86] Case C-467/04, *Criminal proceedings against Giuseppe Francesco Gasparini*, paras. 22–33.

[87] Joined Cases C-187/01 and C-385/01, *Criminal proceedings against Hüseyin Gözütok and Klaus Brügge*, paras. 36–38.

The same test should apply to commitments decisions under Article 9 of Regulation 1/2003. Under Article 9(1), commitments decisions conclude that 'there are no longer grounds for action by the Commission'. Recital 13 clarifies that commitments decision do not determine 'whether or not there has been or still is an infringement' and are 'without prejudice to the powers of competition authorities and courts of the Member States to make such a finding and decide upon the case'. However, if the commitments decision is adopted after a substantive appraisal of the case and after the undertakings concerned have had a full opportunity to exercise their rights of defence, the prohibition of further proceedings and convictions should apply. In *Gözütok and Brügge*, the Court of Justice clearly held that decisions discontinuing the prosecution because the defendants made certain commitments are capable of giving rise to a preclusion.[88] In that case, German law itself considered the decision as triggering the application of the *ne bis in idem* protection.[89] As regards commitments decisions under Article 9 of Regulation 1/2003, while secondary legislation considers such decisions as not constituting a formal conviction, the application of the *ne bis in idem* principle derives directly from Article 50 EU Charter, which is a hierarchically superior norm.

3.4   Setting Aside of an Acquittal or Conviction on Procedural Grounds

In EU law, the setting aside by the EU courts of an infringement decision by the Commission on procedural grounds does not preclude the Commission from resuming the proceedings. Since *PVC (No 2)*, the case law justifies this conclusion on two grounds: a) the annulment of a decision on procedural grounds does not constitute a decision on the merits and is not, therefore an acquittal 'within the meaning given to that expression in penal matters';[90] b) the penalties imposed as a result of the second set of

---

[88] Joined Cases C-187/01 and C-385/01, *Criminal proceedings against Hüseyin Gözütok and Klaus Brügge* [2003] ECR I-1345, para. 27.
[89] Ibid, para. 17.
[90] Joined Cases C-238/99 P, C-244/99 P, C-245/99 P, C-247/99 P, C-250/99 P to C-252/99 P and C-254/99 P, *Limburgse Vinyl Maatschappij NV (LVM)* v. *Commission (PVC No 2)* [2002] ECR I-8375, para. 62; Case T-24/07, *ThyssenKrupp Stainless AG* v. *Commission* [2009] ECR II-2309, para. 190.

proceedings are not added to the previously imposed penalties but replace them.[91] Both strands of reasoning are not fully convincing.

As regards the effect of the judgment setting aside an infringement decision on procedural grounds, it is not obvious that this is the only relevant decision for the purposes of the *ne bis in idem* protection. The relevant decision may well be the annulled decision, which established the infringement and imposed a penalty and which, after the annulment, is no longer amenable to appeal or judicial review and, therefore, final. The doctrinal objection to this argument is that, once a decision has been set aside, it no longer exists and it is, therefore, impossible to say that there is a final acquittal or conviction within the Union according to Article 50 EU Charter. However, it would be equally plausible to argue that a conviction does not simply cease to exist because it has been annulled. While its legal effects are set aside retrospectively, its significance under the *ne bis in idem* principle cannot be cancelled. The reason is that the purpose of the *ne bis in idem* principle is to protect the right of the defendant not to be subject to a second prosecution or punishment once he has already been subjected to proceedings on the merits resulting in a final decision. In the case of procedural annulment of a conviction, the defendant has actually been placed in jeopardy as there was a substantive assessment of the case in proceedings in which he had a full opportunity to exercise his rights of defence. Applying the test proposed in the previous section, it can be argued that such a decision, should bar further proceedings or punishment.

As regards the argument that the second penalty replaces the previously imposed one and is not added to it, it is important to underline that the *ne bis in idem* principle does not protect a right not to be punished twice because the preclusion also applies when the first decision is an acquittal. Therefore, the circumstance that, when the first decision is set aside, the second penalties are not added to the previous ones but replace them, is irrelevant and based on an incorrect understanding of the principle. From the point of view of the defendant, what matters is that the *jus puniendi* of the State or the Union has been already exercised once in proceedings on the merits resulting in a decision no longer amenable to appeal or review. The circumstance that the *jus puniendi* was invalidly exercised should not detract from the protection afforded to the defendant.

---

[91] Joined Cases C-238/99 P, C-244/99 P, C-245/99 P, C-247/99 P, C-250/99 P to C-252/99 P and C-254/99 P, *Limburgse Vinyl Maatschappij NV (LVM)* v. *Commission (PVC No 2)*, para. 62; Case T-24/07, *ThyssenKrupp Stainless AG* v. *Commission*, para. 190.

If, from the perspective of the protection of the fundamental right of the undertakings concerned, there appears to be only a weak doctrinal justification for limiting the *ne bis in idem* principle when the first decision has been set aside, such a justification can be found in the need to ensure the effective enforcement of EU competition law: effective law enforcement requires that procedural defects affecting convictions do not prevent reopening the case, provided that the defect can be cured. The defendant has a right to a procedure according to law and can enforce his right by mounting procedural challenges against a conviction. However, if a procedural challenge is successful, the *ne bis in idem* protection must give way to the public interest in effective law enforcement. Even on this reasoning, however, it could be argued that an unqualified, potentially open-ended possibility of resuming proceedings following the annulment of a conviction on procedural grounds is too draconian an inroad into the *ne bis in idem* right. Furthermore, disciplinary and efficiency considerations suggest that allowing the prosecution to reopen the case time and again notwithstanding serious procedural defects in the proceedings is not desirable from a public interest point of view.

The above considerations suggest that a possible, and probably better, approach to the preclusive effect of a judicial annulment of a conviction on procedural grounds could be to frame a test that balances the protection of the right of the undertakings concerned, the need to safeguard the effective enforcement of EU competition law, and the requirement to ensure that competition authorities act in accordance with the law and in an efficient way on a case-by-case basis. The analysis above suggests that a suitable test could be to allow proceedings to be resumed if: a) the effective enforcement of EU competition law so requires; b) the procedural defect of the decision was either not attributable to the prosecuting authority or, if it was so attributable, was neither in bad faith nor grossly negligent.

3.5   Relationship between EU and National Law Enforcement within the Union

It is uncontroversial that infringement decisions by national competition authorities under EU competition law bar further proceedings under EU competition law by other national competition authorities or the Commission relating to the same facts and the same undertakings.[92] This

---

[92] Joined Cases T-144/07, T-147/07 to T-150/07, and T-154/07, *ThyssenKrupp Liften Ascenseurs NV* v. *Commission* [2011] ECR II-5129. Case T-24/07, *ThyssenKrupp Stainless AG* v. *Commission* [2009] ECR II-2309, para. 162.

chapter has already demonstrated that, as regards the same infringement, the test should be whether the proceedings arise from the same or inextricably linked facts. The problem concerns, therefore, the possibility of parallel proceedings under EU and national competition law. In such a case, even if the national competition authority does not apply EU law, it is still bound by Article 50 EU Charter and by the general EU law principle of *ne bis in idem*. As Advocate General Kokott said in her opinion in *Toshiba*, national competition authorities are only allowed to apply national competition law in accordance with the delimitation of competences set out in Regulation 1/2003. Regulation 1/2003 itself must be interpreted in accordance with Article 50 EU Charter and the general principle of *ne bis in idem*.[93] As a consequence, the application of national competition law must also comply with EU fundamental rights and general principles. In *Toshiba*, the Court did not address specifically the issue and limited itself to the analysis of the temporal application of the *ne bis in idem* principle.[94] However, implicitly, the Court accepted that the *ne bis in idem* principle applies when a national competition authority applies national competition law. This accords with the extensive interpretation of Article 51 EU Charter in *Fransson*[95] and with the case law of the Court of Justice that, since *Walt Wilhelm*,[96] requires a national competition authority applying national competition law to take into account the fines imposed by the Commission on the same undertakings for the same facts.

The question is then whether, at the current stage of development of EU law and of integration of the internal market, a EU competition authority should be prevented from applying EU or national competition law if the same infringement by the same parties is already the subject-matter of a decision on the merits under national or EU competition law, respectively.

In *Walt Wilhelm*, a case dating back to 1969, the Court of Justice ruled that parallel proceedings by the Commission under EU law and by national competition authorities under national law are allowed as long

---

[93] Opinion of AG Kokott in Case C-17/10, *Toshiba Corporation* v. *Úřad pro ochranu hospodářské soutěže*, paras. 105–106.

[94] Case C-17/10, *Toshiba Corporation* v. *Úřad pro ochranu hospodářské soutěže*, para. 95.

[95] Case C-617/10, *Åklagaren* v. *Hans Åkerberg Fransson, nyr.*, paras. 16–31.

[96] Case 14/68, *Walt Wilhelm* v. *Bundeskartellamt, nyr.*; Case C-17/10, *Toshiba Corporation* v. *Úřad pro ochranu hospodářské soutěže*, para. 81; Case C-550/07 P, *Akzo Nobel Chemicals Ltd* v. *Commission* [2010] ECR I-08301, para. 103; Joined Cases C-295/04 to C-298/04, *Vincenzo Manfredi* v. *Lloyd Adriatico Assicurazioni SpA* [2006] ECR I-6619, para. 38.

as the national competition authority respects the primacy of EU law[97] and the previous punishment is taken into account in determining the second sanction.[98]

Walt Wilhelm was decided in a very different context, in which the Court of Justice noted that EU competition law and national competition law have different objectives, the former being concerned with the establishment of the single market and the latter with unspecified 'considerations peculiar to it'.[99] Furthermore, the Court considered it relevant that EU law had not (yet) regulated the relationship between EU and national competition law according to Article 103(2)(e). Both elements in *Walt Wilhelm* apply with much less force today.

It is still true that purely domestic competition law may have objectives that are different from the objectives of EU competition law. However, the reality is that the national competition laws in the Member States are by and large modelled on EU law. Nor is it possible to say that EU competition law is exclusively concerned with the establishment of the internal market while national competition laws pursue wholly different objectives. While the well-functioning of the internal market is the primary objective of EU competition law, the internal market itself has further objectives, including the economic well-being of the peoples of Europe, economic growth and productivity, which are therefore, albeit indirectly, also objectives of EU competition law.[100] Broadly, it is difficult to argue that facilitating trade, promoting economic growth and productivity, and enhancing the economic welfare of the society are not objectives of the national competition laws of the Member States.

Furthermore, Article 3 of Regulation 1/2003 now regulates the relationship between EU competition law and national competition law. In particular, the possibility of parallel proceedings under EU and national law is significantly limited by the duty of national competition authorities to apply Articles 101 and 102 TFEU whenever they apply national competition law to conduct that has an effect on trade between Member States. Save for the application of stricter unilateral conduct rules under

---

[97] Case 14/68, *Walt Wilhelm v. Bundeskartellamt*, paras. 3–9.
[98] Case 14/68, *Walt Wilhelm v. Bundeskartellamt*, para. 11.
[99] Case 14/68, *Walt Wilhelm v. Bundeskartellamt*, para. 3.
[100] R. Nazzini, '*The Foundations of European Union Competition Law: The Objective and Principle of Article 102*' (Oxford: Oxford University Press, 2011), pp. 113–152.

national law, any conflict between EU and national law is expressly prohibited, thus achieving a significant degree of convergence.[101]

Notwithstanding the considerations above, in *Toshiba*, the Grand Chamber of the Court of Justice confirmed the *Walt Wilhelm* approach to parallel EU and national proceedings. In that case, the Czech competition authority had fined the parties to a cartel for the period prior to the accession of the Czech Republic to the EU. The Commission had imposed fines on the same parties for the same cartel. Following the Advocate General, the Court confirmed that EU and national competition law may apply in parallel as they consider restrictions of competition from different angles and have different scopes of application.[102] This, combined with the requirement that the 'legal interest' protected must be the same for two offences to be the same for the purposes of the *ne bis in idem* principle, means that an undertaking can be subject to two fining decisions, one under EU law and one under national law, with the only requirement that the second decision must take into account the previously imposed sanction.

The Court in *Toshiba* even went as far as saying that Article 16(2) of Regulation 1/2003 allows national competition authorities to apply EU and national law after the Commission – and, it would appear to follow *a fortiori*, another national competition authority – has already made a decision with the only limit that a subsequent national decision cannot run counter to a previous decision by the Commission.[103] On this reasoning, an undertaking could be fined by the Commission for a cartel and then fined again by a national competition authority for the same cartel under national law as long as the national decision takes into account the fine imposed by the Commission. The same would apply in the case of abuse of dominance with the additional consideration that, because, under Article 3 of Regulation 1/2003, national law may apply stricter rules than Article 102 to unilateral conduct, it could be argued that a national law decision may even follow a Commission's decision of inapplicability.

The case law of the Court of Justice in *Walt Wilhelm* and *Toshiba* relies on the requirement that two offences are the same only if they

---

[101] F. Louis and G. Accardo, '*Ne Bis in Idem*, Part "*Bis*" ' (2011) 34 *World Competition*, 1, 104.

[102] Case C-17/10, *Toshiba Corporation* v. *Úřad pro ochranu hospodářské soutěže*, paras. 81–83.

[103] Case C-17/10, *Toshiba Corporation* v. *Úřad pro ochranu hospodářské soutěže*, paras. 84–87.

protect the same legal interest. Because, as already argued, this requirement is in breach of Article 50 EU Charter, this case law lacks foundation
and should be overruled at the earliest opportunity. The Court of Justice
should reconsider the position and recognize that when Member States
and the Commission apply national or EU competition law to infringements consisting of the same or inextricably linked facts and committed
by the same undertakings, the *ne bis in idem* principle applies with its full
force barring a second prosecution or punishment. This conclusion is
subject to the sole proviso that a preclusion only arises if the authority
which made the first decision had jurisdiction to make a finding of
infringement in relation to the facts that constitute the offence prosecuted by the second authority. Therefore, in the case of accession States,
a decision under national law is not precluded by a decision of the
Commission concerning the same parties and inextricably linked facts
for the period prior to accession. It was on this simple basis that the
Court of Justice should have decided the reference in *Toshiba*.

3.6   Relationship between Proceedings Within and Outside the EU

As regards the relationship between proceedings in the Union and
previous acquittals or convictions outside the Union, it is settled case
law that the principle of *ne bis in idem* does not apply. The rationale for
the jurisprudence of the EU courts has, however, significantly changed
over time.

   Initially, a first strand of case law represented by *Boehringer Mannheim* v. *Commission* appeared to rely on the different factual matrix
between cartels prosecuted by foreign authorities and cartels prosecuted
within the Union. In particular, the case law seemed to establish a
presumption that the geographical scope of the cases was different and
any punishment imposed in foreign proceedings would not take into
account the anti-competitive effects of the conduct within the Union.[104]

   The subsequent case law moved away from this approach. In *Kyowa
Hakko Kogyo* v. *Commission*, the Court of First Instance construed
Boehringer Mannheim as ruling only that a *hypothetical* duty of the
Commission to take into account a foreign penalty when setting the level
of a fine under EU law could only arise if the facts were identical in the
two sets of proceedings. Since the applicant had not established that it

---

[104] Case 7/72, *Boehringer Mannheim GmbH* v. *Commission* [1972] ECR 1281, paras. 4–8.

was so in that case, the argument failed. *Boehringer Mannheim* had not decided that the Commission had a duty to take into account fines imposed by foreign authorities.[105] On the issue of the application of the principle of *ne bis in idem*, the Court relied on an argument *a fortiori* drawn from the *Walt Wilhelm* case law with: if the *ne bis in idem* principle does not apply in the relationship between EU proceedings and proceedings under the national laws of the Member States, then it cannot apply with respect to foreign proceedings. If EU and national proceedings within the Union pursue different ends, so must EU and foreign proceedings, which aim at protecting different markets.[106] However, the rule that a EU competition authority must take into account the fines already imposed by another EU competition authority on the same undertaking for the same conduct cannot be extended to the relationship between the Commission and foreign authorities. The distinguishing factors are, first, that the relationship between proceedings by the Commission and proceedings by EU national competition authorities is characterized by a special system of concurrent jurisdiction in relation to conduct on the same territory and, second, that there is a close interdependence between the national markets of the EU Member States. Both factors are lacking when it comes to the relationship between proceedings in the Union and foreign proceedings.[107]

Then, when the case law developed a *ne bis in idem* test requiring not only the identity of the facts and the identity of the defendant but also the identity of the legal interest protected by the two offences,[108] a third strand of case law emerged holding that, as regards infringements of foreign competition law and infringements of EU competition law, the requirement of the unity of the legal interest is, by definition, not fulfilled and, therefore, the *ne bis in idem* principle does not apply.[109] Advocate General Tizzano in *Archer Daniels Midlands v. Commission* appears to

---

[105] Case T-223/00, *Kyowa Hakko Kogyo Co Ltd* v. *Commission* [2003] ECR II-2553, paras. 106–114.

[106] Case T-223/00, *Kyowa Hakko Kogyo Co Ltd* v. *Commission*, paras. 100–101. The argument *a fortiori* is now undermined by the implicit acceptance in *Toshiba* that the *ne bis in idem* principle applies in national competition law proceedings: Case C-17/10, *Toshiba Corporation* v. *Úřad pro ochranu hospodářské soutěže*, para. 95.

[107] Case T-223/00, *Kyowa Hakko Kogyo Co Ltd* v. *Commission* [2003] ECR II-2553, paras. 108–111.

[108] Joined Cases C-204/00 P, C-205/00 P, C-211/00 P, C-213/00 P, C-217/00 P and C-219/00 P, *Aalborg Portland A/S* v. *Commission* [2004] ECR I-0123, para. 338.

[109] Case T-224/00, *Archer Daniels Midland* v. *Commission* [2003] ECR II-2597, para. 63.

have followed this approach: after explaining that there is no public international law rule that imposes on the Union institutions a duty to take into account penalties inflicted by foreign authorities, the Advocate General went on to say that, in any event, EU and foreign proceedings aim at protecting different legal interests.[110] The Court of Justice, however, decided the case on a narrow ground, reminiscent of *Boehringer Mannheim*: the applicants had not shown that the facts in the two investigations were identical and, therefore, their appeal failed on this simple ground.[111]

The Court of Justice changed significantly its jurisprudence in *Showa Denko* v. *Commission* and in *SGL Carbon* v. *Commission (No 1)*. In his opinions in both cases, Advocate General Geelhoed had adopted the same approach as Advocate General Tizzano in *Archer Daniels Midlands* relying, first, on the absence of a duty under public international law to take foreign penalties into account and, in any event, on the lack of identity of the legal interest protected.[112] The Court did not follow this reasoning but relied on what appears to be a more fundamental argument: the *ne bis in idem* principle does not apply at all when the previous decision is made by a non-EU authority because foreign and EU competition laws pursue different ends within different geographical scopes of application. In protecting free competition in the internal market, the Union cannot be constrained by decisions of foreign authorities pursuing different objectives. The inapplicability of the principle of *ne bis in idem* in an international context was reaffirmed by the Court of Justice in *SGL Carbon* v. *Commission (No 2)*:[113] proceedings aimed at safeguarding a fundamental objective of the Union cannot be barred by proceedings in non-EU Member States that pursue different interests relevant under foreign law.[114]

The case law of the Court of Justice is correct. In the absence of a public international law norm binding the Union to take into account penalties imposed for competition law infringements outside the Union,

---

[110] Opinion of AG Tizzano in Case C-397/03 P, *Archer Daniels Midlands* v. *Commission*, paras. 92–104.

[111] Case C-397/03 P, *Archer Daniels Midlands* v. *Commission* [2006] ECR I-4429, paras. 46–76.

[112] Case C-289/04 P, *Showa Denko KK* v. *Commission*; Opinion of AG Geelhoed in Case C-308/04 P, *SGL Carbon AG* v. *Commission*, paras. 46–62.

[113] Case C-328/05 P, *SGL Carbon AG* v. *Commission*, para. 28, confirming the approach in the earlier case law: Case C-308/04 P, *SGL Carbon AG* v. *Commission*, paras. 26–32.

[114] Case C-308/04 P, *SGL Carbon AG* v. *Commission*, paras. 26–27.

the matter is one for Union law. Article 50 EU Charter is limited to proceedings within the Union and so is, and should, the general principle of *ne bis in idem*. The effective enforcement of EU competition law plays a fundamental role in this respect: the Union cannot be prevented from pursuing its objectives by the exercise of jurisdiction by foreign authorities. There is a strong presumption – based on the doctrine of international comity – that foreign authorities do not take over the role of punishing and deterring infringements occurring outside their respective jurisdictions.[115] But even if they do, the remedy must be found within the legal systems of those States exercising extraterritorial jurisdiction or in international law norms forbidding the exercise of exorbitant jurisdiction. The exercise of jurisdiction by a non-EU competition authority cannot deprive the Commission or the EU national competition authorities of their power and duty to punish and deter competition infringements within the Union.

4   The Function of the *Ne Bis in Idem* Principle in Limiting Multiple Proceedings and Decisions in EU Competition Law

This chapter argues that the risk of multiple proceedings and convictions in EU competition enforcement is inadequately addressed by the current interpretation of the *ne bis in idem* principle in competition matters.

The review of the case law of the EU courts in the light of this model leads to the following conclusions:

1. The correct position under Article 50 EU Charter and the general EU law principle of *ne bis in idem* is that two infringements are the same offence when they are constituted by the same or inextricably linked facts. The case law of the EU courts on the principle of *ne bis in idem*, which still requires the identity of the legal interest protected, should be reviewed and brought in line with the case law of the Court of Justice on Article 54 CISA and the jurisprudence of the European Court of Human Rights on Article 4 of Protocol no. 7 to the ECHR.

2. A single infringement consisting in the same or inextricably linked facts cannot be subdivided and investigated separately by the Commission and national competition authorities in the Union because the first acquittal or conviction will bar further proceedings.

---

[115] This appears to be implied in Case 7/72, *Boehringer Mannheim GmbH* v. *Commission*, paras. 4–6.

This applies in particular: a) whenever a set of facts gives rise to a single overall infringement, b) whenever the effects of anti-competitive conduct are caused by the same behaviour or are dependent on each other, c) and provided always that the first authority had jurisdiction to investigate the facts that are the subject-matter of the second set of proceedings.

3. At least when the procedure is governed by EU law, provisions allowing proceedings to be closed without a formal acquittal such as those under Article 5 of Regulation 1/2003 (no grounds for action decisions by national competition authorities) or Article 7 of Commission Regulation 773/2004 (complaint rejections by the Commission) must be interpreted as precluding further proceedings if there has been a substantive appraisal of the merits of the case and the defendant has had the opportunity of exercising his rights of defence in full.

4. The EU case law on the reopening of the proceedings following the judicial annulment of a conviction on procedural grounds may be justified by the need to ensure the effective enforcement of EU competition law prevailing over the defendant's right and efficiency considerations. An alternative approach could be to frame a test that balances the protection of the right of the undertakings concerned, the need to safeguard the effective enforcement of EU competition law, and the requirement to ensure that competition authorities act in accordance with the law and in an efficient way on a case-by-case basis. A suitable test could be to allow proceedings to be resumed if: a) the effective enforcement of EU competition law so requires; b) the procedural defect of the decision was not attributable to the prosecuting authority or, if it was so attributable, was neither in bad faith nor grossly negligent.

5. The settled case law holding that national competition authorities may apply national law even if the Commission has already imposed a fine on the same undertakings for the same facts is untenable. Given the substantial degree of convergence between the national competition laws of the Member States and EU competition law achieved in particular after the entry into force of Regulation 1/2003, the correct position under Article 50 EU Charter and the general principle of *ne bis in idem* appears to be that, when Member States and the Commission apply national or EU competition law to infringements consisting in the same or inextricably linked facts and committed by the same undertakings, the *ne bis in idem* principle applies with its full force

barring a second prosecution or punishment. This conclusion is subject to the sole proviso that a preclusion only arises if the authority which made the first decision had jurisdiction to make a finding of infringement in relation to the facts that constitute the offence prosecuted by the second authority.

6. The case law of the EU courts is correct in holding that the *ne bis in idem* principle does not apply when the first acquittal or conviction occurred outside the Union.

In conclusion, the *ne bis in idem* case law of the EU courts in competition law is in need of urgent review. This chapter suggests possible solutions that could allow the principle of *ne bis in idem* to perform more effectively its function of limiting vexatious and inefficient multiple proceedings against the same undertakings for the same alleged infringements of competition law within the Union.

5

Ne Bis in Idem and Tax Offences in EU Law and ECHR Law

PETER J. WATTEL

1 Overview

This chapter on tax offences is divided into the following sections:

2. Possible *bis in idems*
3. Disentangling double jeopardy; *Ne bis puniri* and *ne bis vexari*; credit and finality systems; homogeneity as regards 'idem' and 'criminal proceedings'?
4. Is a punitive tax surcharge a 'criminal proceeding' within the meaning of Article 4 of Protocol no. 7 ECHR and Article 50 of the Charter?
5. The meaning of *Åkerberg Fransson* for tax penalties in the Member States
6. 'idem' issues in tax penalty cases
7. Parallels between (prevention of) international double jeopardy and (prevention of) international double taxation
8. Conclusions

2 Possible Concurrences of Punitive Sanctions for the Same Offence

Four main categories of double jeopardy present themselves: a *bis in idem* in respect of punitive sanctions for the same offence may occur:

 (i) within one national legal system,
 (ii) through concurrence of two or more national legal systems, especially
   (ii)(a) of two EU Member States;
   (ii)(b) of an EU Member State and a third State;
 (iii) between the EU legal system and a Member State's internal law or
 (iv) between the EU legal system and the law of a non-Member State.

2.1   Ad (i): Within One Single EU Member State's Jurisdiction

Under the internal law of several EU Member States, concurrence of two or more punitive sanctions in respect of the same tax offence is not unusual. Especially, the imposition of an administrative fine ('tax penalty'; 'tax surcharge'), may in some Member States be followed by criminal indictment of the taxpayer for the same facts as the surcharge was imposed for, provided that the final total of penalties is not disproportionate to the impugned conduct. Usually, therefore, in such cases of consecutive concurrence, the criminal authorities/the criminal court will take into account, when determining the criminal penalty to be imposed, the tax penalty already imposed by the tax authorities (see Section 3).

Such concurrence of an administrative penalty and a criminal conviction within one single jurisdiction may occur in respect of (i) EU-*harmonized* taxes, such as customs duties, value added tax (VAT), excise duties and capital duty or (ii) *unharmonized* taxes, notably direct taxes. If unharmonized taxes within a wholly internal situation are at issue, then usually the case will not be within the scope of application of EU law, and therefore neither within the scope of Article 50 (*ne bis in idem*) of the Charter of Fundamental rights of the EU (the Charter). Still, such cases may be within the scope of the *ne bis in idem* provision of Article 4 of Protocol no. 7 to the European Convention of Human Rights (ECHR) – provided the Member State involved has ratified that Protocol – which may prohibit a 'bis'.

If penalties in respect of EU-harmonized (indirect) taxes are at issue, even in entirely internal situations, EU law is engaged, and therefore also (Article 50 of) the Charter, at any rate if they feed the 'own resources' of the Union (see Section 5). If penalties in respect of *un*harmonized direct taxes are at issue, then in principle (Article 50 of) the Charter does not apply, as there is no link to EU law in internal situations. Only if a direct tax case has a cross-border aspect which activates the EU free movement rights, if it engages EU State Aid law, or if it concerns one of the rare and rather specific EU Directives on corporate income taxation, it will enter the scope of application of EU law, and with that, the scope of application of (Article 50 of) the Charter (see Subsection 5.1.2). It follows that in respect of penalties for evasion of indirect taxes, the scope of Article 50 of the Charter is much wider (covering both internal and cross-border situations) than in respect of penalties for evasion of unharmonized direct taxes (in principle covering only situations in which the EU free movement rights apply, *that is* in situations featuring some cross-border element).

2.2   Ad (ii)(a): Between the Punitive Systems
of Two Member States

In respect of concurrence between two different Member States' legal systems, the same distinction may be drawn between harmonized and unharmonized taxes, but the sharp contrast which exists in the case of concurrence within one single jurisdiction is reduced considerably. If the punitive systems of two different Member States concur in respect of the same taxable event concerning the same taxpayer, then apparently, an intra-EU cross-border element is present which may imply applicability of one or more of the Union's free movement rights. Applicability of free movement rights in turn engages the EU Charter, as it brings the case within the ambit of application of EU law (see 5.2.2 infra). This means that the legal difference between harmonized (indirect) taxes (which are in principle covered by the Charter) and unharmonized (direct) taxes (which in principle are not covered by the Charter), which exists within one single jurisdiction, is less clear where an intra-EU cross-border element is present, as that element may activate the Charter: in respect of indirect taxes, Article 50 will be applicable anyway because they have been harmonized at EU level and (partly) form own resources of the Union; in respect of direct taxes, Article 50 of the Charter will be applicable where the cross-border element has activated the free movement rights. Unlike Article 4 of Protocol no. 7 to the ECHR, Article 50 of the Charter applies everywhere 'within the Union', *that is* also in two-State situations. It should be observed, however, that punishment of the same tax offence by the same taxpayer in two different jurisdictions is very rare, as almost all taxation is still national. Nevertheless, it is conceivable, in, *for example,* cases of incorrect international transfer pricing (the internal pricing of cross-border transactions and services within international groups of companies determines in which taxing jurisdiction the internal transaction profit falls) or international VAT carrousel-fraud. In competition cases, double jeopardy caused by two national competition authorities (NCAs) is quite conceivable.[1]

---

[1] See Chapter 4 of the present volume. See also, for a stock-taking of possible cross-jurisdictional double jeopardy in competition cases: G. Di Federico, 'EU Competition Law and the principle of Ne Bis in Idem' (2011) 17 *European Public Law*, 2, 241–260, para. 4.

2.3   Ad (ii)(b): Between the Punitive Systems
of a Member State and a Non-Member State

Where one of the two penalizing taxing jurisdictions is a non-Member State, the Charter in principle plays no role, as it flows from Articles 51 and 52 of the Charter that it does not apply to third-State situations, and Article 50 (*ne bis in idem*) explicitly provides that it only applies 'within the Union'. Article 4 of Protocol no. 7 ECHR will be of no help either, as it only applies to double jeopardy within one single State's jurisdiction (paragraph 1). As a rule, therefore, international double jeopardy as regards a tax offence involving a third State will not be eliminated or mitigated, at least not on the basis of EU law or ECHR law (nor on the basis of Article 14(7) of the International Covenant on Civil and Political Rights ICCPR).[2] Possibly, national (constitutional) law of the EU Member State involved provides for mitigation. Again, however, it should be observed that punishment of the same tax offence by the same taxpayer in two different jurisdictions is very rare, the only possible examples springing to mind being incorrect transfer pricing and carrousel-fraud.

2.4   Ad (iii): Between the EU Legal System
and a Member State's National Law

Unlike in the field of competition law, EU law does not confer any powers on the EU institutions to sanction contraventions of tax law. EU law does not even vest any taxing power in the Union's institutions (except for the payroll tax on the Eurocrats' salaries), let alone the power to impose tax surcharges or prosecute offences in respect of these non-existent EU taxes. EU law merely uniformizes, harmonizes or coordinates national tax law. Although EU law may require Member States to penalize certain fraudulent taxpayer behaviour as regards these uniformized or harmonized – but ultimately national – (indirect) taxes, there is no tax administered, levied or collected at EU level by an EU tax authority or administration. Therefore, double jeopardy as a result of concurrence of an EU sanction and a national sanction, which is quite possible in competition law,[3] is not possible in respect of tax offences, not

---

[2] Article 14(7) of the UN International Covenant on Civil and Political Rights of 16 December 1966 also contains a *ne bis in idem* rule, which, however, also only applies within one single Contracting State's jurisdiction.

[3] The paradigm case is Case 14/68 *Walt Wilhelm and Others* v. *Bundeskartellamt*, ECLI:EU: C:1969:4.

even in a completely EU-uniformized area of taxation such as customs duties, the revenue of which is almost entirely transferred, by the Member States, to the Union budget. At the end of the day, all of the individual sanctioning of tax offences is national law.[4]

2.5   Ad (iv): Between the EU Legal System and Third State Law

This category of possible concurrence of sanctions may be a considerable double jeopardy problem in the area of competition fines – which may indeed be concurrently imposed on multinational groups of companies by, *for example*, the Japanese, the EU *and* the US antitrust authorities, but like category (iii), this category is non-existent in tax matters for lack of EU competence in sanctioning tax offences. Moreover, Article 50 of the Charter only applies 'within the Union'.

2.6   Conclusions

From the above stock-taking of possible double jeopardy in respect of tax offences, the following conclusions may be drawn:

First, the categories (ii)(b), (iii) and (iv) of possible double jeopardy listed above do not merit much attention, as they are either non-existent in tax matters (categories (iii) and (iv)), or – if conceivable – non-remediable under either EU (Charter) law or the regular human rights conventions (category (ii)(b)).

Second, double jeopardy in respect of the sanctioning of tax offences is for the most part a one-jurisdictional phenomenon which only engages Article 50 of the Charter if a sufficient link with EU law is present, either because of the fact that EU law has harmonized the tax concerned and requires effective enforcement and collection and/or the tax revenue at stake is an 'own resource' of the Union (indirect taxes), or because some cross-border element brings the matter within the scope of application of the EU free movement rights (direct taxes).

Third, the previous conclusion in turn implies that if a Member State has not (fully) ratified the Seventh Protocol to the ECHR, a large area of

---

[4] The same may be said of EU-harmonized criminal law: even where the EU harmonizes criminal law, *e.g.* in its Framework Decision on environmental crimes, the sanctioning duty falls on Member States. See Articles 82(3) and 83(3) TFEU, confirming that the Member States are the masters of criminal monitoring.

reverse discrimination unfolds: taxpayers submitted to two sanctions in respect of the same tax offence are unable to rely on Article 50 of the Charter if the offence does not relate either to EU-harmonized (indirect) taxes feeding the EU budget, or to direct taxes in a cross-border situation engaging free movement rights. Especially for penalties for direct tax offences, this means that Article 50 of the Charter will only rarely apply. These taxpayers must hope that if they are fined and subsequently also indicted, their country of residence has (fully) ratified Protocol No. 7 to the ECHR.

3   Disentangling Double Jeopardy; *Ne Bis Puniri* and *Ne Bis Vexari*; Credit and Finality Systems; Homogeneity as regards 'Idem' and 'Criminal Proceedings'?

3.1   Ne Bis Puniri *or* Ne Bis Vexari; *Methods for the Prevention of Double Jeopardy*

If one conceives double jeopardy as double *punishment*, and therefore understands the *ne bis in idem* principle as meaning *ne bis puniri*, then two ways of putting the principle into practice are available:

(i) credit the previous penalty against the subsequent second penalty: the court adjudicating the second charge (usually a criminal charge) should, if it considers that charge proven and punishable, take account of the previous penalty already imposed for the same offence (usually an administrative fine) when determining the second penalty for that offence (credit system; *Anrechnungsprinzip*). Several EU Member States, such as Spain, Germany and Sweden, apply this system in respect of, *inter alia*, tax offences, or at least did so until the Court of Justice of the European Union (CJEU)'s judgment in the *Åkerberg Fransson* case,[5] which may have induced these Member States to adjust their policies in this respect. In competition cases, the CJEU itself traditionally also applied this credit system, and *Åkerberg Fransson* does not seem to have changed this for that specific field of law. The paradigm case for competition cases is that of *Walt Wilhelm*.[6] The CJEU does not, however, apply the credit system in respect of competition penalties imposed by third States: EU competition fines are not mitigated to take account of competition fines already imposed for the same cartel

---

[5] CJEU, Case C-617/10, *Åkerberg Fransson*, ECLI:EU:C:2013:105.
[6] CJEU, Case 14/68, *Walt Wilhelm and Others* v. *Bundeskartellamt*, ECLI:EU:C:1969:4.

'or monopoly abuse' by third States.[7] It should be observed that this credit system cannot be applied if the first and the second penalty are unlike: a pecuniary fine cannot be deducted from a detention sentence, nor *vice versa*.

(ii) try the offence as if no previous penalty was imposed for the same offence, and if the trial ends in a conviction or an acquittal, simply cancel the previous penalty. Obviously, such cancellation is only possible in respect of pecuniary penalties (fines), which may be refunded (with interest); a prison sentence cannot be cancelled retrospectively, unless it has not been served yet.

If, by contrast, one perceives the *ne bis in idem* principle as meaning *ne bis vexari* (no second charge),[8] then again, there are two ways of operationalizing the principle:

 (i) the *una via* (one way) system: no administrative fines may be imposed any more – and administrative proceedings with a view to imposing punitive fines must be permanently discontinued – as soon as a criminal indictment is issued for the same (tax) offence, and *vice versa*: if the tax administration has imposed a punitive surcharge (a fine), then – even if it is not final yet because it may be appealed – the public prosecutor is permanently precluded from bringing any subsequent criminal charges against the same person for the same tax offence. Such *una via* system is applied in the Netherlands, in Finland (see Subsection 5.2.1) and will be applied in Sweden (see Subsection 5.2.1);
(ii) the finality system: subsequent punitive proceedings (whether criminal or administrative) must be discontinued – or may not be initiated – once previous punitive proceedings for the same conduct have become final, *that is* have resulted in an irrevocable punitive administrative sanction or criminal sentence (or acquittal).

The latter system is the *ne bis in idem* system of Article 4 of Protocol no. 7 ECHR, which reads as follows (*italics* added):

> No one shall be *liable* to be *tried* or punished *again* in criminal proceedings under the jurisdiction of the same State for an offence for which he

---

[7] CJEU, Case C-289/04P, *Showa Denko*, ECLI:EU:C:2006:431. [2006] ECR I-5859.
[8] B. Van Bockel, *The Ne Bis in Idem Principle in EU law: A Conceptual and Jurisprudential Analysis* (Alphen aan den Rijn: Kluwer Law International, 2010), chapter 4, concludes that the (EU) principle of *ne bis in idem* prohibits double prosecution, and that the prohibition of double punishment is therefore a mere corollary to the first prohibition.

has already been *finally* acquitted or convicted in accordance with the law
and penal procedure of that State.

The European Court of Human Rights (ECtHR) has made it clear in,
inter alia, the *Maresti* case[9] that this provision implies 'ne bis *vexari*'.
That case concerned Mr Maresti, who had drunk too much, abusing and
assaulting bystanders at a bus stop. He was convicted, first, for the
minor offence of 'disorder', to forty days imprisonment under the
Croatian Minor Offences Act; this conviction became final. Subsequently,
Mr Maresti was also charged, under the regular criminal code, for
inflicting physical injury in the course of the same behaviour. For that,
he was sentenced to a one-year prison term. The forty days previously
imposed were deducted from the one-year sentence (credit system).
However, the ECtHR considered that second penalty to be in breach of
the *ne bis in idem* rule of Article 4 of Protocol no. 7 ECHR, as the
crediting of the first conviction against the second conviction 'does not
alter the fact that the applicant was tried twice for the same offence'.
A credit system is not good enough.[10]

The *Maresti* case followed up on the landmark decision of the Grand
Chamber of the ECtHR, earlier that same year, in the *Zolotukhin* case.[11]
That case concerned Mr Sergey Zolotukhin, who had managed to take his
girlfriend unlawfully into a restricted military compound. When they
were apprehended, he was drunk. He verbally abused and (death)
threatened police officers, and tried to escape by pushing away officers
and overturning furniture. On the same day, he was found guilty of an
administrative offence, and sentenced to three days' administrative
detention. That sentence was not amenable to appeal and was effective
immediately. Four months later, Mr Zolutukhin was charged, in respect
of the same behaviour, with three offences under the regular criminal
code. He was acquitted in respect of one of these charges, but convicted
for the remaining two. The Grand Chamber of the ECtHR (seventeen

---

[9] ECtHR, *Maresti* v. *Croatia*, 25 June 2009 (Appl. No. 55759/07), ECLI:CE:
ECHR:2009:0625JUD005575907.

[10] See also the *Tomasovic* case, concerning a 'minor offence' fine, followed by proceedings
on indictment for possession of 0.21 grams of heroin, resulting in a fine which was
reduced by the amount of the previous fine, and a suspended four month imprisonment
sentence: violation of Article 4 of Protocol no. 7: ECtHR, *Tomasovic* v. *Croatia*, 18 October 2011 (Appl. No. 53785/09), ECLI:CE:ECHR:2005:1110JUD000520803.

[11] ECtHR, *Sergey Zolotukhin* v. *Russia*, 10 February 2009 (Appl. No. 14939/03), ECLI:CE:
ECHR:2009:0210JUD001493903.

Justices) unanimously considered this to be a breach of Article 4 of Protocol no. 7, considering, *inter alia*, as follows:

> 107. The Court reiterates that the aim of Article 4 of Protocol no. 7 is to prohibit the repetition of criminal proceedings that have been concluded by a "final" decision . . . .
>
> . . .
>
> 110. . . . , the Court reiterates that Article 4 of Protocol No. 7 is not confined to the right not to be punished twice but extends to the right not to be prosecuted or tried twice (see *Franz Fischer*, cited above, § 29). Were this not the case, it would not have been necessary to add the word "punished" to the word "tried" since this would be mere duplication. Article 4 of Protocol No. 7 applies even where the individual has merely been prosecuted in proceedings that have not resulted in a conviction. The Court reiterates that Article 4 of Protocol No. 7 contains three distinct guarantees and provides that no one shall be (i) liable to be tried, (ii) tried or (iii) punished for the same offence (see *Nikitin*, cited above, § 36).

As will be seen later (Section 4), the fact that Article 4 of Protocol no. 7 uses the term 'criminal' does not imply that a final 'administrative' punitive measure – such as a final tax surcharge – would *not* preclude a subsequent criminal indictment for the same offence. As will also be seen (Subsection 3.2.2), the national legal characterization of the offence – 'criminal' or 'administrative' ('disorder', 'Ordnungswidrigkeit'); 'minor' or 'serious' – and a possible difference in legal interest protected between the two charges are of little importance to the ECtHR. What matters, is whether (i) both sanctions are punitive and (ii) the same factual behaviour is punished twice, whatever its legal classification, and whatever the legal interest protected by the punitive provisions.

The finality system is also the system of Article 54 of the Convention Implementing the Schengen Agreement of 14 June 1985 (CISA), and the system of Article 50 of the Charter of Fundamental Rights of the EU. Article 50 of the Charter reads as follows (emphasis added):

> No one shall be liable to be *tried* or punished again in criminal proceedings for an offence for which he or she has already been *finally* acquitted or convicted within the Union in accordance with the law.

This provision is almost identical to Article 4 of Protocol no. 7 of the ECHR, with the major exception of the term 'within the Union', which replaces the term 'under the jurisdiction of the same State' in Article 4 of Protocol no. 7. This highlights that the application of the *ne bis vexari rule* of the ECHR Protocol is limited to one national jurisdiction (it does not prevent two sentences for the same act imposed by two different national jurisdictions), whereas the Charter's *ne bis vexari* rule applies EU-wide, meaning that whichever Member State is first in (finally) convicting a person, bars punitive proceedings by any other Member State for the same act against the same person (first come, first serve).

Article 54 CISA applies cross-border as well (in the entire *Schengen* area), but it adds an extra requirement before barring a second charge: not only must the first punitive sanction have become final, it must also have been effectuated, or have become Statute-barred (emphasis added):

> A person whose trial has been *finally* disposed of in one Contracting Party may not be *prosecuted* in another Contracting Party for the same acts *provided* that, if a penalty has been imposed, it has been *enforced*, is actually in the process of being enforced or can no longer be enforced under the laws of the sentencing Contracting Party.

This effectuation requirement reflects the reluctance of Member States to mutually recognize the adequateness of each other's punitive systems. It is conceptually identical to a rule of international tax law, to be discussed in Section 7, which is aimed at ensuring effective taxation in at least one jurisdiction and at avoiding that treaties for the prevention of international double taxation have the undesired effect of international non- or token taxation.

3.2   Homogeneity: Article 6 TEU and Article 52(3) Charter

3.2.1   The Homegeneity Rule in the Charter

In principle, the rights and freedoms in the EU Charter of Fundamental Rights are to be understood and applied in the same manner as the corresponding rights and freedoms of the ECHR are understood and applied by the ECtHR, albeit that EU law may offer better protection than the ECHR (see Art. 52(3) Charter). Therefore, in principle, the ECtHR's interpretation of Article 4 of Protocol no. 7 ECHR is leading also for the CJEU where it applies corresponding provisions of the EU Charter, such as the *ne bis vexari* principle enshrined in Article 50 of the Charter. However, Article 4 of Protocol no. 7 has not been (fully) endorsed by all EU Member States. It has not been ratified by Germany, the UK and the Netherlands,[12] and other Member States, such as France,

---

[12] Belgium ratified the Protocol in 2012.

Portugal, Italy, Luxembourg and Austria, have made reservations to it. This rather hinders application of the homogeneity principle of Article 52(3) of the Charter. It bars application, by the CJEU, of the *Sopropé*-solution[13] on the basis of Article 6(3) TEU (stating that ECHR rights 'shall constitute general principles of the Union's law'): these non-ratifications and reservations show that the *ne bis in idem* principle – at least in the manner in which it is understood and applied by the ECtHR: *ne bis vexari*; and 'bis' also including punitive sanctions classified as 'administrative' (see Section 4) – is neither a *general* principle nor a *common* constitutional tradition among the EU Member States. Apparently, many of them wanted to remain free, under the ECHR, to impose 'administrative' penalties such as tax surcharges, and nevertheless be able subsequently to bring criminal charges for the same (tax) offence. This does not seem to have prevented the CJEU, in the *Åkerberg Fransson* case, to follow the ECtHR's interpretation of Article 4 of Protocol no. 7 for tax offences Union-wide (*i.e.* also binding the Member States which have not ratified that Protocol or which have made reservations). On the other hand, the CJEU seems to find legal basis in the diffuse European legal status of that Protocol to depart from the ECtHR's interpretation of the *ne bis vexari* principle in EU competition cases (see Section 6 of this chapter and Chapter 4 of this book).

3.2.2 Homogeneity in Respect of the Concept of 'Idem'?

In its *Zolotukhin* judgment cited in 3.1, the Grand Chamber of the ECtHR extensively argued its finding that the term 'an offence' in Article 4 of Protocol no. 7 does not refer to the national legal classification of the impugned conduct, nor to the legal interest protected by the different provisions penalizing the impugned behaviour, but to the material acts of the charged person. Decisive for the question of whether two charges relate to the same offence (*idem*) for which that person is tried again (*bis*), is the question of whether the second charge arises from identical or substantially the same facts (*e.g.* the same incorrect filing of a tax return) as the first charge. After extensive reasoning and the citing of other (international) legal instruments and of judgments of other Courts, including the CJEU, the Inter-American Court of Human Rights, and the US Supreme Court, it concluded that:

---

[13] Case C-349/07, *Sopropé – Organizações de Calçado Lda* v. *Fazenda Pública*, ECLI:EU:C:2008:746.

81. The Court ... notes that the approach which emphasises the legal characterisation of the two offences is too restrictive on the rights of the individual, for if the Court limits itself to finding that the person was prosecuted for offences having a different legal classification it risks undermining the guarantee enshrined in Article 4 of Protocol No. 7 rather than rendering it practical and effective as required by the Convention (compare *Franz Fischer*, cited above, § 25).

82. Accordingly, the Court takes the view that Article 4 of Protocol No. 7 must be understood as prohibiting the prosecution or trial of a second "offence" in so far as it arises from identical facts or facts which are substantially the same.

...

84. The Court's inquiry should ... focus on those facts which constitute a set of concrete factual circumstances involving the same defendant and inextricably linked together in time and space, the existence of which must be demonstrated in order to secure a conviction or institute criminal proceedings.

The same offence is thus the same material act: (substantially) the same factual conduct, by the same person at the same place and time (*idem factum*); in the present context: the same tax evasion. Therefore, if the authorities have chosen, *for example*, to impose a punitive tax surcharge (an 'administrative' fine) for concealing taxable income or for underdeclaring turnover, based on tax legislation, and such fine has become final, the taxpayer cannot subsequently be charged again for the same false tax declaration under the general or specific fraud provisions or creditor's protection provisions in the criminal code. This interpretation (*idem factum*; the identical or substantially the same factual conduct) is not put into question by the facts that

(i) the applicable punitive provisions in the tax legislation and the criminal code may partly protect different legal interests (promotion of correct tax returns and protection of the State budget on the one hand, and general protection of creditors and of the public at large on the other);

(ii) the tax law provision and the criminal provision may not contain the exact same legal elements to be proven by the punishing authority (as long as the facts which must be demonstrated for both are substantially the same);

(iii) the punishing authority in the first round is not the same authority as in the second round;

(iv) the punitive tax surcharge is not perceived as 'criminal' in nature under national law or

(v) the applicable sanctions under the tax legislation may be different from the sanctions which may be imposed under the criminal code (pecuniary only, or also custodial).

From the later case of *Lucky Dev* v. *Sweden*,[14] it transpires, in keeping with the above, that incorrect fiscal bookkeeping and incorrect filing of a tax return are not the same offence, as underdeclaring or concealing of income or turnover can be committed independent of whether the fiscal accounts have been kept correctly, and *vice versa*: the books may have been tampered with independent of whether the declaration of income or turnover was (in)correct.

The language and reasoning used by the Grand Chamber of the ECtHR in *Zolotukhin*, and the authority cited by it, reveals that the ECtHR intended, in that landmark case, to serve homogeneity in the application of the *ne bis in idem* principle from its side by deciding *Zolotukhin* in keeping with the CJEU's case law on the *ne bis in idem* principle in, especially, Article 54 CISA. Indeed, the ECtHR extensively quoted the CJEU's judgments in the *Kraaijenbrink*[15] case and the *Van Esbroeck*[16] case, and used the same language as the CJEU, which considered, in *Kraaijenbrink*, that:

36. ... Article 54 of the CISA is to be interpreted as meaning that:

– the relevant criterion for the purposes of the application of that article is identity of the material acts, understood as the existence of a set of facts which are inextricably linked together [in time, in space and by their subject-matter; see paragraph 27; *author*], irrespective of the legal classification given to them or the legal interest protected;

– different acts consisting, in particular, first, in holding in one Contracting State the proceeds of drug trafficking and, second, in the exchanging at exchange bureaux in another Contracting State of sums of money also originating from such trafficking should not be regarded as 'the same acts' within the meaning of Article 54 of the CISA merely because the competent national court finds that those acts are linked together by the same criminal intention; ...

---

[14] ECtHR, *Lucky Dev* v. *Sweden*, 27 November 2014 (Appl. No. 7356/10), ECLI:CE: ECHR:2014:1127JUD000735610.
[15] Case C-367/05, *Norma Kraaijenbrink*, ECLI:EU:C:2007:444.
[16] Case C-436/04, *Leopold Henri Van Esbroeck*, ECLI:EU:C:2006:165.

The fact that the Grand Chamber of the ECtHR adhered to the CJEU's interpretation of the *ne bis in idem* principle must have been both pleasing and displeasing to the CJEU. Pleasing, as apparently, the CJEU's reasoning in *Van Esbroeck* and *Kraaijenbrink* convinced the ECtHR and prompted it to harmonize, into one single approach, its three partly overlapping but also partly diverging approaches followed hitherto, thus creating European legal unity and certainty; displeasing, however, as the ECtHR more or less ignored the facts that (i) the CJEU's interpretation of Article 54 CISA is teleologically driven (purposive) in the sense that the CJEU's *idem factum* approach in *Van Esbroeck* and *Kraaijenbrink* was more or less dictated by the explanations relating to Article 50 of the Charter[17] and by the fact that a more formal or legal approach would frustrate free movement of persons within the *Schengen* area[18] and (ii) the CJEU would rather not have been followed by the ECtHR in respect of competition fines. Indeed, in the field of competition fines, the CJEU does not apply the same *idem factum* approach it adopted in *Schengen* matters; in competition cases, it explicitly requires 'a threefold condition of identity': (i) identity of facts, (ii) unity of the offender and (iii) unity of the legal interest protected.[19] The CJEU's reasoning in *Van Esbroeck*[20] shows that its interpretation of the *ne bis in idem* principle in Article 54 CISA is for the most part based on the protection of the free movement of persons and on the fact that for such free movement, *cross-border* double jeopardy must be avoided. The latter purpose is wholly alien to Article 4 of Protocol no. 7, which explicitly applies only within one national jurisdiction. The CJEU considered, in *Van Esbroeck*:

---

[17] These explanations ([2007] O.J. C 303/17) state that if *ne bis in idem* is applied in a cross-border situation, it must be interpreted in line with the EU *acquis*, *i.e.* in accordance with the CJEU case law under the Convention implementing the *Schengen* agreement, whereas if it is applied in a purely internal situation, the principle has the same meaning and scope as Article 4 of Protocol no. 7 ECHR.

[18] See on the *ne bis in idem* principle in Article 54 CISA, a.o., R. Lööf, '5a CISA and the Principles of ne bis in idem', *European Journal of Crime* (2007) 15 *Criminal Law and Criminal Justice*, 3–4, 309–334, who concludes (at 334) that 'it seems more than likely that . . . millions of Europeans . . . would consider it an intolerable absurdity if it was put to them that they not only ran the risk of being tried twice for the same course of action but also that as a result they could be considered guilty in one part of the EU and innocent in another'.

[19] Cases C-204/00P, *Aalborg Portland* (a.k.a. *Cement*), ECLI:EU:C:2004:6, and C-17/10, *Toshiba*, ECLI:EU:C:2012:72.

[20] Case C-436/04, *Leopold Henri Van Esbroeck*, ECLI:EU:C:2006:165.

30. There is a necessary implication in the *ne bis in idem* principle, enshrined in that article, that the Contracting States have mutual trust in their criminal justice systems and that each of them recognises the criminal law in force in the other Contracting States even when the outcome would be different if its own national law were applied ([C-385/01] *Gözütok and Brügge* [[2003] ECR I-1345], paragraph 33).

31. It follows that the possibility of divergent legal classifications of the same acts in two different Contracting States is no obstacle to the application of Article 54 of the CISA.

32. For the same reasons, the criterion of the identity of the protected legal interest cannot be applicable since that criterion is likely to vary from one Contracting State to another.

33. The above findings are further reinforced by the objective of Article 54 of the CISA, which is to ensure that no one is prosecuted for the same acts in several Contracting States on account of his having exercised his right to freedom of movement (*Gözütok and Brügge*, paragraph 38, and Case C-469/03 *Miraglia* [2005] ECR I-2009, paragraph 32).

. . .

35. Because there is no harmonisation of national criminal laws, a criterion based on the legal classification of the acts or on the protected legal interest might create as many barriers to freedom of movement within the Schengen territory as there are penal systems in the Contracting States.

36. In those circumstances, the only relevant criterion for the application of Article 54 of the CISA is identity of the material acts, understood in the sense of the existence of a set of concrete circumstances which are inextricably linked together....

One must conclude that the ECtHR adopted the operative part of *Van Esbroeck* rather than its reasoning, as that reasoning, which is based on the protection of the free cross-border movement of persons, makes little sense for the interpretation of Article 4 of Protocol no. 7 ECHR.

3.2.3   Homogeneity in Respect of the "Criminal" Nature of an Offence?

Article 50 of the Charter, as Article 4 of Protocol no. 7, requires the double jeopardy to threaten to occur in respect of 'criminal proceedings'. That raises the question of which criteria determine whether or not a sanction or a charge is 'criminal' in nature. In that respect, the CJEU considered as follows in the *Åkerberg Fransson* case – which concerned punitive tax surcharges for tax evasion followed by a criminal indictment for the same tax evasion:

33. Application of the *ne bis in idem* principle laid down in Article 50 of the Charter to a prosecution for tax evasion such as that which is the

subject of the main proceedings presupposes that the measures which have already been adopted against the defendant by means of a decision that has become final are of a criminal nature.

34. In this connection, it is to be noted first of all that Article 50 of the Charter does not preclude a Member State from imposing, for the same acts of non-compliance with declaration obligations in the field of VAT, a combination of tax penalties and criminal penalties. In order to ensure that all VAT revenue is collected and, in so doing, that the financial interests of the European Union are protected, the Member States have freedom to choose the applicable penalties (see, to this effect, Case 68/88 *Commission v. Greece* [1989] ECR 2965, paragraph 24; Case C 213/99 *de Andrade* [2000] ECR I 11083, paragraph 19; and Case C-91/02 *Hannl-Hofstetter* [2003] ECR I 12077, paragraph 17). These penalties may therefore take the form of administrative penalties, criminal penalties or a combination of the two. It is only if the tax penalty is criminal in nature for the purposes of Article 50 of the Charter and has become final that that provision precludes criminal proceedings in respect of the same acts from being brought against the same person.

35. Next, three criteria are relevant for the purpose of assessing whether tax penalties are criminal in nature. The first criterion is the legal classification of the offence under national law, the second is the very nature of the offence, and the third is the nature and degree of severity of the penalty that the person concerned is liable to incur (Case C-489/10 *Bonda* [2012] ECR I-0000, paragraph 37).

36. It is for the referring court to determine, in the light of those criteria, whether the combining of tax penalties and criminal penalties that is provided for by national law should be examined in relation to the national standards as referred to in paragraph 29 of the present judgment, which could lead it, as the case may be, to regard their combination as contrary to those standards, as long as the remaining penalties are effective, proportionate and dissuasive (see, to this effect, inter alia *Commission v Greece*, paragraph 24; Case C-326/88 *Hansen* [1990] ECR I-2911, paragraph 17; Case C-167/01 *Inspire Art* [2003] ECR I-10155, paragraph 62; Case C-230/01 *Penycoed* [2004] ECR I-937, paragraph 36; and Joined Cases C-387/02, C-391/02 and C-403/02 *Berlusconi and Others* [2005] ECR I 3565 paragraph 65).

By referring to paragraph 37 of its previous *Bonda* case,[21] the CJEU in fact referred to the *Engel* criteria developed by the ECtHR for determining whether a charge is 'criminal' within the meaning of, especially, Article 6 ECHR (right of a fair hearing for anyone faced with a 'criminal charge') and of Article 4 of Protocol no. 7 ECHR (*ne bis in idem*). Indeed, in para. 37 of *Bonda*, the CJEU considered:

---

[21] Case C-489/10, *Bonda*, ECLI:EU:C:2012:319.

37. According to that case-law [of the ECtHR; *author*], three criteria are relevant in this respect. The first criterion is the legal classification of the offence under national law, the second is the very nature of the offence, and the third is the nature and degree of severity of the penalty that the person concerned is liable to incur (see, inter alia, ECHR, *Engel and Others v. the Netherlands*, 8 June 1976, §§ 80 to 82, Series A no. 22, and *Sergey Zolotukhin v. Russia*, no. 14939/03, §§ 52 and 53, 10 February 2009).

This would seem to imply that full homogeneity exists between Strasbourg and Luxembourg as to the interpretation of the term 'criminal' in both Article 50 of the Charter and Article 4 of Protocol no. 7.

Surprisingly, however, in *Åkerberg Fransson*, the CJEU refrained from applying the *Engel* criteria it declared decisive, leaving that to the referring Swedish court, as if the 'criminal' nature of the tax penalties imposed could still be called into question. That is surprising for two reasons. In the first place, it suggests that, under Article 50 of the Charter, the Member States may still impose both a punitive tax penalty and a criminal penalty successively in respect of the same tax offence, although the case law of the ECtHR offers no discernable room for such position: given the case law of the ECtHR on punitive tax surcharges, especially the *Jussila* case[22] (see Section 4) and the *Janosevic* case[23] (which concerned the exact same Swedish tax surcharges – and to a comparable level – as the ones imposed on Mr Åkerberg Fransson), there can be no reasonable doubt that punitive tax surcharges for tax evasion are 'criminal' for the purposes of Article 6 ECHR, and with that, given the *Zolotukhin* case, also for the purposes of Article 4 of Protocol no. 7 (see Section 4).[24] In the second place, the CJEU had no difficulty applying the *Engel* criteria itself in *Bonda*, characterizing the administrative sanctions imposed on Mr Bonda for overstating his agricultural area to obtain EU subsidies as not 'criminal' in nature.

Possibly, the CJEU's deferential stance in *Åkerberg Fransson* was prompted by a perceived potential for constitutional conflict on the point of *ne bis in idem*.[25] However, the *locus* of such conflict is not immediately

---

[22] ECtHR, *Jussila* v. *Finland*, 23 November 2006 (Appl. No. 73053/01), ECLI:CE: ECHR:2006:1123JUD007305301.

[23] ECtHR, *Janosevic* v. *Sweden*, 23 July 2003 (Appl. No. 34619/97), ECLI:CE: ECHR:2002:0723JUD003461997.

[24] In the same vein: J. Vervaele, 'The Application of the EU Charter of Fundamental Rights and Its Ne bis in idem Principle in the Member States of the EU' (2003) 6 *Review of European Administrative Law*, 1, 133.

[25] See B. van Bockel and P. Wattel, 'New Wine into Old Wineskins: The Scope of the Charter of Fundamental Rights of the EU after Åklagaren v Hans Åkerberg Fransson' (2013) 38 *E.L. Rev.*, 863–880.

obvious in the *Åkerberg Fransson* case, as Sweden has ratified Protocol no. 7 ECHR without reservation. However, the application of the *ne bis in idem* principle in tax evasion matters was the subject of considerable controversy between Swedish courts,[26] and at least two Swedish tax cases on the *ne bis in idem* issue were pending before the ECtHR.[27] Possibly, the CJEU did not wish to get under the ECtHR's feet on this matter and/ or it anticipated that the Swedish judiciary and/or legislature would draw the inevitable conclusion itself anyway. See also the last paragraph of Section 5.2 in Chapter 2 of the present volume. Another explanation might be that the CJEU did not want to prejudice (yet) its traditional and current stance *vis à vis* competition fines, to which it has consistently avoided applying the *Engel* criteria, apparently wishing to consider them as not 'criminal' in nature for the purpose of the *ne bis in idem* principle (despite the *Société Sténuit* case[28] of the ECtHR). Indeed, if the CJEU itself were to declare tax penalties to be 'criminal' in nature for the purposes of *ne bis in idem*, it would seem difficult to explain why competition penalties would not be 'criminal' for those purposes as well. However, we do not quite see how the CJEU is going to avoid, when squarely faced with the question, application of Article 50 of the Charter

---

[26] The Swedish Supreme Court and Supreme Administrative Court ignored the case law of the ECtHR (saw no 'clear support', not even in *Zolotukhin*, for the stance that the Swedish system violated the *ne bis in idem* principle) and only considered relevant whether the total of the administrative and criminal penalties was 'not unreasonable'. Lower Swedish Courts, by contrast, had already conformed to the clear ECtHR case law (see Section 3.1) confirming that *ne bis in idem* in Article 4 of Protocol no. 7 ECHR means *ne bis vexari*, not just the duty to credit the prior penalty against the subsequent penalty to reach a proportionate total. These lower courts refused to hear criminal cases against taxpayers already finally fined by imposition of a tax surcharge. The referral of the *Åkerberg Fransson* case to the CJEU was part of this revolt of the lower Swedish courts. See, a.o., Cécile Brokelind, 'Case Note on Åkerberg Fransson (Case C-617/10)' (2013) 53 *European Taxation*, 6, 282; Joakim Negelius, 'The Nordic States and the European Convention on Human Rights', in: Rainer Arnold (ed.), *The Convergence of the Fundamental Rights protection in Europe* (Springer, 2016), pp. 95–96, and Ulf Bernitz, 'The Scope of the Charter and Its Impact on the Application of the ECHR: The Åkerberg Fransson Case on Ne Bis in Idem in Perspective', in: Sybe de Vries, Ulf Bernitz and Stephen Weatherill (eds.), *The EU Charter of Fundamental Rights as a Binding Instrument* (Hart Publishing, 2015), pp. 167–171.

[27] ECtHR, *Lars Åberg* v. *Sweden*, decided on 21 October 2014 (Appl. No. 57762/10), ECLI: CE:ECHR:2014:1021DEC005776210, and ECtHR, *Björn Henriksson* v. *Sweden,* also decided on 21 October 2014 (Appl. No. 7396/10), ECLI:CE:ECHR:2014:1021-DEC000739610.

[28] ECtHR, *Société Stenuit* v. *France*, 27 February 1992 (Appl. No. 11598/85), ECLI:CE: ECHR:1992:0227JUD001159885.

also to competition fines. In Section 4.3, we offer another possible reason for the CJEU to stand off the issue of whether Article 50 of the Charter precludes Sweden from punishing Mr Åkerberg Fransson a second time.

3.3 Conclusions

The *ne bis in idem* principle in Article 4 of Protocol no. 7 ECHR and in Article 50 of the EU Charter means *ne bis vexari*. A credit system (the first – 'administrative' – penalty is deducted from the subsequent second – 'criminal' – penalty) is not good enough: once the first penalty has become final, any subsequent punitive proceedings for the same offence are prohibited; if already initiated, they must be discontinued. This was made explicitly reiterated in the *Lucky Dev* case cited in Subsection 3.2.2. The question of whether the subsequent proceedings arise from the 'same offence', must be answered on the basis of the material act (do the two proceedings target identical or substantially the same facts/behaviour/conduct?), not on the basis of the legal classification of the two charges, nor on the basis of the legal interests protected by the legal provisions whose violation is being sanctioned. The latter conclusion does not seem to hold, however, in competition cases, as the CJEU seems to stick, notwithstanding *Zolotukhin*, to the 'unity of legal interest protected' requirement. The CJEU further seems to suggest that, despite, *Jussila*, *Zolotukhin* and *Janosevic*, there is still room for considering punitive tax surcharges as not being 'criminal' for the purpose of the application of the *ne bis in idem* principle, but that suggestion seems incorrect to us (see, for elaboration, Section 4).

4 Is a Tax Surcharge a 'Criminal Proceeding' within the Meaning of Article 4 of Protocol no. 7 ECHR and Article 50 of the Charter?

4.1 'Criminal' Has the Same Meaning in Article 6 ECHR and Article 4 of Protocol no. 7 ECHR

From the case law of the ECtHR, especially the *Zolotukhin* case cited earlier in Section 3.1, it appears that the *Engel* criteria, which decide whether an accusation is a 'criminal charge' within the meaning of Article 6 ECHR (fair hearing), also decide whether a measure imposed is a 'criminal proceedings' under Article 4 of Protocol no. 7. These *Engel* criteria are: (i) the legal classification of the offence under national law,

(ii) the very nature of the offence and (iii) the nature and degree of severity of the penalty that the person concerned is liable to incur. The first criterion is not decisive in itself – otherwise States would have the power to switch Article 6 ECHR and Article 4 of Protocol no. 7 on or off at will – and the second and third criteria are alternative and not necessarily cumulative.[29] The unity of interpretation of the term 'criminal' in both Article 6 and in Article 4 of Protocol no. 7, and in fact in the entire ECHR, by the ECtHR also follows from the subsequent *Kurdov et Ivanov* case[30] (only available in French and Croatian):

> 36. A cet égard, la Cour rappelle que la qualification juridique de la procédure en droit interne ne saurait être le seul critère pertinent pour l'applicabilité du principe non bis in idem au regard de l'article 4 § 1 du Protocole no 7. S'il en était autrement, l'application de cette disposition se trouverait subordonnée à l'appréciation des Etats contractants, ce qui risquerait de conduire à des résultats incompatibles avec l'objet et le but de la Convention. Les termes « procédure pénale » employés dans le texte de l'article 4 du Protocole no 7 doivent être interprétés à la lumière des principes généraux applicables aux expressions « accusation en matière pénale » et « peine » figurant respectivement à l'article 6 et à l'article 7 de la Convention (Sergueï Zolotoukhine c. Russie [GC], no 14939/03, § 52 ...

4.2 According to the ECtHR, All Punitive Tax Surcharges Are 'Criminal' in Nature

As with its application of the criteria for establishing whether an 'idem' occurs, the ECtHR was not immediately on one single course in respect of the question of whether tax penalties are 'criminal' in nature for the application of the ECHR and its Protocols. Initially, it was quite outspoken as regards administrative fines, even as regards quite minor ones: these were 'criminal' in nature if the offence was criminal in nature. Paradigm cases are the *Öztürk* case[31] (1984), and the *Lutz* case[32] (1987), concerning German minor traffic offences, not considered as criminal by the German legislator, but as mere *Ordnungswidrigkeiten* (regulatory

---

[29] See, a.o., ECtHR, *Jussila v. Finland*, 23 November 2006 (Appl. No. 73053/01), ECLI:CE: ECHR:2006:1123JUD007305301.

[30] ECtHR, *Kurdov et Ivanov c. Bulgarie*, 31 May 2011 (Appl. No. 16137/04), ECLI:CE: ECHR:2011:0531JUD001613704.

[31] ECtHR, *Öztürk v. Germany*, 2 February 1984 (Appl. No. 8544/79), ECLI:CE: ECHR:1984:0221JUD000854479.

[32] ECtHR, *Lutz v. Germany*, 25 August 1987 (Appl. No. 9912/82), ECLI:CE: ECHR:1987:0825JUD000991282.

offences). The *Öztürk* case concerned a traffic ticket of a mere DM 60 (€ 30), but that did not prevent the ECtHR from considering a 'criminal charge' present, and therefore Article 6 (fair hearing) to be applicable to the question of whether Mr Öztürk was entitled to translation, without cost, of the charge against him into a language he would understand. The German authorities could hardly believe this judgment, and a second judgment in the *Lutz* case – concerning a € 70 traffic fine and the right to reimbursement of the cost of legal counsel – was needed to convince (not only) Germany that the judgment in the *Öztürk* case had not been a judicial error. After *Lutz*, however, it seemed settled case law that administrative fines for traffic offences, and therefore also tax penalties for tax offences, were 'criminal' in nature for the purposes of Article 6 ECHR (fair hearing). The 1994 *Bendenoun* case[33] showed that tax penalties for tax evasion were indeed 'criminal charges', but suggested that such fines needed to be substantial – the tax surcharges imposed on the individual and his company in that case totalled around 1 million FF (€ 160.000) – for the tax offences so sanctioned to be 'criminal' in nature. That suggestion was confirmed in the case of *Morel* v. *France*[34] (2003), concerning a tax penalty of € 678. Mr Morel's application was declared inadmissible because Article 6 ECHR was found not to apply in respect of a 10 per cent tax surcharge which was 'not particularly high' and was therefore 'a long way from the "very substantial" level' needed for it to be classified as criminal. However, two years earlier, in the *Janosevic* case,[35] concerning the same Swedish tax surcharges as in *Åkerberg Fransson*, amounting to SEK 161,261 (€ 17,284), the ECtHR made no reference to *Bendenoun* or its particular approach (requiring substantial penalties) but proceeded squarely on the basis of the *Engel* criteria, considering the nature of the offence to be 'criminal'. *Morel* did not refer to *Janosevic*, and *Janosevic* did not refer to *Bendenoun*. Things were becoming unclear, producing legal uncertainty. Therefore, the Grand Chamber of the ECtHR undertook to throw light on the Court's position on tax penalties.

---

[33] ECtHR, *Bendenoun* v. *France*, 24 February 1994 (Appl. No. 12547/86), ECLI:CE: ECHR:1994:0224JUD001254786.

[34] ECtHR, *Morel* v. *France*, 6 June 2000 (Appl. No. 54559/00), ECLI:CE:ECHR:2003:0603-DEC005455900.

[35] ECtHR, *Janosevic* v. *Sweden*, 23 July 2002 (Appl. No. 34619/97), ECLI:CE: ECHR:2002:0723JUD003461997. On the same day, the similar case of ECtHR, *Västberga Taxi Aktiebolag and Vulic* v. *Sweden*, 23 July 2002 (Appl. No. 36985/97), ECLI:CE: ECHR:2002:0723JUD003698597, was decided.

It did so in the *Jussila* case (2006),[36] concerning a tax fine of a mere € 309 for poor VAT-bookkeeping. The ECtHR considered *Morel* v. *France* to be the odd one out, to which no importance should be attached. (All) tax penalties are criminal charges. The ECtHR considered:

34. ... *Morel* is an exception among the reported cases in that it relies on the lack of severity of the penalty as removing the case from the ambit of Article 6, although the other criteria (general rule, not compensatory in nature, deterrent and punitive purpose) had clearly been fulfilled.

35. The Grand Chamber agrees with the approach adopted in the *Janosevic* case, which gives a detailed analysis of the issues in a judgment on the merits after the benefit of hearing argument from the parties (cf. *Morel* which was a decision on inadmissibility). No established or authoritative basis has therefore emerged in the case-law for holding that the minor nature of the penalty, in taxation proceedings or otherwise, may be decisive in removing an offence, otherwise criminal by nature, from the scope of Article 6.

36. Furthermore, the Court is not persuaded that the nature of tax surcharge proceedings is such that they fall, or should fall, outside the protection of Article 6. Arguments to that effect have also failed in the context of prison disciplinary and minor traffic offences (see, variously, *Ezeh and Connors* and *Öztürk*, cited above). While there is no doubt as to the importance of tax to the effective functioning of the State, the Court is not convinced that removing procedural safeguards in the imposition of punitive penalties in that sphere is necessary to maintain the efficacy of the fiscal system or indeed can be regarded as consonant with the spirit and purpose of the Convention. In this case the Court will therefore apply the *Engel* criteria as identified above.

37. Turning to the first criterion, it is apparent that the tax surcharges in this case were not classified as criminal but as part of the fiscal regime. This is however not decisive.

38. The second criterion, the nature of the offence, is the more important. The Court observes that, as in the *Janosevic* and *Bendenoun* cases, it may be said that the tax surcharges were imposed by general legal provisions applying to taxpayers generally. It is not persuaded by the Government's argument that VAT applies to only a limited group with a special status: as in the previously-mentioned cases, the applicant was liable in his capacity as a taxpayer. The fact that he opted for VAT registration for business purposes does not detract from this position. Further, as acknowledged by the Government, the tax surcharges were not intended as pecuniary compensation for damage but as a punishment to deter re-offending. It may therefore be concluded that the surcharges were

---

[36] ECtHR, *Jussila* v. *Finland*, 23 November 2006 (Appl. No. 73053/01), ECLI:CE: ECHR:2006:1123JUD007305301.

imposed by a rule whose purpose was deterrent and punitive. Without more, the Court considers that this establishes the criminal nature of the offence. The minor nature of the penalty renders this case different from Janosevic and Bendenoun as regards the third *Engel* criterion but does not remove the matter from the scope of Article 6. Hence, Article 6 applies under its criminal head notwithstanding the minor nature of the tax surcharge.

The Court reiterated, dismissing *Morel* and *Bendenoun* in that respect, that only the *Engel* criteria – ((i) national classification, (ii) the very nature of the offence and (iii) the nature severity of penalty possibly incurred) – remain decisive for the determination of the 'criminal' character of a charge or penalty, that of these criteria the first one is of modest relevance and the other two are alternative and not necessarily cumulative, and that the second criterion (the nature of the offence) is the more important one.

4.3   Differentiation in the Level of Fair Trial Protection Depending on the Seriousness of the Charge and of the Possible Penalty

Although considering a € 309 administrative fine for insufficient tax bookkeeping a 'criminal charge', the court in *Jussila* went on to differentiate in the solidity of the fair hearing requirements of Article 6 ECHR depending on the seriousness of the criminal charge. It thus held that although the tax penalty imposed on Mr Jussila was criminal in nature, Article 6 had not been breached by the Finnish court's decision that an oral and public hearing of Mr Jussila's appeal was unnecessary since both the tax inspector and Mr Jussila, as well as an expert witness of Mr Jussila's choice, had had – and had used - the opportunity to submit written observations, and to reply to each other's observations. Explicitly, the ECtHR made a distinction between 'the hard core of criminal law' and more peripheral or non-traditional criminal charges, to which the criminal-head guarantees of Article 6 ECHR do not necessarily fully apply:

> 4.3 ... Notwithstanding the consideration that a certain gravity attaches to criminal proceedings, which are concerned with the allocation of criminal responsibility and the imposition of a punitive and deterrent sanction, it is self-evident that there are criminal cases which do not carry any significant degree of stigma. There are clearly 'criminal charges' of differing weight. What is more, the autonomous interpretation adopted by the Convention institutions of the notion of a 'criminal charge' by

applying the *Engel* criteria have underpinned a gradual broadening of the criminal head to cases not strictly belonging to the traditional categories of the criminal law, for example administrative penalties (Öztürk v. Germany), prison disciplinary proceedings (Campbell and Fell v. the United Kingdom, judgment of 28 June 1984, Series A, no. 80), customs law (Salabiaku v. France, judgment of 7 October 1988, Series A no 141-A), competition law (Société Stenuit v. France, judgment of 27 February 1992, Series A no. 232-A) and penalties imposed by a court with jurisdiction in financial matters (Guisset v. France, no. 33933/96, ECHR 2000-IX). Tax surcharges differ from the hard core of criminal law; consequently, the criminal-head guarantees will not necessarily apply with their full stringency (see Bendenoun and Janosevic, § 46 and § 81 respectively, where it was found compatible with Article 6 § 1 for criminal penalties to be imposed, in the first instance, by an administrative or non-judicial body: *a contrario*, Findlay v. the United Kingdom, cited above).

This implies a differentiating approach to the requirements of Article 6 ECHR under its criminal heading depending on the severity of the penalty risked by the charged person and the degree of stigma associated with it. Possibly, this differentiation, especially the distinction between 'hard core' criminal charges and other criminal charges (the latter apparently including both competition fines and tax penalties) may have inspired the CJEU to exercise restraint in *Åkerberg Fransson*.[37] Indeed, if not all requirements of Article 6 ECHR need to be met in all proceedings on criminal charges because of the relative insignificance of what is at stake for the defendant, then maybe neither does the *ne bis in idem* principle of Article 4 of Protocol no. 7 need to be applied in all rigour in all instances of double jeopardy, *for example*, not in petty cases such as the traffic *Ordnungswidirgkeiten* at issue in *Öztürk* and *Lutz*. On the other hand: (i) the less significant a criminal charge, the less justification seems to be present to bother rigging up a second punitive measure if the first penalty has become final; (ii) it is unclear to us how Article 50 of the Charter should be applied without its 'full stringency' in non-hard core criminal cases, as there seems nothing in between one criminal proceeding and two criminal proceedings for the same offence (one-and-a-half proceedings?) and (iii) Article 4 of Protocol no. 7 is only a minimum standard (see Article 52(3)(2nd sentence)) for the EU, but admittedly, that is a problematic statement in respect of an ECHR provision which has not been (fully) ratified by all EU Member States.

---

[37] For further speculations as to the reasons for the CJEU's stand-offishness in *Åkerberg Fransson*, see Section 3.2.3 (last paragraph).

4.4 More Conclusions

Since the *Jussila, Zolotukhin* and *Kurdov and Ivanov* judgments of the ECtHR there can be no doubt that the imposition of punitive tax surcharges produces both a 'criminal charge' within the meaning of Article 6 ECHR (fair hearing) and 'criminal proceedings' within the meaning of Article 4 of Protocol no. 7 ECHR (*ne bis in idem*), and with that, also – given Article 52(3) of the EU Charter – 'criminal proceedings' within the meaning of Article 50 of the Charter. However, there are sizes and measures in 'criminal charges', some belonging to 'hard core' criminal law and some belonging to more peripheral punitive law, such as administrative penalties, especially for petty traffic offences, disciplinary measures, tax penalties and competition fines. Although for these non-hardcore criminal cases not all requirements *of Article 6 ECHR* (and with that, of *Article 47 of the Charter*) necessarily apply with their 'full stringency', it seems unlikely to us that *Article 4 of Protocol no. 7* and *Article 50 of the EU Charter* could be applied with less than their 'full stringency', as under a *ne bis vexari* interpretation of the *ne bis in idem* principle a second accusation for the same facts is either acceptable (if one of the accusations is not 'criminal', or the second one is not a 'bis') or it is not. Under a *ne bis puniri* interpretation of the *ne bis in idem* principle, by contrast, an important role is reserved for the proportionality principle, and one could argue that *Jussila* somewhat enlarges the Contracting States' margin of appreciation as regards their proportionality assessment of the total of punishments for the same offence.

5   The Meaning of *Åkerberg Fransson* for Tax Penalties in the Member States

5.1   *The Åkerberg Fransson case*

5.1.1   Introduction

The *Åkerberg Fransson* case[38] concerned a Swedish fisherman who was accused of providing false information in his tax returns to evade income tax, value added tax (VAT) and employer's contributions. Mr Åkerberg Fransson was ordered to pay additional assessments to correct his underpayments, and also to pay, on top of that, punitive tax surcharges in the amount of € 11,250 for evading income tax, € 1,800 for evading

---

[38] Case C-617/10, *Åklagaren v. Hans Åkerberg Fransson*, ECLI:EU:C:2013:105.

employers' contributions, and € 1,025 for evading VAT. These surcharges were not contested by Mr Åkerberg Fransson and thus became final. Meanwhile, criminal proceedings were brought against him, based on the same acts of providing false tax information.

The local Swedish criminal court handling the case preliminarily asked the CJEU, *inter alia*, whether the bringing of criminal proceedings after the imposition of tax surcharges in respect of 'the same act of providing false information' comes under the *ne bis in idem* principle of Article 4 of Protocol no. 7 ECHR and of Article 50 of the Charter of Fundamental Rights. This referral was part of the revolt of the lower Swedish courts against the case law of the Swedish Supreme Courts (the *Högsta Domstolen* and the *Högsta förvaltningsdomstolen*), which did not consider the ECtHR case law to provide 'clear support' for vitiating the Swedish double punishment system.

Two main hurdles had to be taken: (i) the Charter needed to be applicable to the fining and prosecution of Mr Åkerberg Fransson's tax offences (for that, Article 51(1) requires that Sweden, when fining and prosecuting Mr Åkerberg Fransson for these offences, was 'implementing Union law') and (ii) the tax surcharges needed to constitute 'criminal proceedings' within the meaning of Article 50 of the Charter (and, via Article 52(3), also within the meaning of Article 4 of Protocol no. 7 ECtHR).

5.1.2   Applicability of the Charter; 'Implementing Union Law'

As to the question of the applicability of the Charter, we only summarize the judgment here, as this issue and its implications are discussed at length elsewhere in this volume. The applicability of the Charter was not obvious, as the case seemed entirely domestic and devoid of any 'implementation' of EU law, and therefore outside the scope of (Article 50 of) the Charter: neither profit taxation nor employer's contributions have been regulated at EU level, and the facts of the case revealed no cross-border element that might have engaged the EU free movement rights. The only connection with EU law seemed to be the Sixth VAT-Directive (Directive 77/388/EEC), which harmonizes the tax base of turnover taxation in the Member States ('common system of value added tax'),[39] but which does not contain provisions on the (manner of) enforcement of VAT, let alone any provisions on (modes of) penalties. Both the tax

---

[39] Now replaced by the Recast VAT Directive 2006/112/EC on the common system of value added tax (OJ 2006, L 347, p. 1).

surcharges and the criminal proceedings were national law, and moreover mainly concerned the unharmonized income tax and employer's contributions, all in a purely internal situation. Further, the questions referred to the CJEU primarily concerned the case law of the ECtHR on Article 4 of Protocol no.7 ECHR.

(Also) for these reasons, several Member States intervened in order to plead non-applicability of the Charter. They found the Commission on their side, and, as it appeared, also Advocate General Cruz Villalón, who considered the questions referred to be inadmissible for lack of a sufficient link to EU law. Indeed, (Article 50 of) the Charter only applies to the Member States 'when they are implementing Union law' (see Article 51(1) of the Charter).

The Court disagreed, however, with the Advocate General and the Commission; it considered the case to fall within the scope of (Article 50 of) the Charter on the basis of, first, the finding that 'implementing Union law' covers any situation within the scope of application of EU law, which meant that '[t]he applicability of EU law entails applicability of the fundamental rights guaranteed by the Charter' (so: if EU law applies, the Charter applies), and, second, the finding that the case had a sufficient link with EU law for three, apparently cumulative, reasons: (i) the VAT Directives 77/388/EEC and 2006/11/EC obliged Member States 'to take all legislative and administrative measures appropriate for ensuring collection of all the VAT due on its territory and for preventing evasion', (ii) the same obligation flows from Article 4(3) TEU (sincere cooperation) and (iii) Article 325 TFEU requires Member States to 'counter illegal activities affecting the financial interests of the EU'.[40] The court noted that VAT is part of the EU's own resources, and that this provides 'a direct link between the collection of VAT revenue in compliance with the European Union law applicable and the availability to the European Union budget of the corresponding VAT resources'.[41]

For these reasons, both the tax surcharges imposed on Mr Akerberg Fransson and the criminal proceedings brought against him 'consitute implementation ... of European Union law' for the purposes of Article 51(1) of the Charter. It should be noted that this conclusion could only be reached in respect of Mr Åkerberg Fransson's VAT offences; not in respect of his income tax and employer's contribution offences.

---

[40] Paragraph 25.   [41] Paragraph 26.

5.1.3   The *Ne Bis in Idem* Issue

The (partial) applicability of the Charter thus having been established, the Court turned to the *ne bis in idem* questions, which, as observed, boiled down to the question of whether the VAT surcharges imposed were 'criminal' in nature. In this respect, the Court in fact did nothing but indirectly repeat the ECtHR's *Engel* criteria and refer that question back to the referring Swedish court:

> 35. . . . , three criteria are relevant for the purpose of assessing whether tax penalties are criminal in nature. The first criterion is the legal classification of the offence under national law, the second is the very nature of the offence, and the third is the nature and degree of severity of the penalty that the person concerned is liable to incur (Case C-489/10 *Bonda* [2012] ECR I-0000, paragraph 37).
>
> 36. It is for the referring court to determine, in the light of those criteria, whether the combining of tax penalties and criminal penalties that is provided for by national law should be examined in relation to the national standards as referred to in paragraph 29 of the present judgment, which could lead it, as the case may be, to regard their combination as contrary to those standards, as long as the remaining penalties are effective, proportionate and dissuasive (see, to this effect, inter alia *Commission v Greece*, paragraph 24; Case C-326/88 *Hansen* [1990] ECR I-2911, paragraph 17; Case C-167/01 *Inspire Art* [2003] ECR I-10155, paragraph 62; Case C-230/01 *Penycoed* [2004] ECR I-937, paragraph 36; and Joined Cases C-387/02, C-391/02 and C-403/02 *Berlusconi and Others* [2005] ECR I-3565 paragraph 65).
>
> 37. It follows from the foregoing considerations that the answer to the second, third and fourth questions is that the *ne bis in idem* principle laid down in Article 50 of the Charter does not preclude a Member State from imposing successively, for the same acts of non-compliance with declaration obligations in the field of VAT, a tax penalty and a criminal penalty in so far as the first penalty is not criminal in nature, a matter which is for the national court to determine.

In Section 3.2.3 (last paragraph) and Section 4.3, we speculated on the reasons for the CJEU's stand-offishness as regards the question of whether Mr Åkerberg Fransson's prosecution was a *bis in idem* prohibited under Article 50 of the Charter. See also the last paragraph of Section 5.2 in Chapter 2 of the present volume.

5.1.4   'Clear Support'

The referring Swedish court also enquired as to the compatibility with EU law of the Swedish national law requirement that there must be 'clear support' in the ECHR, the Charter, or the case law of the ECtHR or the

CJEU, in order for a Swedish court to be able to disapply national provisions that could infringe the rights set out in the ECHR and in the Charter.[42] Given the *Zolotukhin, Janosevic* and *Jussila* judgments of the ECtHR cited earlier, one cannot but wonder how much clarity could be required as to the incompatibility of the Swedish credit system with Article 4 of Protocol no. 7. The Swedish Supreme Court nevertheless stuck to its guns,[43] considering that the ECtHR's admissibility decision in the *Nilsson* v. *Sweden* Case[44] (still) offered room for combining tax penalties and criminal prosecution, as that decision accepted that after a final punitive judgment, another measure such as the temporary withdrawal of a driving license is imposed by another authority if there is a sufficiently close connection between them in substance and in time. We submit that this admissibility decision does not shed much light on the issue of double punishment of tax offences, as (i) the *Nilsson* decision does not concern the 'idem' issue, but only the 'bis' issue; as such, it only *confirms* that the *same* offence was at issue in both proceedings and (ii) measures such as the withdrawal of a driving license (or the impounding of illegal substances) are not (just) punitive, but (also) based on public order and safety.

It comes as no surprise that the CJEU did not accept this Swedish judicial rule, as it limits a national court's power to assess the compatibility of national law with the Charter in situations within the scope of application of EU law. It would thus run counter to the effectiveness and uniform application of EU (Charter) law. However, this does raise the question as to whether the 'wide margin of appreciation' the ECtHR grants the Member States, especially in matters of social and economic policy such as tax matters, does not exist if the case enters the scope of application of EU law. At any rate, this creates a difference between a Swedish taxpayer who can only rely on the ECHR ('clear support' required) and a Swedish taxpayer who can also invoke the Charter because his case (also) concerns VAT or customs duties (no 'clear support' required). One would hope that such difference, which is difficult to explain to taxpayers in materially identical situations, will not be accepted by the ECtHR under Article 14 (nondiscrimination) *juncto*

---

[42] We note that to our knowledge, this rule has never been applied by Swedish courts in direct connection to EU law, but only as regards the ECHR.

[43] NJA (Nytt Juridiskt Arkiv) 2010, 168, and NJA 2011, 444.

[44] ECtHR, *Nilsson* v. *Sweden*, 13 December 2005 (Appl. No. 73661/01), ECLI:CE: ECHR:2005:1213DEC007366101.

Article 1 Protocol 1 (right to property) ECHR and Protocol 12 ECHR (nondiscrimination). Precisely the 'wide margin of appreciation' the ECtHR leaves the States in tax matters may, however, prevent the ECtHR from intervening. In Sweden, such intervention will not be necessary as regards tax surcharges, as the Swedish Supreme Court made amends after the CJEU's *Åkerberg Fransson* judgment, in two judgments of June and July 2013,[45] not only holding the Swedish double proceedings and double sanctions system to be incompatible with the *ne bis in idem* principle and granting persons both fined and convicted for the same tax offence the right to a rehearing of their cases (leading to many tax fraud convicts to be released from custody and many criminal proceedings to be discontinued[46]), but also holding that ECHR-protection against double jeopardy should not be less comprehensive than the protection afforded under Article 50 of the EU Charter[47] (homogeneity). In its reasoning, it referred to fundamental principles of foreseeability and equal treatment. In November of the same year (2013), the Swedish Supreme Administrative Court followed suit. See, for elaboration, Section 5.2 of Chapter 2 of the present volume.

5.2   What Does Åkerberg Fransson *Mean for National Tax (Penalty) Law?*

5.2.1   What Does This Mean for Mr Åkerberg Fransson's Case and for Swedish Law?[48]

The referring Swedish court had to apply the Charter to the double jeopardy situation in respect of Mr Åkerberg Fransson's VAT offences. For that, it had to assess, on the basis of the *Engel* criteria, whether the tax surcharges imposed (in respect of the VAT offences) were 'criminal' in nature. Since Mr Åkerberg Fransson's evasion of income tax and employer's contributions had no link with EU law, the tax penalties imposed therefor did not enter the scope of application of EU law; therefore,

---

[45] NJA 2013, 502 and NJA 2013, 746.

[46] See Joakim Negelius, 'The Nordic States and the European Convention on Human Rights', in: Rainer Arnold (ed.), *The Convergence of the Fundamental Rights Protection in Europe* (Springer, 2016), p. 96.

[47] See Ulf Bernitz, 'The Scope of the Charter and Its Impact on the Application of the ECHR: The *Åkerberg Fransson* Case on *Ne Bis in Idem* in Perspective', in: Sybe de Vries, Ulf Bernitz and Stephen Weatherill (eds.), *The EU Charter of Fundamental Rights as a Binding Instrument*, (Hart Publishing, 2015), p. 168.

[48] See also the last two paragraphs of Section 5.3 of Chapter 2 of this volume.

neither did the Charter apply to them.[49] This left Mr Åkerberg Fransson in a rather awkward legal position: Article 50 of the Charter only protected him from double jeopardy in respect of his evasion of VAT; for the major part of his double jeopardy (for the penalties for evading profit taxation and employer's contribution), he could not rely on the Charter. For these non-VAT double jeopardies, he could only invoke national (constitutional) law or, if his State of residence has ratified Protocol No. 7, the *ne bis in idem* principle enshrined in Article 4 of that Protocol. Sweden has in fact ratified Protocol no. 7 to the ECHR, so in principle, one would expect Mr Åkerberg Fransson to be able to obtain equivalent protection under the ECHR. In the *Dereçi* case,[50] an immigration case in which the CJEU considered Article 7 of the Charter (respect for family life) not to be applicable for lack of a sufficient link with EU law, that Court explicitly observed that the fact that the Charter does not apply, does not take away the national court's obligation to apply the corresponding provision in the ECHR:

> 72. Thus, . . . , if the referring court . . . takes the view that that situation is not covered by European Union law, it must undertake that examination in the light of Article 8(1) of the ECHR.
>
> 73. All the Member States are, after all, parties to the ECHR which enshrines the right to respect for private and family life in Article 8.

Although this reasoning does not fly in respect of the *ne bis in idem* principle in Member States which have not (fully) ratified Protocol No. 7, it is valid as regards Sweden, which did ratify that Protocol without reservations. As observed in Section 5.1.4, however, this fact had not precluded the Swedish Supreme Courts from allowing double jeopardy in respect of the same tax offence – provided that the total of the tax penalty and the criminal conviction for that same fact was not unreasonable (credit system), apparently on the basis of the 'clear support' doctrine explained in Section 5.1.4, even though the combination of *Janosevic, Jussila, Maresti* and *Zolotukhin* would seem quite clear enough to consider a 'double penalty with credit' – system such as the Swedish one to be a violation of Article 4 of Protocol no. 7. As also observed (Section 3.2.3): in *Åkerberg Fransson*, the CJEU seems to suggest that the *Engel* criteria leave room for not (always) considering the Swedish tax

---

[49] See, for elaboration: C. Brokelind, 'Case Note on Akerberg Fransson (Case C-617/10)' (2013) 53 *European Taxation*, 6, 284–285.

[50] Case C-256/11, *Murat Dereci a.o. v. Bundesministerium für Inneres*, ECLI:EU:C:2011:734.

surcharges to be 'criminal' within the meaning of Article 50 of the Charter and of Article 4 of Protocol no. 7 ECHR. We submit that the *Engel* criteria to which the CJEU refers in *Åkerberg Fransson* and *Bonda* must be the same *Engel* criteria as applied by the ECtHR in *Zolotukhin* and *Maresti*, and therefore that no such room exists; the credit system applied in Sweden is at odds with the *ne bis vexari* rule of Article 4 of Protocol no. 7; only the finality system is acceptable. Therefore, in our opinion, the Swedish referring court had no choice, given *Zolotukhin*, but to acquit Mr Åkerberg Fransson from all criminal indictments brought against him which had already been punished by way of tax penalties, also the criminal indictments relating to evasion of profit taxation and employer's contributions; although the latter are not within the scope of Article 50 of the Charter for lack of a link with EU law, they *are* covered by Article 4 of Protocol no. 7 ECHR.

The *Finnish* Supreme Court (*Korkein oikeus*) went even further, adopting the *una via* system explained in Section 3.1, in a ruling of 5 July 2013, KKO:2013:59. That case concerned an estimated additional assessment and tax penalties imposed on an entrepreneur in 2005. After rejection of his appeal, the tax surcharges became final in 2010. In 2008, the taxpayer was also criminally charged for tax fraud on the basis of the same undeclared income. Changing its previous case law,[51] the *Korkein oikeus* held that Article 4 of Protocol no. 7 prevents the *starting* or *continuing* of a criminal procedure once a tax penalty has been imposed (or has been waived by the tax administration in a decision), irrespective of whether it has become final in the sense that it cannot be appealed any more: its preventive effect as regards criminal prosecution is immediately upon imposition. The *Korkein oikeus* considered this interpretation to advance best the fulfilment of human rights under both the ECHR and the Finnish Constitution. Sub- and consequently, Finland changed its law, which since 1 December 2013 provides that the tax administration is not required any more to impose a tax penalty immediately when deciding a tax matter; it may be imposed by subsequent

---

[51] *Korkein oikeus*, judgments of 29 June 2010, KKO:2010:45 and KKO:2010:46. In these previous cases, the Finnish Supreme Court had decided that, although not being criminal under domestic law, a tax surcharge constitutes a criminal charge under the ECHR, covered by the *ne bis in idem* rule; but also that the *ne bis in idem* rule had to be interpreted thus that it prevented a criminal prosecution for the same tax offence only if the tax surcharge had become final (under Finnish tax procedure law, a taxpayer may appeal a decision of the tax administration until five years after the end of the year of assessment).

separate decision, to be issued at the latest by the end of the year following the year in which the tax matter was decided, provided that no criminal prosecution has been initiated on the basis of the same facts. As from the moment of imposition of a tax penalty, the public prosecutor is precluded from bringing criminal proceedings against the same taxpayer, unless evidence of new facts emerges.

As observed in Section 5.1.4, also the Swedish Supreme Court in 2013 inferred from *Åkerberg Fransson* that there should be equal protection against double jeopardy under both the Charter and Article 4 of Protocol no. 7, and it reversed its case law. Everyone fined for a tax offence and also convicted for that same offence after the date of the ECtHR's *Zolotukhin* case could apply for a retrial. Thus, a finality system was introduced. Subsequently, the Swedish legislator also set out to change Statute law and went even further: as of 1 January 2016, an *una via* system like the Netherlands' and the Finnish tax penalties sytems will apply also in Sweden.[52] The Swedish Tax Offences Act (*Skattebrottslagen 1971:69*) and Tax Procedure Act (*Skatteförfarandelagen 2011:1244*) have been amended and a new Tax Surcharges Act (*Lag om talan om skattetillägg i vissa fall 2015:632*) has been introduced.

5.2.2 (Other) Implications for Member States' Tax (Penalty) Law

The CJEU held, in *Åkerberg Fransson*, that '(t)he applicability of EU law entails applicability of the fundamental rights guaranteed by the Charter'. Thus, if EU law is activated, the Charter is also activated. This means that the Charter not only applies to situations in which Member States 'implement' EU law in the sense that they are 'acting as agents of EU law' (*e.g.* implementing EU Directives and enforcing EU Regulations), but in every situation which enters the scope of application of EU law. The Court thus has cast the net of the Charter rather widely, and we believe it was wise to do so. The restrictive position taken by the Commission, the Advocate General, and five Member States in *Åkerberg Fransson* could have yielded strange results, such as the applicability of the Charter to harmonized indirect taxation and, at the same time, the non-applicability of the Charter to unharmonized direct taxes violating

---

[52] See Eleonor Kristoffersson, 'The Future of the Swedish tax Sanction System After Ne Bis in Idem', in: Joakim Nergelius and Eleonor Kristofferson (eds.), *Human Rights in Contemporary European Law* (Hart Publishing, 2015), ch. 12.

free movement rights or State aid rules.[53] A narrower application of the Charter than the scope of application of EU law itself would also have led to discrepancies between the scope of the general principles of EU law and that of the rights protected by the Charter. After *Åkerberg Fransson*, the (tax) courts of the Member States are confronted with only two possibilities: situations falling within and situations outside the scope of application of EU law *and* of the Charter; these two are already difficult enough to distinguish.

Thus, not only cases involving EU-harmonized indirect taxes feeding the EU budget are covered (VAT and customs duties), but all tax cases which activate EU law, therefore also cases concerning *un*harmonized direct taxation such as individual and corporate income taxation, provided that another link to EU law (than harmonization and the EU budget) is present. This means that as regards unharmonized direct taxes, the Charter will (only) apply if some cross-border element is present which activates the free movement rights enshrined in the Treaty on the Functioning of the Union or the EU State aid rules. Such direct tax cases would include, notably: (i) exit taxation upon emigration of individuals or companies, (ii) discriminatory taxation of foreign-source income, (iii) discriminatory taxation of nonresidents and (iv) tax rulings which constitute a selective advantage for (a) certain undertaking(s). If, *for example,* a company relocating its mind and management to another Member State makes false statements in its emigration tax return about its unrealized capital gains, it may be either fined or indicted, but not both (more precise: it may be both fined and prosecuted, but once one of these proceedings has come to a final penalty (or acquittal), the other proceedings must be discontinued[54]). Apparently, the German *BundesVerfassungsGericht* (Constitutional Court) disagrees with this interpretation and wants to confine the scope of *Åkerberg Fransson* according to the 'distinctive features of the law on

---

[53] R. Palma, 'Åklagaran v Hans Åkerberg Fransson: Charter(ing) new territory' (2013) 2 *British Tax Review*, 137–145, seems to suggest that the Member State involved should have an intention to 'give effect to EU law' (p. 141) or that the national measure in question should at least have some EU law implementing effect (p. 142). But where a Member State restricts EU free movement rights by way of a tax measure, there is no such intention, nor such implementing effect. Nevertheless, we submit that the Charter is applicable, as the national measure frustrating EU free movement rights clearly enters the scope of application of EU law.

[54] See, most clearly, ECtHR, *Lucky Dev* v. *Sweden*, 27 November 2014 (Appl. No. 7356/10), ECLI:CE:ECHR:2014:1127JUD000735610.

value added tax'.[55] It should be observed that there is *some* harmonization of specific aspects of corporate income taxation in respect of
cross-border intragroup dividend, interest and royalty payments[56] and
cross-border mergers and divisions.[57] It would seem the Charter applies
where these Directives apply, even though they do not contain provisions comparable to those in the VAT Directives requiring Member
States to take all legislative and administrative measures appropriate for
ensuring collection of tax due on their territory and for preventing
evasion. The same will go for the pending Anti Tax Avoidance Directive
proposed by the Commission[58] if it will be adopted by the Council.

If *un*harmonized (direct) taxes in an *internal* situation are at issue,
then the case will not enter the scope of application of EU law for want of
a link with EU law, and therefore (Article 50 of) the Charter will not
apply. Still, such cases may be within the scope of Article 4 of Protocol
no. 7 (if the Member State involved has ratified that Protocol), which
may still prohibit a 'bis', as that provision applies (only) in internal
situations within one jurisdiction. By contrast, if penalties in respect of
EU-*harmonized* (indirect) taxes are at issue, it is irrelevant whether or
not the case is internal within one Member State, as *Åkerberg Fransson*
shows that if EU law is engaged, also (Article 50 of) the Charter
is engaged, especially if the harmonized tax which has been evaded is
labelled as 'own resources' of the Union.

It follows that in respect of penalties for evasion of indirect taxes, the
scope of Article 50 of the Charter is much wider (covering penalties in

---

[55] See the BVerfG press release no. 31/2013 of 24 April 2013 which accompanies its
judgment BVerfG, 1 BvR 1215/07, 24 April 2013 at [91]. See also the editorial comments
on that press release in: 'Ultra vires – has the Bundesverfassungsgericht shown its teeth?',
CMLRev (50), 925–930.

[56] Council Directive 2011/96/EU of 30 November 2011 on the common system of taxation
applicable in the case of parent companies and subsidiaries of different Member States,
OJ L 345, 29 December 2011, pp. 8–16, as amended, and Council Directive 2003/49/EC of
3 June 2003 on a common system of taxation applicable to interest and royalty payments
made between associated companies of different Member States, OJ L 157 of 26 June
2003, p. 49.

[57] Council Directive 2009/133/EC of 19 October 2009 on the common system of
taxation applicable to mergers, divisions, partial divisions, transfers of assets and
exchanges of shares concerning companies of different Member States and to the
transfer of the registered office of an SE or SCE between Member States, OJ L 310,
25 November 2009.

[58] Proposal for a Council Directive laying down rules against tax avoidance practices that
directly affect the functioning of the internal market, COM/2016/026 final – 2016/
011 (CNS).

both internal and cross-border situations) than in respect of penalties for evasion of unharmonized direct taxes (in principle covering only (i) situations in which the EU free movement rights apply, *that is* in situations featuring some cross-border element, (ii) situations in which EU State aid rules apply and (iii) situations in which one of the few and specific corporate income tax Directives apply).

We do observe, however, that the CJEU held that VAT being part of the EU's own resources provides 'a direct link between the collection of VAT revenue in compliance with the European Union law applicable and the availability to the European Union budget of the corresponding VAT resources'. If *that* link is sufficient for entering the scope of application of EU law (and therefore of the Charter), then *all* national taxation, including unharmonized direct taxation, enters that scope, also in all internal situations. Indeed, the Union's own resources stem from three sources:[59] (i) the proceeds of the Common Customs Tariff duties and levies under the common organization of the market for sugar (therefore, customs penalties are also within the scope of the *ne bis in idem* principle of Article 50); (ii) a percentage of the national VAT base, capped at a percentage of gross national income and (iii) a percentage of gross national income. The latter EU income is obviously paid out of total national tax revenue. Therefore, that contribution to the EU budget includes (the same percentage of) *all* taxes. That would seem to produce, as the Court put it in *Åkerberg Fransson*, not only for VAT, but also for direct taxes a 'direct link' between the collection of taxes and 'the availability to the European Union budget' of the corresponding part of national tax revenue. Since (total) national tax revenue *as such* is thus a source of the Union's own resources, Article 4(3) TEU (sincere cooperation) and Article 325 TFEU (requiring Member States to counter illegal activities affecting the financial interests of the EU) would seem to apply to *all* national taxation in the same way as it does to VAT and customs duties. The only ground missing from the CJEU's three grounds for finding a sufficient link with EU law in *Åkerberg Fransson*, is thus the fact that, unlike VAT and customs duties, direct taxation has not been harmonized (apart from the few specific corporate income taxation Directives aforementioned), let alone uniformized.

We conclude that penalties in respect of evasion of other taxes than VAT and customs duties only rarely enter the scope of application of the

---

[59] Council Decision 2007/436/EC, Euratom of 7 June 2007 on the system of the European Communities' own resources.

Charter. Without a cross-border element activating EU free movement law, the link between unharmonized (direct) taxation and EU law will generally be too vague and indirect. We believe this conclusion is supported by the *Sindicato dos Bancários do Norte* Case,[60] which shows that not just any link with EU law is sufficient to engage the Charter, not even if EU rules are being implemented. The case concerned Portuguese bank personnel litigating against their employer, a nationalized bank, which had drastically reduced their wages to comply with the national budget law providing for wage reduction in respect of all civil servants with a view to meeting the requirements of the EU Stability and Growth Pact (SGP). The referring Portuguese court doubted whether this legislation was compatible with the prohibition of discrimination and the right to working conditions respecting the workers' dignity (Articles 20, 21 and 31 of the Charter). Even though the wage measures taken ultimately flowed from Portugal's EU obligations under the SGP, the CJEU did not see any 'implementation' of EU law within the meaning of Article 51 of the Charter and considered itself, therefore, by *ordonnance*, 'manifestement incompétente' to answer the questions.[61] We observe that in the light of *Åkerberg Fransson*, it is not obvious why the implementation of the SGP should fall outside the scope of the Charter, but if the Court had ruled differently, this could have brought every national cutback law, and maybe every national tax law, within the scope of the Charter, and therefore within the scrutiny of the Court of Justice. Such an outcome (all national taxation, irrespective of any direct link with EU (budget) law or any cross-border element, comes within the scope of the Charter and CJEU scrutiny) would not seem acceptable in the light of the subsidiarity principle laid down in Articles 6(1) TEU and 51(2) of the Charter.

We agree with Vervaele that *Åkerberg Fransson* implies that 'Article 50 de facto sets aside the non-ratification [and] reservations [of/to Protocol No. 7; authors], as long as the Charter applies in a domestic situation ... In such a situation all Member States should apply the substance of Article 50.'[62] We again stress, however, that Article 50 of the Charter only applies in domestic situations involving tax penalties if

---

[60] Case C-128/12, *Sindicato dos Bancários do Norte a.o. v. Banco Português de Negócios SA*, ECLI:EU:C:2013:149.

[61] The CJEU reached the same conclusion in Case C-264/12, *Sindicato Nacional dos Profissionais de Seguros e Afins*, ECLI:EU:C:2014:2327.

[62] J. Vervaele, 'The Application of the EU Charter of Fundamental Rights and its Ne bis in idem Principle in the Member States of the EU' (2013) 6 *Review of European Administrative Law*, 134.

the latter have been imposed for VAT or customs duties offences. Article 50 of the Charter will have little impact in respect of tax penalties for direct taxes: it will only impact cross-border situations in which a free movement right is at issue and situations in which either the EU State Aid prohibition or one of the few and rather specific EU Directives on corporate income taxation are at issue.

The importance of the Court's decision to interpret the term 'implementing Union law' in Article 51 of the Charter widely, as 'within the scope of application of EU law', also in tax matters transcends the field of *ne bis in idem*. To give just one example: the ECtHR has consistently held that proceedings concerning, *inter alia*, taxation[63] and aliens[64] are not covered by Article 6 ECHR (the right to a fair and public hearing without undue delay), as they do not concern a criminal charge or civil rights and obligations. In contract, its sister provision in the Charter, Article 47, does not limit the reach of its fair hearing requirements to litigation concerning criminal charges and civil rights and obligations. It therefore also covers all tax litigation and all immigration litigation, provided that there is a link with EU law (*e.g.* with free movement rights), without distinguishing between harmonized and unharmonized taxes. We applaud this result, as it would have been difficult to explain why a dispute before a national Court on indirect taxation violating the Recast VAT Directive or the Union Customs Code would merit a fair hearing without undue delay, and disputes before the same national Court on direct taxation violating, *for example*, the freedom of establishment, would not. It would be equally difficult to explain why, in a dispute before a national court on harmonized indirect taxation, the right of property (Article 17 of the Charter) should be respected if, in a dispute before the same national court on unharmonized direct taxation violating the Treaty freedoms, the rights protected by the Charter could be ignored.

The question arises as to the relation between (Article 50 of) the Charter and the general principle of effectiveness of material EU law. What if the tax penalty imposed on Mr Åkerberg Fransson were to be considered insufficiently 'effective, proportionate and dissuasive' to protect the EU's own resources and to dissuade Mr Åkerberg Fransson and

---

[63] ECtHR, *Ferrazzini* v. *Italy*, 12 July 2001 (Appl. No. 44759/98), ECLI:CE:ECHR:2001:0712JUD004475998.

[64] ECtHR, *Maaouia* v. *France*, 5 October 2000 (Appl. No. 39652/98), ECLI:CE:ECHR:2000:1005JUD003965298.

other entrepreneurs from (further) VAT evasion? In *Zolotukhin*, the ECtHR unambiguously held that *any* second prosecution will violate Article 4 Protocol no. 7 ECHR after the outcome of the first prosecution has become final. The principle of effectiveness of EU law, however, may require the Member State involved to bring a second prosecution if the first charge was insufficiently effective. Given its nature as a fundamental right, we submit that the effectiveness principle ought to be trumped by the Charter and, despite the possible ineffectiveness of the first and final penalty, no second charge ought to be possible, irrespective of the possibly unobjectionable proportionality of a supplementary sanction.

This stance is supported by the *Belvedere Costruzioni* judgment,[65] concerning the Italian statutory rule that after ten years of litigation, tax claims may be waived against payment of 5 per cent of their nominal amount, if the litigating taxpayer was successful at first and second judicial instance. Such a rule clearly runs counter to the effectiveness of EU VAT rules, EU customs duties law, and EU excise duties law. Nevertheless, the Court held (paragraphs 22–23) that:

> it follows from Articles 2 and 22 of the Sixth Directive and Article 4(3) TEU that every Member State is under an obligation to take all legislative and administrative measures appropriate for ensuring collection of all the VAT due on its territory. In that regard, Member States are required to check taxable persons' returns, accounts and other relevant documents, and to calculate and collect the tax due. Under the common system of VAT, the Member States are required to ensure compliance with the obligations to which taxable persons are subject, and they enjoy in that respect a certain measure of latitude, inter alia, as to how they use the means at their disposal. That latitude is nevertheless limited by the obligation to ensure effective collection of the European Union's own resources and not to create significant differences in the manner in which taxable persons are treated, either within a Member State or throughout the Member States. . . . However in the first place, the obligation to ensure effective collection of European Union resources cannot run counter to compliance with the principle that judgment should be given within a reasonable time, which, under the second paragraph of Article 47 of the Charter of Fundamental Rights of the European Union, must be observed by the Member States when they implement European Union law, and must also be observed under Article 6(1) of the ECHR.

---

[65] Case C-500/10, *Uffucio IVA di Piacenza* v. *Belvedere Costruzioni Srl*, ECLI:EU: C:2012:186.

Thus, the effectiveness of EU law includes the effectiveness of the EU Charter rights, which may trump substantive EU law, as fundamental rights trump other law in national legal orders as well. This does not take away the fact, however, that the Member State involved in such a case has an obligation to either raise its tax penalties to an effective and dissuasive level, or to bring criminal proceedings instead at the outset. If it does not, the Commission may take it to Court.

6 'Idem' Issues in Tax Penalty (and Competition) Cases

As explained earlier (Section 3.2.2), the CJEU and the ECtHR in general agree – at least outside the area of competition penalties – that 'the same offence' is the same material act, *that is* substantially the same factual conduct, by the same person at the same place and time (*idem factum*), 'irrespective of the legal classification or the legal interest protected'; in the present context: the same tax evasion. Once the taxpayer has been fined for that material act and that pecuniary penalty has become final (or the taxpayer has been acquitted), no second charge for that material act is acceptable. In the field of competition law, however, the CJEU hitherto has stipulated 'a threefold condition of identity': (i) identity of facts, (ii) unity of the offender, and (iii) unity of the legal interest protected. Thus, in competition cases, the same person *may* be punished twice for the same material act (for a 'single course of conduct') if the two legal provisions on which the two charges are based, are not designed to protect the same legal asset.[66] Among many others, Wils,[67] Van Bockel[68] and Advocate General Kokott[69] argue that no such variance according to the legal interest protected should exist, neither between different fields of law, nor between Strasbourg and Luxembourg. Their main arguments are that (i) legal certainty, (ii) the homogeneity principle and (iii) the fact that Article 4 of Protocol no. 7 ECHR is a minimum standard, require uniform *ne bis in idem* conditions across the board. The ECJ, however, despite Advocate General Kokott's Opinion in that case, reiterated its deviating 'threefold condition of identity' for application of the *ne bis in*

---

[66] Case C-204/00P, *Aalborg Portland* (a.k.a. *Cement*), ECLI:EU:C:2004:6.

[67] W. Wils, 'The Principle of Ne Bis in Idem in EC Antitrust Enforcement: A Legal and Ecocnomic Analysis' (2003) 26 *World Competition*, 131, 143.

[68] B. Van Bockel, *The Ne Bis in Idem Principle in EU Law: A Conceptual and Jurisprudential Analysis* (Leiden: Ipskamp Drukkers, 2009).

[69] Opinion in Case C-17/10, *Toshiba*.

idem principle in competition matters in Case C-17/10, *Toshiba*. In this respect, the CJEU maintains that EU competition law does not protect the same legal interest as national competition law and competition law of third States, without, however, discernably clarifying this in terms of different geographical or product/service markets or other clarifying criteria. The fact that the EU competition rules address cartels capable of affecting trade between Member States, whereas this is not a condition for national competition penalties, to us does not explain this case law. Indeed, a cartel agreement does not need to be viewed as one single course of action. If it concerns more than one national market within the EU (which it would if the Commission is engaged) and/or more than one (not interchangeable) product or service on that geographical market (which also implies a different (product) market), then in our view there are as many offences. Only if it is the same product on the same geographical market, it is the same offence, and can the same cartelist not be punished again after a previous penalty by either the Commission or the national competition authority. Possibly the CJEU wants to retain the possibility for both the national authority and the Commission to 'top up' a penalty for an international cartel agreement already imposed by the other party in order to effect a higher level of antitrust protection. Indeed, if Member States or the Commission remain free to apply a stricter norm, they should logically also be free to apply harsher penalties, if necessary by instituting a second proceeding.[70] At any rate, this case law does not conform to the CJEU's case law in other fields on *ne bis in idem*.[71]

Lenaerts and Gutiérrez-Fons[72] present the CJEU's and ECtHR's inter-pretation of the *ne bis in idem* principle as 'an example of convergence' of the approaches of the CJEU and the ECtHR, but they are silent about the area of competition fines. One can but speculate as to the CJEU's reasons for its 'unity of legal interest' requirement in competition cases. Possibly, the Court wants to avoid the Commission having to yield to – or take account of – competition fines imposed (or more importantly: acquittals

---

[70] Cf., in the context of minimum harmonization, B. Van Bockel, *The Ne Bis in Idem Principle in EU Law: A Conceptual and Jurisprudential Analysis* (Leiden: Ipskamp Drukkers, 2009), chapter 6.

[71] Cf. M. Frese, *Sanctions in EU Competition Law: Principles and Practice* (Amsterdam: Bloombury Publishers, 2012), pp. 97–99.

[72] K. Lenaerts and J. Gutiérrez-Fons, 'The Place of the Charter in the EU Institutional Edifice', in S. Peers, T. Hervey, J. Kenner and A. Ward (eds.), *The EU Charter of Fundamental Rights: A Commentary* (Oxford: Hart Publishing, 2014).

handed down) in third States in global competition cases, even though Advocate General Kokott in *Toshiba* pointed out and elaborated on the fact that Article 50 Charter limits its *ne bis in idem* rule to 'within the Union'.

Competition fines and tax surcharges have many characteristics in common, as neither of them belong to what the ECtHR calls 'hard core' or 'traditional' criminal law (see Section 4.3); both are imposed for economic offences aimed at illegal pecuniary benefit which distorts equality and the level playing field; both produce little moral stigma. This raises the question of whether the CJEU may follow its narrow 'threefold identity' approach also in respect of tax surcharges, or will group such surcharges in the *Kraaijenbrink* and *Zolotukhin* category ('same material act'). To illustrate the importance of the classification, (*that is* the importance of the question of whether or not there is 'unity of the legal interest protected'), we give the example of a taxpayer filing a VAT return in which he provides false information with a view to paying less VAT than required by law, and in which he states that he has provided full and correct answers. In many Member States, no less than three penalties may be imposed: (i) a punitive tax surcharge, (ii) a criminal sentence for a criminal offence defined in the tax code and (iii) a criminal sentence for a criminal offence defined in the general criminal code (possibly even for three such regular offences: fraud, deceit and/or defrauding creditors). If the 'same material act' approach is adopted, the finality of a penalty (or an acquittal) for any of these legal classifications will preclude the imposition of a penalty for any other classification, and will end any possible parallel proceedings in respect of any of the other legal classifications. If, on the other hand, the 'legal interest protected' approach is chosen, it would seem that all of these penalties may be combined (provided that the resulting total penalty is not disproportionate to the (lack of) seriousness of ... the material act!), as they all seem to protect a (more or less) different legal interest, such as protection of the smooth administrative process of levying and collection of taxes, protection of the public budget for collective expenditure, protection of creditors in general, and protection of the public at large.

We submit that either the 'legal interest protected' approach should be abandoned by the CJEU also for competition fines, or it should explicitly be confined to that field of law, under a detailed explanation of the (categories of) cases in which it cannot be missed for the sake of the effectiveness of competition law. We observe that if the Union wishes competition fines to be effective and to be more uniform in their effect

Union-wide, EU law should provide uniformly that such fines are not in any way deductible as business expenses for national profit taxation purposes.

In tax cases, also the 'unity of the offender' requirement may raise questions, especially in cases where a single shareholder/director of a closely held company files incorrect tax returns for the company, concealing (i) sales, (ii) wages paid out and (iii) profits made, and withdrawing the resulting 'black' money for his personal benefit from the company, obviously also without declaring it in his personal income tax return. These are at least five different tax offences (for turnover tax, wage withholding tax, corporate income tax, dividend withholding tax and individual income tax; additionally, there may be separate penalties for incorrect tax accounting or making false accounts available for inspection), all of which may be both administratively punished (at least five different tax surcharges) and prosecuted on criminal indictment (at least five counts). Since any pecuniary penalty imposed on the company will affect the personal means of the sole shareholder/director in the exact same amount – the value of his shares drops by the same amount – the question arises whether and if so, to what extent a closely held company and its shareholder/director may or must be identified in a case such as this. At any rate, the proportionality principle can scarcely be missed in a case like this.

Lastly, we draw attention to two situations in which taxation itself may amount to a penalty, producing the effect of materially punishing twice the same fiscal conduct. The first situation involves the intergovernmental Convention on the Elimination of Double Taxation in Connection with the Adjustment of Profits of Associated Enterprises (the Arbitration Convention),[73] which is part of the *acquis*, meaning that it has been ratified by all Member States and that any new Member acceding must also ratify it. It provides for (first a mutual agreement procedure, and if that does not work) an arbitration procedure in case of unresolved transfer pricing disputes between the tax administrations of different Member States. Such disputes cause international double taxation for the international groups of companies involved, as a different pricing of the same intragroup transaction between two associated enterprises in two different taxing jurisdictions causes (part of) the profit on that cross-border transaction to be taxed in both jurisdictions. Referring the case for

---

[73] Convention 90/463/EEC of 23 July 1990, OJ 1990 No. L 225/10.

arbitration does not prevent the Contracting States from commencing or continuing administrative or criminal proceedings in respect of the transactions giving rise to the price correction (Art. 7(2)), and arbitration does not even need to be initiated or may be discontinued if one of the enterprises is made subject to a 'serious penalty' for the allegedly incorrect pricing of the internal transactions (Art. 8(1) and (2)). The latter provision has the effect of enabling the Contracting States to stay or pre-empt arbitration – thus perpetuating double taxation – by criminally indicting or administratively fining one of the associated enterprises involved. To us, it is not self-evident that international double taxation, possibly in the amount of millions of euros, may be left unrelieved solely because penalties are imposed. Indeed, not eliminating the double taxation on the grounds that a penalty was imposed amounts to a second penalty for the same offence already sanctioned. We submit that fraud and irregularities should attract criminal or administrative sanctions, but no arbitrary double taxation. We further submit that, as the only reason for maintaining such arbitrary double burden is apparently the fact that tax penalties were imposed or an indictment was issued in respect of the transactions giving rise to the profit adjustment, such deliberate double taxation could be regarded as a 'criminal charge' under both Article 6 ECHR and Article 4 of Protocol no. 7 ECHR. We admit, however, that it is hard to say which of the two States involved is doing the double charging, as, precisely because of the abortion of the arbitration procedure, it remains unclear how the taxing rights should be divided over the two States involved. At any rate, the case is in principle within the reach of Article 50 of the Charter, as by definition, transfer pricing disputes concern cross-border trade or services within a group of companies which has secondarily established itself abroad.

The second situation in which taxation itself may be the second penalty arises from application of Article 236 of the Community Customs Code, which provides that the entitlement to a refund of customs duties paid but not due is forfeited if the taxpayer's conduct leading to the payment of customs duties was fraudulent. The result of the application of such a provision is that a non-existent tax claim is nevertheless effected, although the same material fact (the fraudulent conduct) is already subject to tax penalties (and possibly, on top of that, also to criminal indictment; in that case, a *three*fold jeopardy presents itself). Again, the case is within the scope of application of the Charter, as customs duties form 'own resources' of the Union.

7 Parallels between (Prevention of) International Double Jeopardy and (Prevention of) International Double Taxation

As observed earlier (Section 3.2.2), the CJEU in *Schengen* matters explicitly based its interpretation of Article 54 CISA (international *ne bis vexari*) also on free movement rights, preventing double jeopardy by guaranteeing single proceedings and mutual recognition of convictions and acquittals. International double taxation is at least as effective in obstructing free movement as international double indictment. It is mainly caused by the fact that the residence State of the taxpayer applies the residence principle for defining its taxing jurisdiction, therefore taxing the worldwide income of its residents, and the source State of the income applies the source principle, taxing nonresident taxpayers for the income sourced within its territory (compare the *lex loci delicti* in international criminal law). There is a successful international public law remedy for the resulting double taxation on the sourced income: almost all bilateral relationships between EU Member States are covered by double tax conventions following the OECD Model Tax Convention.[74] However, because of disparities and mismatches, these conventions do not always fully take away international double taxation, and some bilateral relations are not yet covered by such convention. Remaining double taxation cannot be declared incompatible with the EU free movement rights, as neither of the two States involved distinguishes between domestic and comparable cross-border situations, and EU law is silent on the question of which State must yield to which other State's determination of taxing jurisdiction. EU law does not contain clues as to whether the source principle or the residence principle is better. For lack of indications in EU law on the division of taxing power among the Member States, the ECJ accepts this – what it calls – 'exercise in parallel' of taxing jurisdiction.[75] Double taxation thus persists. EU law does not offer any *ne bis in idem* rule in international taxation. Although it is obvious that international double taxation frustrates free movement, there is no basis for designating the culprit who should undo it if neither State involved distinguishes between the cross-border and the comparable internal situation.

---

[74] Model Tax Convention on Income and on Capital, OECD, Paris.
[75] Case C-513/04, *Kerckhaert-Morres*, ECLI:EU:C:2006:713; Case C-128/08, *Damseaux*, ECLI:EU:C:2009:471; and Case C-67/08, *Block*, ECLI:EU:C:2009:92.

Article 293 of the former EC Treaty called for negotiations between the Member States to secure for their residents 'the abolition of double taxation within the Community', but it had no direct effect.[76] Moreover, Article 293 EC mysteriously vanished at the end of the Lisbon Treaty negotiations; hitherto it has not been clarified why.

As EU law does not clear up which jurisdictional claim is better (source or residence?),[77] mutual recognition does not work: which State is to recognize which other State's taxing rights? In international double jeopardy cases, it would have been the same, as States regard the exercise of their national criminal jurisdiction just as much as an expression of their sovereignty as they do the exercise of their taxing jurisdiction, were it not for the fact that *ne bis in idem* in criminal matters is a human right. Therefore, in criminal matters, it is clear(er) which State must yield under the *ne bis in idem* principle: first come, first serve; the jurisdiction of the first conviction or acquittal to become final prevails over the other jurisdiction which then must abstain fully. However, in competition fine cases, especially those involving also third States, the Union takes the same position as national taxing jurisdictions: it sees no reason why it should yield to the jurisdiction assumed by any third State.

Another parallel between international double indictment and international double taxation is the following: in international tax law, two main methods for the prevention of double taxation are applied: the exemption method and the credit method. The first exempts foreign source income from home State taxation and is thus based on mutual recognition of the source State's prior right to tax. It thus resembles the finality system of preventing international double jeopardy (*ne bis vexari*) which the CJEU adheres to in its *Schengen* case law on Article 54 CISA. Under the credit method for the prevention of international double taxation, the foreign source income is fully included in the domestic tax base, but the resulting tax claim is reduced by the tax already paid abroad on that foreign source income. This method thus closely resembles the credit method for the prevention of double jeopardy (*ne bis puniri*) the CJEU adheres to in competition law cases.

A last parallel is the following: in double tax conventions and in national tax law, the State obliged to prevent double taxation (usually

---

[76] Case C-336/96, *époux Gilly*, ECLI:EU:C:1998:221.

[77] Some States apply also nationality as a tax connecting factor, especially for inheritance and gift taxation. For companies, not only residence, but often also the law of incorporation is used as a tax connecting factor.

the residence State) often requires *effective* taxation in the source State to which the income is allocated. Especially the credit method for the prevention of double taxation explained earlier is geared to effective overall taxation at home State level (capital export neutrality), but also exemption States apply *switch over* clauses, meaning that the foreign source income will not be exempted if it has not been subject to effective taxation in the source State at a specified minimum level, but only a credit will be extended for the amount effectively paid. Article 1(1) of the EU Intragroup Interest and Royalty Directive[78] also requires effective taxation in the creditor State as a condition for the debtor State to waive its withholding tax on the outbound interest and royalty payments. Article 54 CISA does exactly the same: it only requires the second prosecuting State to abstain if the penalty imposed in the first prosecuting State has become final *and* it is effective, in the sense that it has been enforced, is actually in the process of being enforced or can no longer be enforced due to the Statute of limitations. That too is a parallel, for that matter: also tax, even though effectively *levied*, cannot be *collected* any more after expiry of the statutory time limit for recovery.

8   Summary and Conclusions

International *bis in idem* is a much larger problem in respect of taxation itself (international double taxation) than it is in respect of penalties for tax offences. Double jeopardy in respect of the sanctioning of tax offences is mostly a one-jurisdictional (internal) phenomenon which only engages Article 50 of the Charter if a sufficient link with EU law is present. That is the case (i) if the tax concerned has been harmonized at EU level and EU law requires effective collection and/or designates its revenue as an 'own resource' of the Union (this is the case for VAT and customs duties) or (ii) if some cross-border element brings the tax concerned within the scope of application of the EU free movement rights (this is the – relatively rare – case for unharmonized direct taxes in situations involving, notably, exit taxation, discriminatory taxation of foreign-source income, and discriminatory taxation of nonresidents). In respect of penalties for evasion of indirect taxes, the scope of Article 50 of the Charter is thus much wider (covering penalties in both internal and

---

[78] Council Directive 2003/49/EC on a common system of taxation applicable to interest and royalty payments made between associated companies of different Member States, OJ 2003 No. L157/49.

cross-border situations) than in respect of penalties for evasion of unhar-monized direct taxes (in principle covering only situations in which the EU free movement rights apply).

If the Member State concerned has not (fully) ratified the Seventh Protocol to the ECHR, a large area of reverse discrimination exists. Indeed, if that Protocol has not been (fully) ratified, taxpayers exposed to two punitive charges in respect of the same tax course of action can only rely on Article 50 of the Charter, which, however, only applies if a sufficient link with EU law is present. Especially for penalties for offences in respect of unharmonized direct taxes not designated as own resources of the Union, this means that *ne bis in idem* will only rarely apply, as all internal situations within one jurisdiction are excluded for direct taxes, unlike for harmonized indirect taxes. Taxpayers committing offences in respect of direct taxes should therefore be advised to live in Member States which have (fully) ratified Protocol No. 7 to the ECHR.

The *ne bis in idem* principle in both Article 4 of Protocol no. 7 ECHR and Article 50 of the EU Charter means *ne bis vexari*. A credit system which subtracts the prior penalty from the subsequent penalty is not good enough. Once the first penalty – or acquittal – has become final, any subsequent (continuation of) punitive proceedings for the same offence is/are prohibited (finality system). At least three EU Member States, the Netherlands, Finland and Sweden, go even further, applying an *una via* system. In such a system, the very imposition of a tax surcharge or the very criminal indictment in respect of a tax offence already precludes or terminates the other proceedings. Whether or not the first penalty has already become final is irrelevant; its imposition or charge is already decisive.

The question of whether the subsequent proceedings arise from the 'same offence', must be answered on the basis of the material act (do the two proceedings target identical or substantially the same facts/behav-iour/conduct/course of action?), rather than on the basis of the legal classification of the two charges or the legal interests protected. This conclusion does not seem to hold, however, in competition cases, as the CJEU seems to stick to its 'unity of legal interest protected' requirement in competition cases.

The CJEU in *Åkerberg Fransson* seemed to suggest that there is still room for considering punitive tax surcharges as not being 'criminal' for the purpose of the application of the *ne bis in idem* principle, but such suggestion seems incorrect to us and is probably explained by the fact that the CJEU wished to leave the execution of the death sentence for the

Swedish double jeopardy system to either the ECtHR in two at that time pending Swedish cases or to the national Swedish courts. Indeed, since the *Janosevic, Jussila, Radu* and *Zolotukhin* judgments of the ECtHR there could be no doubt that the imposition of punitive tax surcharges produces both a 'criminal charge' within the meaning of Article 6 ECHR (fair hearing) and 'criminal proceedings' within the meaning of Article 4 of Protocol no. 7 ECHR (*ne bis in idem*), and with that – given Article 52(3) of the Charter – also produces 'criminal proceedings' within the meaning of Article 50 of the Charter. This does not mean that all 'criminal charges' are the same, as according to the ECtHR, some belong to 'hard core' criminal law and some belong to more peripheral punitive law, such as administrative penalties, tax penalties and competition fines. Although for these non-hardcore criminal cases not all requirements *of Article 6 ECHR* (and with that, of *Article 47 of the Charter*) necessarily apply with their 'full stringency', it seems unlikely to us that *Article 4 of Protocol no. 7* and *Article 50 of the EU Charter* could be applied with less than their 'full stringency', as under a *ne bis vexari* interpretation of the *ne bis in idem* principle a second accusation for the same facts is either acceptable (if one of the accusations is not 'criminal', or the second one is not a 'bis') or it is not.

We believe that the Swedish referring court in *Åkerberg Fransson* had little choice, given *Zolotukhin*, but to acquit Mr Åkerberg Fransson from all criminal indictments brought against him which have already been punished by way of tax penalties, including the criminal indictments relating to evasion of profit taxation and employer's contributions; although the latter are not within the scope of Article 50 of the Charter for lack of a link with EU law, they *are* covered by Article 4 of Protocol no. 7 ECHR, and in our view (and eventually also of the Swedish Supreme Courts), there is an ample 'clear support' for holding the Swedish credit system applied until 2013 to violate Article 4 of Protocol no. 7.

The relevance of *Åkerberg Fransson* also in tax matters transcends the field of *ne bis in idem* by far. Litigation concerning taxation is now, via Article 47 of the Charter, covered by Article 6 ECHR, as Article 47, unlike Article 6, does not limit the reach of its fair hearing requirements to litigation concerning criminal charges and civil rights and obligations, provided that there is a link with EU law (*e.g.* with free movement rights). We applaud this result, as it is difficult to explain why a dispute before a national Court on indirect taxation violating the Recast VAT Directive would merit a fair hearing, and disputes before the same national Court on direct taxation violating, *for example*, the freedom of establishment would not. It would be equally difficult to explain why, in a dispute before a national court on harmonized indirect taxation, the right of property (Art. 17 of the Charter) should be respected if, in a dispute before the same national court on unharmonized direct taxation violating the Treaty freedoms, the rights protected by the Charter could be ignored.

The principle of effectiveness of EU law may require a Member State to bring a second prosecution if the first penalty was insufficiently effective and dissuasive. However, given the Charter's nature as a catalogue of fundamental rights, we submit that it should trump the principle of effectiveness of substantive EU law.

As competition fines and tax surcharges have many characteristics in common, the question rises whether the CJEU may follow the narrow 'threefold identity' approach it applies in competition cases also in respect of tax surcharges, or will group such surcharges in the *Kraaijenbrink* and *Zolotukhin* category ('same material act'). We believe that either the 'legal interest protected' approach should be abandoned also for competition fines, or it should be confined to that field of law, under a detailed explanation why it cannot be missed for the effectiveness of competition law. We observe that if the Union wants competition fines to be effective it should provide that such fines are not deductible as business expenses for national profit taxation purposes.

International double jeopardy and international double taxation show many parallels. Most importantly, in both cases, some criterion must decide which jurisdiction takes priority. In double jeopardy cases, the rule is first come, first serve: the jurisdiction of the first conviction or acquittal to become final prevails over the other jurisdiction which then must abstain fully. In double taxation cases, States usually bilaterally agree on source country entitlement to the taxable income, but still, national taxing jurisdictions frequently see no reason why they should yield to the jurisdiction assumed by another State. The exemption method for the prevention of double taxation is based on mutual recognition of the source State's prior right to tax and thus resembles the finality system of preventing international double jeopardy (*ne bis vexari*) the CJEU adheres to in CISA cases. Under the credit method for the prevention of international double taxation, the foreign tax is merely deducted from the own taxation by the residence State, and it thus closely resembles the credit method for the prevention of double jeopardy (*ne bis puniri*) the CJEU adheres to in competition law cases. A last parallel is that both international tax law and Article 54 CISA require *effective* taxation and punishment, respectively, before the other jurisdiction is prepared to abstain from exercising its taxing jurisdiction or its criminal jurisdiction, respectively.

6

Ne Bis in Idem Issues Under
the Single Supervisory Mechanism

BAS VAN BOCKEL

1 Introduction

This chapter addresses potential issues of *ne bis in idem* under the Single Supervisory Mechanism (SSM), both in the relation between the different types of instruments available to the European Central Bank (ECB) and National Competent Authorities (NCAs) as well as in the interaction with national (criminal) laws. Actual infringements of the *ne bis in idem* principle occur on a case-by-case basis, and there are at the time of writing no cases beforehand enabling us to assess all potential aspects of the issue. The question addressed here is therefore not whether an infringement of the *ne bis in idem* principle is *possible* under SSM, but whether the SSM Regulation (SSMR) carries a kind of 'built-in risk' of violations of *ne bis in idem* in certain types of situations.

When compared to the enforcement set-up in competition law under Regulation 1/2003 (the procedural regulation for competition law) discussed in Chapter 4, it appears that potential *ne bis in idem* issues for the SSMR are not necessarily similar. The nature of the rules enforced by the ECB and NCAs in general, and the division of tasks between the ECB and the NCAs on the basis of the distinction between 'significant' and 'less significant' banks in particular, mitigate the risk of violations of the *ne bis in idem* principle. The decentralized enforcement architecture of Regulation 1/2003 hinges on Article 3(2) of that Regulation, which does lead to a risk of violations of the *ne bis in idem* principle, however, these are usually avoided in practice.

The SSMR does however raise some *ne bis in idem* concerns, for instance in the interaction with national criminal law. This may be exacerbated by the diversity of criminal law responses to financial

The research for this chapter was financed through a Legal Research Grant from the European Central Bank.

misconduct that have emerged during and after the past financial crisis. In some cases, aspects of situations falling under the supervisory competences of the ECB and the NCAs will also constitute criminal offences under the laws of some Member States. Such instances do not necessarily fall within the scope of application of the Charter of Fundamental Rights of the EU (the 'Charter') and will not therefore violate the *ne bis in idem* principle as a matter of EU law. There is, however, a growing body of EU legislation in the field of criminal law, which has the effect of widening the scope of application of the Charter also in respect of pre-existing national criminal laws. In the following paragraphs, the enforcement instruments set out in the SSMR are briefly discussed, in as far as relevant (i.e. the competences to impose fines and to take other enforcement measures with potential *ne bis in idem* relevance). After that, the potential for violations of the *ne bis in idem* principle in the SSMR is assessed in more detail, and some conclusions are drawn.

2   Enforcement Measures Under the SSMR

2.1   Introduction

The economic and financial crisis demonstrated that the system of banking oversight based on national supervision provided insufficient protection.[1] The European legislator adopted a new set-up for a common level of supervision in the Euro area, the SSM.[2] Under the SSM, the ECB assumes the role of European Prudential Supervisor, taking over some of the functions of national authorities where 'significant' banks are concerned. All other credit institutions in the Eurozone-countries continue to be supervised by the NCAs, but the ECB can decide at any time to exercise direct supervision over any one of these credit institutions in order to ensure the consistent application of high supervisory standards.[3]

---

[1] *Preambule*, SSM Regulation, in p. 2. See, amongst others: B. Wolfers and Th. Voland, 'Level the playing field: the new supervision of credit institutions by the European Central Bank', 51 *CMLRev* (2014), p. 1463.

[2] G. Lo Schiavo, 'From national banking supervision to a centralized model of prudential supervision in Europe: The stability function of prudential supervision in Europe' (2014) 21 *MJ*,1, 111.

[3] Art. 6 SSM Regulation; Wolfers and Voland, cited *supra* note 2, p. 1468. The significance of an institution will be assessed on the basis of five alternative criteria: i) size, ii) relevance for the economy of the EU or any participating Member State, iii) volume of cross-border activities, iv) ranking amongst the three most significant institutions in a participating

The powers of the ECB are extensive, ranging from administrative powers to authorize credit institutions and assess administrative holdings to powers concerning compliance and sanctioning.[4] *Inter alia*, the ECB has the competence to ensure compliance with the minimum capital requirements, to safeguard the adequacy of internal capital in relation to the risk profile of a credit institution, and to enforce compliance with provisions on leverage and liquidity.[5] The ECB may take early intervention measures where capital requirements are violated, request information from credit institutions and conduct all necessary investigations,[6] including on-site inspections.[7] National supervisory authorities play a significant role, and EU financial regulation takes shape in a joined effort between the ECB and national supervisory authorities. In the end, however, the ECB alone is responsible for the effective and consistent functioning of the SSM. The supervisory powers and tasks of the ECB (Art. 16 SSMR) in respect of which administrative penalties can be applied (Art. 18 SSMR) are determined in accordance with the objectives of the SSMR, including the rules contained in the so-called CRD IV/CRR (which includes Directive 2013/36/EU, the 'CR Directive' and Regulation EU 575/2013, the 'CR Regulation') as well as in the light of any relevant case law of the EU courts.

2.2 Penalties

Several aspects of the SSMR carry potential *ne bis in idem* relevance, in particular the competence of the ECB to impose fines directly upon credit institutions,[8] and the possibility of the withdrawal of a license. Three types of decision can be identified in this regard:

- Administrative pecuniary penalties (Art. 18(1) Reg. 1024/2013) of up to twice the amount of profits gained or losses avoided or up to 10 per cent of annual turnover;
- Sanctions in accordance with Regulation (EC) 2532/98 for 'failure to comply with ECB decisions or regulations' (Art. 18(7) Reg. 1024/2013); and
- The withdrawal of authorization (Art. 14 (4) Reg. 1024/2013).

Member State and v) direct public assistance. A credit institution will not be deemed 'less significant' if the value of its assets exceeds EUR 30 billion.

[4] Art. 4 SSM Regulation.   [5] Art. 5 SSM Regulation.
[6] Art. 10 SSM Regulation; Art. 11 SSM Regulation.   [7] Art. 12 SSM Regulation.
[8] Art. 18 SSM Regulation.

The ECB has the exclusive competence to open infringement proceedings against and impose administrative penalties on 'significant supervised entities'. NCAs have the exclusive competence to open infringement proceedings against and impose administrative penalties on less significant supervised entities.[9] In situations covered by Art. 18(5) SSMR (breach of national law), the ECB cannot impose administrative pecuniary penalties, but it can require NCAs to open proceedings against significant supervised entities leading to the imposition of sanctions. The ECB has no competence to impose sanctions on natural persons, but the NCAs are competent to impose administrative penalties on natural persons and to impose administrative penalties where there is a breach of national law, including a national law transposing a directive. As regards the sanctions of Art. 18(7) SSMR, these sanctions will usually concern significant supervised entities, but an ECB regulation or decision may also apply to a less significant entity. In this case, the ECB retains the exclusive competence to impose sanctions.

As for the extent to which each of the aforementioned sanctions can be considered as 'punitive' within the meaning of the *Engel/Bonda* criteria, it can be concluded that each of these sanctions – including the withdrawal of a license – *potentially* fall within its scope of the *Engel/Bonda* and therefore carry *ne bis in idem* relevance.[10] In *Nilsson* v. *Sweden*, the Court found that the temporary suspension of a driving license belonged to the criminal law sphere in that case because the suspension was not an 'automatic' or 'immediate and foreseeable' consequence of the subject's conviction for a serious road traffic offence. Because some time passed between the time of the subject's conviction and the moment his driving license was suspended, the Court concluded that the measure must have been, at least in part, punitive in nature. It held that 'prevention and deterrence for the protection of the safety of road users could not have been the only purposes of the measure; retribution must also have been a major consideration'.[11] In the *Haarvig* case, the temporary revocation of a medical license was considered not to be of a 'criminal law nature' given that the provision in question laid down a professional standard and did not aim to punish and deter, but only to prevent further damage to the

---

[9] *Public consultation on a Draft Regulation of the ECB*, p. 18.

[10] As discussed later on in this paper there can be little doubt that the first and second types of sanctions belong to the 'sphere of criminal law' within the meaning of the *Engel/Bonda* doctrine, and may consequently trigger *ne bis in idem* protection.

[11] *Nilsson* v. *Sweden*, ECtHR 13 December 2005, appl. no. 73661/01.

subjects' patients.[12] Similarly, minor disciplinary proceedings against lawyers merely leading to a warning have been held to fall outside of the scope of the notion of 'criminal charge'. A finding of a criminal charge may be based on a combination of factors. In the *Matyjek* case, the Court considered that a ban from taking certain government positions was sufficiently serious to constitute a criminal charge, even though not accompanied by a fine or any other form of punishment.[13] The reason for this was, according to the Court, that 'the prohibition on practicing certain professions (political or legal) for a long period of time may have a very serious impact on a person, depriving him or her of the possibility of continuing professional life. ... This sanction should thus be regarded as having at least partly punitive and deterrent character.'[14] In the context of the SSMR, the conclusion from this is that the withdrawal of authorization can under circumstances constitute a criminal charge and therefore trigger the application of the *ne bis in idem* principle in relation to other penalties under the SSMR. Whether the same holds true for the removal by the ECB of 'members from the management body of credit institutions' pursuant to Art. 16(2)(m) SSMR is not all that certain as those members will not be 'banned' from practicing their profession like in the *Matyek* case. All the while, there is no doubt that such a decision may have a 'significant impact' on the person in question so that the observance of at least the minimum requisite procedural safeguards under the ECHR appears advisable, regardless of whether such decision will trigger the *Engel* doctrine in every case.

2.3   The Architecture of Enforcement of the SSMR

Similarly to Regulation 1/2003, the SSMR neither contains a *ne bis in idem* provision nor any 'hard', legal rules coordinating enforcement action between the ECB and the NCAs. For the SSM, the 'Framework Regulation' (Regulation EU 468/2014) establishes the rules and procedures governing the cooperation between the ECB and NCAs to ensure a good functioning of the SSM. Pursuant to Art. 6(7) SSMR the Framework Regulation sets out (see Art. 1 Framework Regulation):

---

[12] *Knut Haarvig* v. *Norway*, ECtHR 11 December 2007 (admissibility), appl. no. 11187/05.
[13] *Matyjek* v. *Poland*, ECtHR 30 May 2006 (admissibility), appl. no. 38184/03.
[14] Para. 55 of the decision.

(a) the methodology for assessing and reviewing the criteria laid down in the SSMR for determining whether a credit institution is significant or not;
(b) the procedures governing the cooperation between the ECB and NCAs as regards the supervision of significant credit institutions; and
(c) the procedures governing the cooperation between the ECB and NCAs as regards the supervision of less significant credit institutions.

Under the Framework Regulation, the ECB and the NCAs are under a duty to cooperate in good faith and to exchange information (Art. 20 Framework Regulation). Under Art. 22 of the Framework Regulation the ECB has the right to instruct the NCAs and to take action where the ECB has a supervisory task, but no accompanying powers to take enforcement measures. Here, there is a clear difference with competition law, which reflects the more centralized nature of the system of enforcement of the SSMR and follows logically from the nature of prudential supervision. In many other ways, the enforcement architecture of the SSM is reminiscent of that of Regulation 1/2003.

Both 'administrative pecuniary sanctions' (Art. 18(1) SSMR) and sanctions for "failure to comply with ECB decisions or regulations" (Art. 18(7) SSMR) are comparable in size and nature to the equivalent sanctions in EU competition law. An important difference with competition law lies in the third category of sanctions: the withdrawal of authorization. No such sanction is available in the enforcement of the competition rules.

The SSMR provides little information on the extent to which the different types of sanctions could interact in practice. The CR Directive is also inconclusive in this regard, but may nevertheless shed some further light on these issues. According to Art. 64(1) of the CR Directive:

> (c)ompetent authorities shall be given all supervisory powers to intervene in the activity of institutions that are necessary for the exercise of their function, including in particular the right to withdraw an authorisation in accordance with Article 18, the powers required in accordance with Article 102 and the powers set out in Articles 104 and 105.

Art. 65(1) of the CR Directive further specifies that

> without prejudice to the supervisory powers of competent authorities referred to in Article 64 and the right of Member States to provide for and impose criminal penalties, Member States shall lay down rules on administrative penalties and other administrative measures in respect of

breaches of national provisions transposing this Directive and of Regulation (EU) No 575/2013 and shall take all measures necessary to ensure that they are implemented. Where Member States decide not to lay down rules for administrative penalties for breaches which are subject to national criminal law they shall communicate to the Commission the relevant criminal law provisions.

2.4 Scope for Parallel Enforcement in Respect of the Same Infringement

A preliminary assessment of the extent to which *ne bis in idem* situations may arise under the SSMR shows that many questions could be raised on the point of who does what within the SSM, and many important procedural details are unclear or purposively left for the ECB to deal with in more detail at a later time.

The considerations of the SSMR provide several clues. Point 86 of the considerations affirms the respect for fundamental rights and principles and mentions the protection of personal data, the freedom to conduct a business, the right to an effective remedy and to a fair trial, but does not mention the *ne bis in idem* principle (which is perhaps somewhat unfortunate as it could convey the impression that potential problems in this connection were not duly considered in drafting the Regulation). Several other points raise interest, in particular point 36:

> In order to ensure that supervisory rules and decisions are applied ... effective, proportionate and dissuasive penalties should be imposed in case of a breach. In accordance with Article 132(3) TFEU and Council Regulation (EC) No 2532/98 of 23 November 1998 concerning the powers of the European Central Bank to impose sanctions, the ECB is entitled to impose fines or periodic penalty payments on undertakings for failure to comply with obligations under its regulations and decisions. Moreover, in order to enable the ECB to effectively carry out its tasks relating to the enforcement of supervisory rules set out in directly applicable Union law, the ECB should be empowered to impose pecuniary penalties on credit institutions, financial holding companies and mixed financial holding companies for breaches of such rules. National authorities *should remain able to apply penalties in case of failure to comply with obligations stemming from national law transposing Union Directives* (italics added). Where the ECB considers it appropriate for the fulfillment of its tasks that a penalty is applied for such breaches, it should be able to refer the matter to national competent authorities for those purposes.

The main difference with competition law is that the ECB is the first and foremost party responsible for the overall functioning of the system, and the SSMR is built around this central role. Art. 4(1) SSMR confirms that the ECB is attributed exclusive competence for prudential supervisory purposes in respect of all banks, and Art. 6 SSMR sets forth a delegation of prudential supervisory competences from the ECB to the NCAs in respect to less significant banks. This, however, does not however *disqualify* the ECB as the main competent authority for *both significant and less significant banks*. Point 36 of the Considerations confirms that this system does not necessarily exclude the possibility of parallel or consecutive sanctions imposed by the ECB and the NCAs in respect of the same, or related infringements. The same follows from paragraphs 1 and 5 of Article 18 of the Regulation, which read as follows:

(1.) For the purpose of carrying out the tasks conferred on it by this Regulation, where credit institutions, financial holding companies, or mixed financial holding companies, intentionally or negligently, breach a requirement under relevant directly applicable acts of Union law in relation to which administrative pecuniary penalties shall be made available to competent authorities under the relevant Union law, the ECB may impose administrative pecuniary penalties of up to twice the amount of the profits gained or losses avoided because of the breach where those can be determined, or up to 10 % of the total annual turnover, as defined in relevant Union law, of a legal person in the preceding business year or such other pecuniary penalties as may be provided for in relevant Union law.

. . .

(5.) In the cases not covered by paragraph 1 of this Article, where necessary for the purpose of carrying out the tasks conferred on it by this Regulation, the ECB may require national competent authorities to open proceedings with a view to taking action in order to ensure that appropriate penalties are imposed in accordance with the acts referred to in the first subparagraph of Article 4(3) and any relevant national legislation which confers specific powers which are currently not required by Union law. The penalties applied by national competent authorities shall be effective, proportionate and dissuasive. The first subparagraph of this paragraph shall be applicable in particular to pecuniary penalties to be imposed on credit institutions, financial holding companies or mixed financial holding companies for breaches of national law transposing relevant Directives, and to any administrative penalties or measures to be imposed

on members of the management board of a credit institution,
financial holding company or mixed financial holding company or
any other individuals who under national law are responsible for a
breach by a credit institution, financial holding company or mixed
financial holding company.

It does not follow from this that the NCAs competences are automatically suspended or withdrawn when the ECB acts or has acted with respect
to a certain credit institution. Furthermore, it is sufficiently clear that
enforcement action *of a different nature* is not taken into account in the
SSMR. The SSMR would therefore *prima facie* seem to leave room for
national authorities to act in various types situations in which there may
be a risk of the violation of the *ne bis in idem* principle.

Some features of the SSM-R mitigate the risk of infringements of the
ne bis in idem principle. The coordinating function of the distinction
between 'significant' and 'less significant' institutions in Art. 6 SSMR may
be sufficient to avoid any *ne bis in idem* situations as far as administrative
pecuniary penalties under Art. 18(1) SSM-R are concerned, but there are
no guarantees in the SSM-R itself. A difference with competition law is
that penalties under the SSMR reflect the gains had by the institution
from the infringement and are not somehow divided up according to the
supposed harm inflicted on different national markets for the purpose
of the calculation of fines by different national authorities, as is presently
the case in competition enforcement practice. Under the SSMR, it is clear
that the NCAs are fully competent to impose any penalties available in
respect of the entities supervised by them, whereas it was discussed in
Chapter 4 of this study that competition law is more ambiguous in that it
is thought that the national authorities *are only competent as far as their
own national markets are concerned.*[15]

Three other categories of situations can be distinguished: i) situations
in which there are penalties available under the SSMR and under national
law, *implementing EU legislation* in the field of financial supervision; ii)
situations in which there are penalties available under the SSMR and
under national law, *not (directly) related* to EU legislation in the field of
financial supervision; and: iii) situations in which a license is withdrawn
and a penalty is simultaneously or consecutively imposed by either the

---

[15] This (unwritten) 'rule' in competition law is paradoxical because it relies on national
(market) boundaries which competition law and EU law as a whole precisely aim to
remove. This aspect of the method of decentralized fine-setting arguably reveals a
deficiency in the enforcement architecture of Regulation 1/2003.

ECB or an NCA. Both situations in which the ECB acts, as well as situations in which the NCAs act (applying both EU law and national law, implementing EU law) ostensibly fall within the scope of the Charter. The same is true for situations in which options were exercised in national legislation, regardless of the extent of discretion available to the national legislature in exercising those options. Questions may arise in situations in which the ECB for instance acts under the rules of the European Stability Mechanism, but it would seem certain that the Charter will also apply in those instances because it is an EU institution (the ECB) that acts. In addition, although the Charter applies in such situations, the legal situation of a supervised entity in proceedings before a national court (e.g. in situations in which an NCA acted under the instruction of the ECB subject to Art. 4(1) jo. 6(1) SSMR) may in practice be quite different from that in which a decision by the ECB can be challenged directly by the supervised institution before the EU courts. Large parts of the Charter remain untouched by the case law of the CJEU, so that much is left to the particular attitudes of the national judiciary in applying Charter rights and/or referring questions to the CJEU.

An interesting question may present itself in Art. 18(5) SSMR, where it states that the ECB may require NCAs to open proceedings 'with a view to taking action in order to ensure that appropriate penalties are imposed in accordance with . . . any national legislation which confers specific powers which are currently not required by Union law'. By doing so, the ECB would arguably be bringing those national laws within the scope of EU law and therefore within that of the Charter, even though those national laws themselves may not be connected to EU law in any way.

The SSMR provides for the unique possibility that an EU institution may apply national law in Article 4(3) SSMR:

> For the purpose of carrying out the tasks conferred on it by this Regulation, and with the objective of ensuring high standards of supervision, the ECB shall apply all relevant Union law, and where this Union law is composed of Directives, the national legislation transposing those Directives. Where the relevant Union law is composed of Regulations and where currently those Regulations explicitly grant options for Member States, the ECB shall apply also the national legislation exercising those options.

It arguably follows (*inter alia* from the *Åkerberg Fransson*[16] and *Melloni*[17] judgments) that if an EU institution or other EU body applies

---

[16] Case C-617/10, *Åkerberg Fransson*, EU:C:2013:280.
[17] Case C-399/11, *Melloni*, EU:C:2013:107.

national law, *implementing* EU law directly, that institution will also be bound by any relevant higher national standards of fundamental rights protection in situations in which those national laws are not 'entirely determined' by EU law. The ECB may therefore be required, (also) *as a matter of EU law*, to take certain national constitutional rights into account when applying national legislation under Art. 4(3) SSMR. This could raise tricky questions of national constitutional interpretation. As for the degree to which such will (or can) deviate from the standard of protection provided in the Charter, there is much uncertainty after *Åkerberg Fransson* and *Melloni*. The question we are left with is when it is that the 'primacy, unity and effectiveness' of EU law are not 'compromised', and therefore how the Court weighs the interest of the protection of fundamental rights against that of the enforcement of material provisions of EU law.[18]

3   Analysis

The coordinating function of the distinction between significant and less significant institutions from Art. 6 SSMR forms an important first safeguard against conflicts of jurisdiction and violations of the *ne bis in idem* principle, but the SSMR itself does not *verbatim* exclude the possibility of infringements of the *ne bis in idem* principle. It has been pointed out that many questions remain open where the details of enforcement procedures of the SSMR is concerned so that some conclusions from this chapter must remain somewhat tentative.

It has been pointed out at several points in this study that the *Walt Wilhelm* judgment is no longer 'good law', and will not therefore work to prevent violations of *ne bis in idem* in relation to the SSMR. As discussed in particular in Chapter 1, the only logically defensible position by now is that 'the identity of the legal interest protected' from the competition cases discussed in Chapters 1 and 4 of this study must be understood as meaning the very same thing as the 'scope of EU law' from the *Åkerberg Fransson* judgment. Otherwise, the Court would have to find a way to distinguish between the 'scope of EU law' and the scope of the 'legal interest protected' by EU law (which appears to make no sense).

---

[18] The question whether the CJEU is taking human rights 'seriously' has lingered ever since the birth of fundamental rights protection through 'general principles' in the case law of the CJEU.

One could perhaps speculate that the sanctions under Art. 18(7) SSMR (a maximum amount of EUR 500.000) might not be sufficient to meet the *Engel/Bonda* criteria given the kinds of sums that supervised entities normally work with, but there is hardly a shred of tangible evidence in the case law of the ECtHR to support such a claim. In the following, the different situations which may give rise to violations of the *ne bis in idem* principle are examined in more detail, and conclusions are drawn where possible.

3.1   The Interaction between a Penalty and the Withdrawal of a License under the SSMR

According to Recital 20 of the SSMR,

> prior authorisation for taking up the business of credit institutions is a key prudential technique to ensure that only operators with a sound economic basis, an organisation capable of dealing with the specific risks inherent to deposit taking and credit provision, and suitable directors carry out those activities. The ECB should therefore have the task of authorising credit institutions that are to be established in a participating Member State and should be responsible for the withdrawal of authorisations.

The aim of this type of decision (for which the ECB *is* exclusively competent) is therefore not necessarily *punitive*. Although it must nevertheless be assumed that the withdrawal of a license will, in principle, fall within the *Engel/Bonda* criteria, it follows from the case law that:

i) the decision withdrawing a license as such is not *always* necessarily punitive in nature, and different circumstances may even lead to different findings in individual cases;
ii) the concurrence of the withdrawal of a license and the imposition of a fine is not necessarily problematic as long as the *withdrawal of the license* (and therefore not the imposition of a fine, due to its necessarily punitive nature) forms the *immediate and foreseeable consequence* of a decision sanctioning certain conduct which gives rise to a fine.

Here, the boundaries of the *Engel* doctrine and the requirement of the finality of the previous sentence as they appear from the case law of the ECtHR are somewhat blurred. It is for instance not certain whether the withdrawal of a license which is per se punitive but also forms the 'immediate and foreseeable consequence' of the decision to impose a fine or another sanction is caught by the *ne bis in idem* principle, or not. From the case law of the ECtHR we know that if the revocation of a driving license automatically follows a conviction for a road traffic offence this is not problematic, but if sufficient time has passed between the initial conviction and the revocation of the license, and the latter was at least in part based on a separate assessment of the facts of the case, this provides some indication of the (partially) punitive nature of the latter decision. From the wording of the SSMR too little can be inferred with sufficient certainty on the interaction between the procedures for adopting decisions under Articles 14 and 18 SSMR to make a full assessment on this point, although it can safely be assumed that those provisions will by their nature prove relevant in the same real-life situations. The ECB is well advised to carefully coordinate the procedures leading to a decision to withdraw the license of a credit institution with the imposition of any administrative pecuniary penalties under Art. 18(1) SSMR.

A final possibility worth mentioning is the interaction of a withdrawal of a license and enforcement of national law, not connected to prudential supervision under the SSMR. In such situations there is typically no risk of a violation of the *ne bis in idem* principle of Art. 50 of the Charter, because the Charter typically doesn't apply to both procedures in such situations. This is different if the national law at issue is brought "within the scope of EU law" through EU legislation not directly linked to the SSM (for instance: the Money Laundering Directive in the Area of Freedom Security and Justice). In such situations, violations of the *ne bis in idem* principle may prove hard to avoid through enforcement coordination. The CJEU has, however, not had occasion to rule on any issues along these lines. From the case law discussed in Section 2 of this chapter, it appears that there is a possibility that it will find grounds to rule that such a situation does not violate the *ne bis in idem* principle as a matter of EU law.

3.2 Potential Issues in the Interaction with Other Sanctions and Procedures under National Law

The SSMR doesn't as such mention national criminal laws, tax laws or national laws of any other kind. The only provision which may provide some indication on this point is Art. 3(10) of Regulation (EC) 2532/98, which reads as follows:

> If an infringement also relates to one or more areas outside the competence of the ESCB, the right to initiate an infringement procedure on the basis of this Regulation shall be independent of any right of a competent

national authority to initiate separate procedures in relation to such areas outside the competence of the ESCB. This provision shall be *without prejudice to the application of criminal law* (italics added) and to prudential supervisory competencies in participating Member States.

Although there is apparently some discussion on the question of the extent to which this provision is still relevant after the adoption of the SSM-R, its wording doesn't augur well for *ne bis in idem* issues. A variety of national legislative responses to financial misconduct emerged during and after the recent financial crisis, and a range of potential issues could be identified on this point. The complexity of the questions that may arise in this connection makes it difficult to arrive at general conclusions. It is worth pointing out that such issues only arise if it is indeed the legal entity – the bank or other credit institution itself – that is penalized and not its CEOs or employees. This isn't equally the case in all Member States, because not every Member State recognizes criminal law responsibility of legal persons. In situations in which a CEO or employee is prosecuted, this does not trigger *ne bis in idem* protection for the legal entity, and *vice versa*. At least, so it must be (and is generally) assumed, as there is at present no judgment from either court confirming this. There is a difference between the Charter and the ECHR on this point. It should be recalled that such a combination of sanctions is only a potential issue of *ne bis in idem* as a matter of EU law, if *both* decisions (sanctions) fall within the scope of the Charter. Although the influence of EU law on national criminal law and therefore the extent to which the Charter applies in situations governed by national law is steadily growing, the vast majority of criminal cases are and will likely always remain outside of the scope of application of EU law and the Charter. In financial criminal law, however, there is more relevant EU legislation to consider than in many other fields of criminal law. The possibility of the occurrence of a situation in which a single infringement triggers different enforcement responses by the ECB and/ or an NCA as well as national prosecutors is therefore not imaginary. In situations in which both instances of prosecution are (sufficiently) connected to EU law, this may violate Art. 50 of the Charter. Direct taxation on the other hand is not harmonized at all on the EU level, so that the risk of a violation of art 50 Charter through the concurrence of a tax penalty and a penalty under the SSMR for the same conduct seems negligible or non-existent.

Outside of the scope of the Charter, there are various national *ne bis in idem* provisions that must be taken into account in addition to Art. 4P7

ECHR, which (to further complicate matters) was not ratified by all Member States. Here, there is considerable uncertainty. What seems certain is that NCAs are bound by the Convention, both when they apply national law and/or EU law on their own accord, as well as when acting under instruction of the ECB.

No lessons can be drawn from competition law as the types of questions that may arise here don't really present themselves in the context of competition law enforcement. Competition laws in the Member States are (supposedly) the fruit of a process of 'spontaneous harmonization', raising the question whether the Charter applies to national competition law at all, in situations not affecting trade between the Member States – although there are good grounds to assume that it does. What the SSM, competition law, and many other areas of EU law have in common is that there is scope for conflict between requirements of effective and dissuasive measures under EU law and Convention obligations for the Member States, and the *Åkerberg Fransson* and *Bonda* judgments provide some clear examples.

In the case of *Lucky Dev* the ECtHR held that bookkeeping fraud and the filing of an incorrect tax statement are sufficiently separate to constitute separate facts for the application of the *ne bis in idem* principle.[19] For prudential supervision this is an important judgment which will no doubt help to take the edge off *ne bis in idem* issues in case of complex financial infringements by banks and other credit institutions, which are more easily divided up into separate wrongdoing than most other criminal acts.

4 Conclusions

The question raised in this chapter is not whether an infringement of the *ne bis in idem* principle is possible under SSM, but whether there is, to borrow a familiar term from the field of financial regulation, a *systemic risk* of violations of that principle. This chapter has examined whether the enforcement architecture of the SSMR is conducive to violations of the *ne bis in idem* principle in certain situations and competition law was used as a point of reference where possible. The conclusion is that the SSM is *prima facie* more '*ne bis in idem* proof' than Regulation 1/2003, but that there are also *caveats*.

---

[19] *Lucky Dev*, ECtHR 27 November 2014, appl. no. 7356/10.

There is no provision on *ne bis in idem* in the SSM package and the regulation itself does not preempt violations of the *ne bis in idem* principle. The same is true for Regulation 1/2003, but the actual problems for competition law are hardly comparable to those found in prudential banking supervision. One familiar *ne bis in idem* issue in competition law is that the internal market is in practice 'divided up' into national markets overlooked by national competition authorities. Because of this the architecture of EU competition law enforcement is conducive to infringements of the *ne bis in idem* principle, which are in practice prevented through coordination and cooperation within the ECN. Fines imposed by ECB or NCAs on the other hand do not supposedly reflect the impact of an infringement on affected markets, but are determined according to the subjective gain had by a bank through the infringement. This differences in practice limits the potential for *ne bis in idem* violations.

From the foregoing it should not be concluded that the lack of a formal division of tasks and competences between the members of the SSM in the SSMR doesn't raise any potential issues. Indeed, more legal clarity on this point in the SSMR itself may have been preferable from a fundamental rights perspective. An issue that was already identified is that enforcement requires effective judicial remedies, which may not be equally available before national and EU courts in all types of situations: situations in which the ECB applies EU and/or national law, situations in which NCAs act under the instruction of the ECB, and situations in which the NCAs act in other situations. Such issues are however beyond the remit of this contribution to further address.

A possible *ne bis in idem* issue that can be identified within the SSMR is the interaction of an administrative pecuniary penalty and the withdrawal of a license. No parallel can be drawn here with competition law; it is a problem specific to the SSM-R. It should be practically possible to avoid *ne bis in idem* infringements in this type of situation, but the Regulation does not provide any particular mechanism on this point so that this must be achieved through coordination of the withdrawal of a license and the imposition of a administrative penalty. From the ECtHR case law discussed earlier in this contribution, however, it follows that the withdrawal of a license must be the immediate and foreseeable consequence of an investigation or a decision also imposing or leading up to the imposition of a penalty. It is possible that, applying the rule from the *Jussilla* judgment,[20] the ECtHR will show itself to be more lenient in this regard where it concerns banks and other large enterprises but there has been so far no case concerning the *ne bis in idem* principle specifically to confirm this.

A clear parallel with competition law exists only as regards to sanctions for 'failure to comply with ECB decisions or regulations' (Art. 18(7) SSMR). For reasons similar to those in competition law, those types of sanction will not typically give rise to *ne bis in idem* trouble. For one, each sanction requires a specific individual 'failure to comply', and a continued failure to comply can thus be divided up into different infringements by adopting a series of decisions, which is not possible in respect of infringement in connection with sanction under Art. 18(1) SSMR. Although the possibility that a single historical infringement may give rise to the possibility of sanctions of several types cannot *a priori* be excluded, competition enforcement practice shows that this is probably very rare (or at least that it has not so-far surfaced in competition proceedings before the EU courts.

Other issues may also present themselves, in particular in the interaction:

 i) with national criminal and possibly tax law and
 ii) between the withdrawal of authorization and the imposition of an administrative pecuniary penalty.

The potential for such issues will necessarily vary from one Member State to another. Such situations will not typically fall within the scope of EU law and of the Charter due to the limited extent to which national criminal law is harmonized at the EU level. The same applies to tax law, due to the wholly unharmonized nature of direct taxation in the EU. This however leaves the potential for violations of Member States' obligations under Art. 4P7 ECHR. Although the ECHR is formally (still) not binding on the EU such violations nevertheless deserve consideration in the context of the SSMR. Many potential *ne bis in idem* issues signalled in this chapter are only avoided through gaps in the protection afforded by Art. 50 Charter, which only applies in situations falling 'within the scope of EU law', and Art. 4P7 ECHR, which only applies within one and the same Member State and was not ratified by all Member States. What subjects are left with is the possibility of some form of *ne bis in idem*

---

[20] ECtHR, *Jusilla* v. *Finland*, 23 November 2006, appl. no. 73053/01.

protection under national law in situations in which the ECB (or an NCA) imposed a fine *first*, after which proceedings of a different nature were brought under national law and this will necessarily vary from Member State to Member State. All and all, the (potential) *ne bis in idem* questions raised by the SSMR in relation to proceedings under national law clearly show that the system of fundamental rights protection in the EU is at present exceedingly complex, and far from perfect.

~

Conclusions

The Changing Geometry of Fundamental Rights
Protection in the EU

BAS VAN BOCKEL

This chapter aims to bring the various observations from the previous chapters together and to draw some conclusions. Particular attention is given to the question what the jurisprudential developments discussed in the different chapters of this study can tell us about the direction that the system of fundamental rights protection in the EU is taking. Important aspects of the recent case law of the Court of Justice of the European Union (CJEU) seem to revolve around the question of who shall have the final say in fundamental rights protection matters in the EU. In the last part of this Chapter, some of the main findings from this study are presented, and conclusions are drawn.

As Sarmiento wrote at the start of Chapter 3 of this volume, 'the *ne bis in idem* principle is everywhere in EU law, its influence touches every area of EU policy, but the definition of its precise contours is still subject to considerable discussion'. The case law of different European courts on the *ne bis in idem* principle illustrates the difficulty of reconciling constitutional pluralism[1] with the need to maintain doctrinal coherence across different strands of case law of different European courts. As also discussed in Chapter 3, the CJEU has struggled to develop a coherent doctrine governing the relationship between EU fundamental rights, the European Court of Human Rights (ECtHR) and national 'constitutional traditions'. At present it is not evident from the case law discussed in this study that the CJEU still strives to establish such a doctrine. There are indications in the case law that the Court may opt for

---

[1] Understood here as the 'plurality of constitutional sources and claims of final authority which create a context for potential constitutional conflicts that are not hierarchically regulated', M. Poiares Maduro, 'Three claims of constitutional pluralism' (working paper, available from: www.wzb.eu/sites/default/files/veranstaltungen/the-promise-of-constitutional-pluralism/miguelmadurothreeclaimsofconstitutionalpluralismhu-collmay152012.pdf)

a more practical rather than legal-formal division of tasks between itself, the ECtHR and national constitutional courts. To give one example of this: it was already pointed out in Section 3 of Chapter 2 that in the case of *Åkerberg Fransson* the CJEU chose to leave the actual determination of whether there had been an infringement of a Charter right to the referring court, omitting any reference to the relevant case law of the ECtHR. This contrasts with the *Bonda* judgment in which the Court found no difficulty in settling essentially the same point of law itself and *did* refer to the relevant case law of the ECtHR. Several other cases have been discussed at various points in this study in which the Court either referred to the case law of the ECtHR or precisely omitted any references to it. From these a pattern appears to emerge that could be interpreted as indicative of a strategy on the part of the Court to leave sufficient space for national courts to make their own determination of fundamental rights questions in situations involving the Charter. If this is indeed the case, this is in itself perhaps hardly novel or surprising given that fundamental rights protection in the EU has always primarily rested with the judiciary in the Member States. It makes sense for the CJEU to exercise a degree of judicial deference in relation to the judiciary in the Member States in situations involving the Charter because national courts are increasingly faced with complex questions in the interaction between national constitutional rights, Charter rights and obligations under the European Convention of Human Rights (ECHR) that the CJEU may not always wish to engage in their finer detail. Furthermore, these cases reach Luxembourg exclusively in preliminary proceedings, and the exact level of fundamental rights protection in each of the Member States is not necessarily amongst the Court's primary concerns as long as the 'primacy, unity and effectiveness of EU law' are not compromised and the minimum standards from the Charter are respected.

At the same time, it follows from the relevant considerations of the *Åkerberg Fransson* judgment that the Court will not maintain this position if it deems that the 'primacy, unity and effectiveness of EU law' *are* endangered. The relevant considerations of the judgment are reminiscent of the wording of the famous *Solange II* judgment of the German *Bundesverfassungsgericht*, in which that Court held that '(a)s long as the European Communities, in particular European Court case law, generally ensure effective protection of fundamental rights as against the sovereign powers of the Communities which is to be regarded as substantially similar to the protection of fundamental rights required unconditionally by the Constitution'.[2]

A more controversial aspect of the approach of the CJEU may be its apparent resolve to cede as little as possible of its position as the EU's highest fundamental rights court to the ECtHR. Recent cases like *Schrems*[3]*Digital Rights Ireland*[4] and most recently the case of *Front Polisario* v. *Council*[5] the CJEU has shown itself to be a strong and active defender of fundamental rights in situations in which the validity of EU law is challenged directly on grounds of incompatibility of fundamental rights guaranteed within the EU legal order. The foundations for these developments in the case law of the CJEU appear to have been laid in the seminal *Åkerberg Fransson* and *Melloni* judgments discussed in several chapters of this study. These judgments may incidentally also shed some more light on the possible reasons for the CJEU's (perhaps) surprising rejection of the accession agreement of the EU to the ECHR in Opinion 2/2014.[6] It is, however, also possible that these developments had gradually begun to take shape in the case law of the CJEU already some time before the cases of *Åkerberg Fransson* and *Melloni* provided a suitable opportunity to clarify its foundations in relation to national (constitutional) law.

It remains to be seen whether such a 'decentralized' system of EU fundamental rights governance is feasible. Some key challenges it could be faced with could be: i) the highly internalized nature of ECHR rights in the EU legal order and ii) the special relationship between the CJEU, the ECtHR and national constitutional courts. As for the first challenge (the highly internalized nature of ECHR rights in the EU legal order) it should be pointed out that although the CJEU has managed to block accession of the EU to the ECHR, it has so far not managed to overcome Article 52(3) of the Charter (the 'homogeneity clause') in its case law – or at least not convincingly. It is sufficiently clear that the CJEU cannot always avoid recourse to the case law of the ECtHR in interpreting Charter rights as well other rights under EU law, and it will therefore likely be forced to fundamentally address the relationship between Convention and Charter rights at some point in its case law. To give an

---

[2] ECLI:DE:BVerfG:2000:ls20000607.2bvl000197(*unofficial translation*).
[3] Case C-362/14, *Schrems*, EU:C:2015:650.
[4] Case C-293/12, *Digital Rights Ireland*, EU:C:2014:238.
[5] Case T-512/12, *Front Polisario v. Council*, EU:T:2015:953.
[6] Opinion 2/2014, EU:C:2014:2454.

example: it was pointed out in Chapter 2, Section 4.3 that it is difficult to deny that the starting point of the relevant considerations of the *Åkerberg Fransson* case is formed by the *Engel*-criteria, which the CJEU clearly enumerates in that judgment even though no explicit reference to the case law of the ECtHR is made. The CJEU therefore appears to push for a higher degree of judicial autonomy for the CJEU *vis-à-vis* the case law of the ECtHR than it actually enjoys. EU law and the ECHR have become deeply intertwined and this is a reality that the CJEU cannot fully overcome (for example by omitting references to the case law of the ECtHR in some cases). In addition, it remains to be seen what the effect of the impending reform of the court will be in this regard, as scrutiny by the ECtHR may prove to be a practical and political necessity for an enlarged and otherwise constitutionally unsupervised EU court.

As for the second potential challenge, the special relationship between the CJEU, the ECtHR and national constitutional courts, the picture is more complex. In its *Bosphorus* judgment, the ECtHR developed the doctrine of equivalent protection, which establishes the conditions under which a Member State is responsible for a breach of the ECHR arising from (then) EC law, or its national implementing laws.[7] There are similarities (and also some differences) between the *Bosphorus*, *Åkerberg Fransson/Melloni* and *Solange II* doctrines. The result is a remarkable triangular relationship of conditionality between the CJEU, the ECtHR and the *Bundesverfassungsgericht*. Each of those courts appears to demand a form of 'equivalent' (constitutional) protection from one of the others in return for a commitment to refrain from giving the fullest effect to the Charter, the ECHR, and the German *Grundgesetz*, respectively, in situations involving the jurisdiction of one of the others. Evidently, accession of the EU to the ECHR could have upset this delicate 'constitutional balance' as far as the CJEU is concerned. It requires a mutual ability for each of the parties involved to impose balanced constraints on each of the others on equal (constitutional) footing, in order for it to work. If any of the parties involved in such a balancing act lay claim to a form of *final* authority as the CJEU arguably does in Opinion 2/14 in respect of the EU legal order, this could prompt the others to do the same, upsetting the balance. The stacking up of claims to final authority could certainly erode the foundations of this uniquely complex and fragile system of European fundamental rights protection. It

---

[7] *Bosphorus Hava Yolları Turizm ve Ticaret Anonim Sirketi* v. *Ireland*, ECtHR 30 June 2005, app. no. 45036/98.

may therefore be that the CJEU will have to be more forthcoming towards the case law of the ECtHR in recognition of the conditional nature of their relationship for its own sake, as well as in the interest of the further development and maintenance of a balanced system of fundamental rights protection in the EU. All the while, requirements of legal certainty may in the longer run require a more formal doctrine due to the nature and importance of EU fundamental rights protection and the described complexity of the relationship between the different 'European' courts.

From the foregoing it is sufficiently clear that idea of a 'judicial dialogue' between courts through mutual doctrinal influence and persuasion only captures some aspects of the complex interaction between the ECJ, the ECtHR and national constitutional courts in the field of fundamental rights protection. Other factors, in particular considerations of judicial autonomy and conditionality *vis-à-vis* other European courts – as well as undeniable mutual interdependence – may shape developments in 'European' human rights jurisprudence, and these considerations pull in opposite directions. There does not at present appear to be any established theory or concept available to scholars of European integration capable of explaining the full dynamic presently witnessed in the case law discussed in this study. A promising possibility (and one that may follow from the observations made in this study) may be the notion of a 'constitutional balance', which captures both the attracting and the opposing forces seen at work in the case law (which include, but are not limited to, some form of a judicial dialogue on the substance of the rights to be realized).[8]

Interpretative questions and inconsistencies in the case law of different 'European' courts on the *ne bis in idem* principle have been identified and discussed in every chapter of this study, although there is some overlap. In Chapter 1 it was agued that whilst it may be necessary to differentiate the interpretation of a right like the *ne bis in idem* principle somewhat according to the specific characteristics of different EU policy areas, the CJEU will have to find some doctrinal justification for the inconsistencies between the case law on the *ne bis in idem* principle in the Area of Freedom, Security and Justice and in competition law in particular.[9]

---

[8] An example of how this concept could be developed further in the EU context is: M. Dawson and F. de Witte, 'Constitutional Balance in the EU after the Euro-crisis', (2013) *Modern Law Review* 76(5), 817–844.

[9] These inconsistencies were identified and discussed in more particular in Chapters 2 and 4.

Otherwise, the national judiciary may not always be persuaded to follow the CJEU, especially in situations in which national constitutional rights or Convention rights are at stake. As for the inconsistencies within the case law of the CJEU, it appears increasingly difficult to maintain that the requirement of the 'identity of the legal interest protected' from the competition law cases can mean anything other than 'the scope of EU law' as laid down in Article 51 of the Charter. In the *Åkerberg Fransson* judgment, it was held that the scope of the Charter coincides with that of EU law itself. In the light of the requirement of the 'identity of the legal interest protected', this raises the question what other 'legal interest' could be at stake other than that of EU law in general, in situations falling within the scope of the Charter. The same follows, *mutatis mutandis*, from the *Walt Wilhelm* judgment in which the requirement of the identity of the protected legal interest was originally introduced by the CJEU. If there is indeed only one possible 'legal interest' to be considered for the purposes of *'idem'* in situations falling within the scope of EU law (and this conclusion appears inevitable) this causes the 'threefold requirement' from the competition cases to collapse into the twofold *Zolotukhin* test. That is, unless the CJEU finds some other acceptable doctrinal justification for its differentiated interpretation of the element of *idem*, capable of withstanding the weight of doctrinal logic.

As for the proposition from Chapter 2 that uniformity isn't the sole cure for the ailments of the system of EU fundamental rights protection, the *Zoran Spasic* case discussed in Chapter 1 provides a clear illustration.[10] In that case, the CJEU adopted an approach which doesn't follow from the wording of the Charter, and which appears unnecessary for the outcome. The CJEU sanctioned the approach followed by the German *Bundesverfassungsgericht* in an earlier case, while at the same time avoiding the ECtHR's 'template'. What this case illustrates is that the dynamic interaction between the CJEU, the ECtHR and (in this case, but not surprisingly) the German *Bundesverfassungsgericht* doesn't necessarily contribute to greater uniformity or coherence in the substantive interpretation of fundamental rights, but it can lead to higher level of fundamental rights protection (not only on the national, but also on the EU level). As discussed earlier, this results from a situation of mutual interdependence in which each European court enjoys a limited degree of

---

[10] Case C-129/14 PPU, *Spasic*, EU:C:2014:586.

interpretative autonomy *vis-a-vis* the others, but none really has the final say where the interpretation of a fundamental right like the *ne bis in idem* principle is concerned. Although perhaps not ideal for a system of fundamental rights protection due to the complexity and legal uncertainty that results from it, the surprising conclusion is therefore that there are important benefits, as it can be seen to lead to a higher level of protection of fundamental rights in practice.

In Chapter 6, it was concluded that many potential *ne bis in idem* issues under the SSM are in practice only avoided through gaps in the protection afforded by Article 50 of the Charter, which only applies in situations falling 'within the scope of EU law', and Article 4 of Protocol no. 7 ECHR, which only applies within one and the same Member State and was not ratified by all Member States. The clear resulting gaps in protection could have been partially remedied by accession of the EU to the ECHR, but Opinion 2/14 has prevented this. What subjects are left with is the possibility of some form of *ne bis in idem* protection under national law in situations in which the ECB (or an NCA) imposed a fine *first*, after which proceedings of a different nature were brought under national law, and this will necessarily vary from Member State to Member State. What this perhaps illustrates is that the system of fundamental rights protection in the EU is at present far from perfect, and that the *ne bis in idem* principle forms a very suitable litmus test bringing to light its many shortcomings in keeping with the aim of this study.

INDEX

CPSIA information can be obtained
at www.ICGtesting.com
Printed in the USA
LVHW04s2229240718
584768LV00003B/171/P

9 781107 451841